A Man's Work

Is Never Done

A Man's Work Is Never Done

A Man's Work Is Never Done

A Novel
About Mentoring Our Sons

James Cloughley

First Published in Canada 2011 by Influence Publishing

Author's Photo: Linda Warren

Cover Design: Greg Salisbury

This book is dedicated to the memory of John Fraser, my dearest friend who was a much greater inspiration than he could have known. I miss his humour, his perspective but more than anything I miss his humanity.

A Man's Work Is Never Done

Testimonials

As a physician who deals with families of every description I see a strong role for literature such as this and room for so many other works that help us raise our children.

I would recommend this book to fathers, grandfathers, mentors and all men who work with boys and teens.

I think mothers and grandmothers will find this book of interest as they understand the unique role that men have in passing on tradition and wisdom from one generation to the next. Some knowledge can only be passed on from one man to the next without our involvement.

A Man's Work Is Never Done. . . could easily serve as a small group book study, focus for a mens' workshop, basis for a lecture and discussion series and could be used in individual counselling among men, particularly with traumatic backgrounds, addiction histories or absent father figures in their life.

In reading A Man's Work is Never Done I have come to understand some of the things my son requires only his father can give to him. I respect more fully the integral role fathers play in shaping their son's transition to manhood.

Amanda Bell, BArtsSc, MD,FCFP
Family Physician
Port Colborne, Ontario

Jim Cloughley poses a challenging question to all 21st century men. What is the mark you will leave once your life is done? Through his narrative he weaves the questions and answers men must confront in a shifting paradigm of what and who exactly a man is to be in our modern world. What are the rules for conduct at work, at home, and in society? I would recommend this book for anyone with a young man in their life — whether it be a family member or in your role as a professional in order to gain a glimpse into the competing expectations placed before men today.

Barclay Walker, Hon. B.Sc., B.Ed., O.C.T.

"The book is an insightful read into the mind of a man. And yes, I thought I had it all figured out before I had read the book! It brought sensitivity and understanding into the 'why and how' of the every day actions and thoughts of our male counterparts. As I was reading, I could feel myself questioning some of my own actions and assessments of men. I truly read a different aspect of the male mind.

The symbolism of the front porch allowed me to evaluate my current relationship with my spouse, giving us both a discerning understanding of why things happen in our own lives.

Our lives are built on relationships and having the power to understand them is a gift. Jim has this gift and relays that through his story."

Sherri Cousineau
Wife and mother of two

"I found this book clearly laid out issues that, not only young men but adult men as well, struggle with regularly. The author deals with them in a step by step approach within the context of a story that more than held my interest. You could read this book a chapter at a time or as a continuous read—either way is impactful. This is a must read for single parents, co-parents, young men who question their place in todays society, teachers, professionals and anyone else who is interested in not only understanding what is happening in the world for men currently but for those truly wanting to learn how to support and assist them in this time of uncertainty. It will benefit all. The timing of this book is perfect."

Phil Durrant, MSW, RSW
Coordinator of Social Service Worker Program
Niagara College,
Welland, Ontario

Male clients of today would benefit from the wisdom in this book. Men need role models which are often non-existent in their lives. Jim's book would be a great resource for men in my practice but young men overall today. Great Work Jim.

Roxanne Derhodge B.Sc., M.Sc.,
Psychotherapist/Consultant.

Defining manhood is a serious issue in the modern world. What does it mean to be a man, and how do we mentor young males into manhood when many are being raised - as I was in an earlier generation - without significant male influences in their lives? In "A Man's Work Is Never Done: A Novel About Mentoring Our Sons," Jim Cloughley tackles this question head-on, in novel form, as he helps a troubled young neighbour understand what it is to be a man, and in the process learns as much about himself and the meaning and purpose of his own life as he teaches his protege. Whether male or female, young or old, this book will help you understand more fully the process of growing into manhood, and the importance of having strong role models and mentors to help along the way.

Rev. Steven Davis B.A., M.Div.

A Man's Work Is Never Done

Acknowledgements

Ken Kirkby well known Canadian artist, for his time, energy and his insightful comments in articulating the philosophy of the book.

Phil Durrant for his positive look at the early manuscript and his encouragement and support.

Julie Salisbury of Influence Publishing for her professionalism and expertise and belief in my ideas. The members of the Spiritual Author's Circle for their caring and support.

Hammie Schilstra for her dedication, support and feedback to help organize what I couldn't.

Nancy Geddie who edited this manuscript and made it read, look and sound like I knew what I was doing.

Linda Rosier and the good people at Wee Gates Inc. in Erin, Ontario who were very generous with their time and allowed me to use The Inukshuk Story to explain what the book is all about.

Linda Warren who offered her professionalism and expertise in helping to get the word out on the social media platforms.

And those friends and colleagues who showed their interest in my work and the topic.

A Man's Work Is Never Done

Contents

Foreward

Throughout history, the relationship between fathers and sons has been an uneasy one. These tensions appear to be more pronounced in western societies, especially those most technologically advanced and financially well off. Over the last few decades the ever-widening distance between the generations has become toxic. I think it is fair to say that changes that have taken place in recent time are unparalleled in human history, and not only the changes but the speed with which they have taken place.

Some 70 years ago, when I was born, the human population of our planet was less than half of what it is today. Most of those alive at that time populated rural areas, villages and small towns. Many, if not most, were engaged in some aspect of farming. The most common family grouping comprised grandparents, parents and grandchildren. The various roles were reasonably long standing and clearly defined.

The massive upheaval brought about by the Industrial Revolution, followed by our even more explosive technological revolution, has served to all but eviscerate long-standing traditions. Life on the land close to the natural world was abandoned in favour of work in the ever-bloated compressions of our cities. The traditional family scattered. Loyalty to the group and each other dissolved. The individual became king in a headlong rush to financial wealth and material possessions. It is not only that we want these possessions; we want them right now! Tomorrow they will in all likelihood be obsolete. Added to this, if we do not look like the person staring back at us from the cover of this or that magazine or electronic screen, we feel less than desirable and will need to seek salvation in medication.

What a strange and dark irony it is when we stop to consider that until recently North America was mostly populated by immigrants from the far reaches of Russia to the slums of Europe with less than nothing. In little more than a blink of an eye, we have more material wealth than any one could ever imagined, but here we are anorexic, bulimic, stressed and depressed in this age of entitlement and anxiety.

Can there be any wonder that our children are the big losers?

The family, such as it is now, is as often as not made up of a single parent working at one, two or even three jobs just to make ends meet. This situation is also occurring at a time of rapidly diminishing salaries, the shortfall between what is coming in and what is going out frequently resulting in the accumulation of debt. When at home, the parent is usually exhausted and not present, so the child is mostly left to his own devices, leading generally to the child sitting in front of a computer screen for hours on end. The key messages being relentlessly broadcast are that success in life is spelled MONEY and that our one and only true responsibility is to consume the products of a machine which churns them out at a rate of tons a minute.

Boys, it seems, are particularly susceptible to these messages. Boys also develop and mature more slowly than girls and need more attention from fully engaged fathers. When this relationship is missing, as it so often is, it is not too hard to see why boys would seek out the male companionship of others, not infrequently in gangs — some of them criminal — in a misguided attempt to satisfy a deep-seated hunger.

Boys without fully engaged fathers as models, guides and mentors are set adrift without a rudder or a sense of direction.

Boys do not learn much from words; rather, they learn by example. In other words, don't tell me; show me!

Ken Kirkby
Canadian Painter
Son of an exceptional father and father of a fine son

Glossary of Terms

(Definitions from Webster's New World Dictionary & The Free Dictionary-Online)

1. Androgyny:
   a. I am using this word in this way: to illustrate or refer to a blending of masculine or feminine roles and traits that distinguish neither gender

2. Characteristic:
   a. (adj) Being a feature that helps to distinguish a person or thing: for example: "I heard this characteristic laugh" or "The stripes that are characteristic of the zebra."
   b. A distinguishing trait, feature, or quality a peculiarity
   c. (n) A distinguishing feature or quality. For example: Generosity is his chief characteristic.

3. Competent:
   a. Well qualified; capable; fit

4. Confident:
   a. Assured; certain of oneself

5. Contentment:
   a. The state, quality, or fact of being contented; satisfying or being satisfied

6. Culture
   a. The ideas, customs, skills, etc. of a given people in a given period; civilization

7. Gender:
   a. Describes a social role
   b. A reference to "he" or "she" meaning male or female

    c. A gender role-a set of perceived behavioural norms associated particularly with males and females in a given group or system. It can be a form of division of labour by gender.

8. Homogenous:
   a. Having similarity in structure because of common descent

9. Humanity:
   a. The fact or quality of being human; human nature; human qualities and characteristics.

10. Innate:
    a. Existing naturally rather than acquired
    b. That which seems to have been in one since birth
    c. That which belongs to something as a part of its nature or constitution

11. Instincts:
    a. An inborn tendency to behave in a way characteristic of a species (human in this case); natural; not an acquired mode of response to stimuli. For example, suckling, as an infant; spawning, as with salmon; birds that fly south without ever having travelled that route before; blinking when something comes near our eyes
    b. An innate capability or aptitude
    c. An inherited tendency of an organism to behave in a certain way, usually in reaction to its environment and for the purpose of fulfilling a specific need.

12. Intrinsic:
    a. belonging to the real nature of a thing; not dependent on external circumstances; essential; inherent
    b. located within, or exclusively of, a part Intuition:
    c. The direct knowing or learning (as in become aware of) something without conscious use of reasoning; immediate comprehension or understanding

    d. (n) a keen and quick insight

    e. The quality or ability of having such direct perception or quick insight

    f. Pure, untaught, non-inferential knowledge

    g. A sense of something not evident or deductible; an impression

13. Manhood:

    a. The state or time of being a man; manly character or qualities such as virility, courage, resolution, etc.; men collectively

14. Misogynist:

    a. Someone who has a hatred of women especially by a man

15. Primal:

    a. first in time; original; primitive; primeval

    b. first in importance; chief; primary

16. Resolution:

    a. resolving, or determining; deciding;

    b. the thing determined upon; a decision as to future action; resolve

17. Sexes:

    a. All the attributes by which males and females are divided

18. Trait:

    a. A distinguishing quality or characteristic, as of personality

The Back Cover and Its Significance

All the while I was writing this book, I believed the moment would come when I would know what to put on its cover... that I would be guided to something beyond what I alone could conceive. And I was right.

On a motorcycle trip up North with my buddy, coming around a particularly beautiful corner of the road, I saw a figure made of stone – one that looked like a human with its arms outstretched ... welcoming, inviting and meaningful.

Instantly I knew that this was the image that must be on the cover for it conveyed to me of all the messages and understandings I wanted to share.

I couldn't wait to find out more about this powerful, peaceful figure that presented itself as my answer. It was an Inukshuk ... and here is what I found out from a small company called Wee Gates – dedicated to helping people and our environment: Inukshuk, pronounced in-ook-shook, are stone monuments erected in the image of humans. One of their purposes was to communicate direction in the harsh and desolate Arctic. As such they were instruments for survival, and symbolic of the unselfish acts of a nomadic people – the Inuit – who built them as guides to make the way easier and safer for those who followed.

The hands of many and the efforts of an entire group were required to build these massive stone sculptures. They are the result of a consensus of purpose, of focused action by a group united in its goal and labour. The Inukshuk are the product of cooperation, teaching us that as good as our individual efforts may be, together we can do even greater things.

Each stone in an Inukshuk is a separate entity. Each supports, and is supported by the one above and the below it... no piece is any more, or less important than the next. Its strength lies in its unity. Its significance comes from its meaning as a whole. What is true about the Inukshuk is true about people. Each individual alone has significance. As part of a team or family, each of us supports and is supported by another. As human beings we are united by our common goals and together we are part of a greater whole.

The stones that make up the Inukshuk are secured through balance. They are chosen for how well they fit together. Looking at the structure it can be easily seen that the removal of even one stone will destroy the integrity of the whole. So, too, with a team or family. Each individual is necessary for the realization of the groups' purpose. The removal of even one person will result in the weakening of the structure. What holds the team/family together is the balance – the complementary nature of the individual skills.

The Inukshuk are a symbol of the human spirit. They recognize our ability to succeed with others, where we would fail alone. They remind us of our need to belong to something greater than ourselves. They reinforce our ability to commit to common goals.

The Inukshuk celebrate our working together. They continue to remind us of our inter-dependent responsibilities to invest our efforts today, to direct a better way for all of us tomorrow.

Today, the Inukshuk are a tangible symbol of communication – a universal means of speaking about our concerns for one another, and our dependence on one another. Because of their history, they convey the importance of personal contribution, responsible environmental leadership, and an invitation to speak with one another on a higher level about what really matters.

Everyone needs to know they are making a difference… in their jobs, to their colleagues, to whatever tasks they devote their time, energy and enthusiasm. Inukshuk act as a reminder to all of us that our efforts are appreciated, and that

> *"The difference we make today counts in all our tomorrows."*
> C.H. Pearce

I am truly grateful for the journey that the writing of this book has offered me.

May you be inspired by the journey it may take you on, and may we all be Inukshuk in our families and relationships.

Preface

TRUE: Men are very confused about the role(s) they play in today's world. Our socially ingrained roles are those of the protector, provider, hunter, competitor and the warrior. Men are expected to take the "bullet" for the family. Yet those roles and their importance to men as a natural content of who they are are changing faster than they can evolve or adapt. They are left with unanswered questions about their importance and value in their homes and communities.

Where do they fit in now? They are expected to be warriors in the workplace and work to better the standards for their families and themselves, yet also be caregivers and nurturers in the family home.

There is no blame attached to this statement. This is not about "us and them" or who is at fault because they, as men, are confused about their roles in their society. There is no "right or wrong" or "good or bad" to be decided. This is simply a statement expressing concern about what is happening currently, and it is not good for any of us.

Consequently, men are responding in one of three ways:

1. Many are choosing to ignore the roles that have been a part of them since time began. They are less involved with family and often just walk away because of the inner turmoil of not fulfilling their male destinies, while at the same time, being encouraged to behave as someone other than who they are.
2. Some men have just given up trying to maintain, so they "give in to get along" and in doing so don't experience that sense of value and connectedness and leadership in their families that is vital to the male ego, which is likely one of the three most fragile things in the world today.
3. Still others, who have decided to stay and fight the ever-changing expectations, become polarized and aggressive. Some become violent in their opposition to change. Some, in the extreme, become misogynistic.

Change is inevitable. It is the only constant I can think of. As men in the world, they have tried a variety of ways to get by. In truth, the only way for them to get by is to stop complaining about how things are and begin to change how they choose to deal with the "new rules." There is much that can be done. Todays men can change how they see the world they live in and how they live in the world they see. Attitudes such as tolerance and acceptance can be learned and practiced. This doesn't mean giving in or giving up anything. It means moving on and sharing the world with those around them. Men, at any time, can decide to live their lives with a focus on their time granted roles and do it with dignity, passion, compassion and self-respect. They can decide that happiness is a way of being and not a way of living.

After many years of doing this work, I have come to understand there are four areas of life that can be seen as life altering. Those choosing to work at changing how they function in those areas are likely to experience more peace, happiness and fulfillment in their daily lives.

If it is good for us, it will be good for those around us.

All the best,
Jim

Who Knew? Would You Be Ready?

Why Me And Why Now?

The phone rang and rang. It seemed as though I had just nicely closed my eyes and it started. I picked it up and growled, "It's your dime . . ." There was dead silence and then I heard the words that would change the course of my life as I had known it. He had my attention. He said it again and I thought that this was a joke of some kind – and a poor one at that.

It is amazing how fast your mind can process information – especially the type that is unwanted – and there is nowhere to hide in your head. Finally I settled on the idea that this was, indeed, a dream or a nightmare, whichever, and that I needed to do something to wake up and end it all. So I bit myself and watched as a trickle of blood came to the surface. My hands stopped working. I dropped the phone on the floor as I realized that this was no dream or nightmare. This was real, and the message was real too.

I stooped to pick up the phone as my friend and personal physician, John, said it one more time. "I'm so sorry Jim. I have checked the results three times and each report said the same thing. It is the kind of thing that will not produce a great deal of discomfort but it will happen and there is nothing to be done about it. I can and will, of course, do all I can to make it easier but 12 to 18 months is tops. There is no question. I'm shocked and so sorry. I need you to . . ."

I hung up the phone at that point. I had no idea of where to go, what to do, whom to see or not see. How does one prepare to die? Really. I did what most would do I guess and asked aloud, "Why me and why now?" Should I be angry and at whom? Should I feel sorry for myself? What will it be like?

I passed the rest of the afternoon sitting on my front porch watching the world go by and seeing nothing. How many afternoons do I have left? There is nowhere to run.

I looked up the street and saw the cruiser coming this way. It stopped in front of the next door neighbours' house. The officer got out and let the guy in the back seat out as well. I watched him shake his head at the passenger and then escort him up the walk to the front door. It was the kid who lived next door with his mother. Nice woman, a single parent, with her hands full of trouble. The problem moving up the walk was called Jacob, her son. She opened the door and began to speak. Nothing came out. She just stood there and then turned around to go back into the house.

This was not the first time he had come home like this and I doubted it would be the last. The officer said something to Jacob and then returned to his car and drove off. Jacob noticed me then. He looked at me, shrugged his shoulders with kind of a smirk as if to say, "No big deal." I felt as though I wanted to walk over to him and cuff him upside his head and say to him, "Hey, you little twit. Do you have any idea of the precious gift you are wasting? If you don't want it, give it to me. I'll gladly take it." Obviously, I couldn't do that, but I sure wanted to.

The days began to roll by. I thought of all the ways I could to try to slow down time, but we know that that can't be done. I began to settle into a state of reality mixed with a modicum of acceptance.

A good friend became aware of the situation and was very helpful, although he would never know just how helpful. He asked me one day when we were sitting out front if I had identified "my mark."

"Yeah," he said, "You know: How do you want to be seen by others? How do you want to be remembered by your peers? Hey, sorry. I'm not trying to embarrass you or upset you. I always understood that it was important to identify your mark, to think about what contribution to the world you feel good about making during your time here?"

I was incredulous to say the least. "What! I'm still here yet you ask me that! Isn't that for the world to determine AFTER I am no longer taking a breath on the planet?" I asked.

He simply looked at me and said, "Actually, no, it's not. It's up to you to decide BEFORE you leave us." With that, he said, "I have to go, but think about it."

I began to consider men that I had known who had given up on their dreams. Most went on to be resentful, angry, non-caring even violent people who believed they had nothing to pass on to their families and especially their sons.

Over the next few days I continued to think about his remark. That was all I thought about actually, and he was right. It was the best question that anyone could have asked me, as it turned out.

What's So Important About Leaving My Mark?

As a man, I have come to understand the importance of leaving a 'mark' on the world I live in. It is primal in its nature and a driving force for many of us. How do I want to be remembered by those I leave behind? Did my life mean anything? Did I make any kind of contribution to the community I lived in? Did I leave this earth in any way better than how I found it?

Our purpose, then, is to have purpose. As a man I need to go knowing that I accomplished this in some way. I hope it will make my passing easier and in some way gratifying. I'm not looking forward to the day, but I know it will come.

As I was focused on this thought, Annie, the woman next door, came out of her house, went down the sidewalk and started to walk toward me. Lately, I had begun to notice the beauty in the simplest things like flowers and clouds and children playing and squealing with delight and excitement. Even the rain was beautiful. So I noticed how attractive Annie was, yet she walked with the burden of ages upon her. Up my sidewalk she walked and then stopped at the top of the stairs. She was nervous and a bit embarrassed, it seemed.

"Have a seat" I said. "Can I get you something?" She just sat there quietly, so I let her have all the time she needed. Finally she said, "I have this question to ask you and I'm not sure how to ask it."

"Well, the easiest way would be to just put it out there," I remarked.

But she couldn't do it. Instead she began to talk about what it is like being a single parent and a mother and how difficult it is trying to be all things to her son, Jacob. She spoke about how she came to be a single parent three years ago and how Jacob had taken the news.

"That's when it all began," she said. "He has been so angry and so uncaring ever since then. He has forgotten how to be a kid. He has marched right into a form of adulthood that he is ill-equipped to deal with. I am frightened for him, yet I don't know any way to love him more or how to ease his pain. He is becoming a man and I can't help him now."

I was beginning to get an odd feeling about where all this was going, but I let her continue. She rattled on for a bit about the police bringing him home at all hours and his not attending school. Then she said, with a mixture of dread and embarrassment in her voice, "He is only

11

seventeen, soon to be eighteen, but he thinks he is a man now, and part of what he needs to do is look after me."

And then she just rolled it out so quickly that I had to ask her to repeat what she had just said. So she repeated it: "Would you talk to him and try to make him see that he needs to do something different?"

I felt like saying are you nuts, lady? I don't know him and from what I have seen of him, I don't like him much either.

I knew I couldn't say that, of course, but I sure wanted to. Outside of a few close friends, I hadn't mentioned my fate to anyone, so there was no way she could know what was going on with me and just how full my plate really was, so I blurted out, "Well, what is it you had in mind exactly? I mean, why would he listen to me about anything especially given what you have just mentioned? I'm nothing to him and I'm not sure he'd really care to have me say anything."

We bandied about for a while and finally reached an agreement. I could see the desperation in her eyes. She was not going to take no for an answer, at least not without twisting my arm in a variety of different ways before giving up on the idea.

We agreed that she would talk to him and, if he agreed to talk to me, would I do it? I said I would, and she got up to leave. She looked at me as if she had just been tossed a life jacket in a raging sea. The panic was gone and the sadness had been replaced by hope.

What was I in for, I wondered? I thought about how I could get out of doing what I had agreed to do. I had too many other things that were more important now. Little did I know that that was just not true.

Days went by with no Jacob. Then a week and then another. I was beginning to feel as though I had dodged a bullet when, lo and behold, he showed up on my porch one afternoon. There he was waiting for me before I had returned from seeing John. I was not in a mood to see anyone, let alone this kid, but my word is my word so I asked "What, no school today?"

He came back without missing a beat. "What's that to you? he snapped. "I knew this was a bogus idea. See ya."

Again that attitude. He wore it like an armour of sorts. He kept the world at arm's length with it. He started to get up, and I said, "You're here now and you came for something. Have a seat. Sorry to jump on you. Just a bad day, I guess."

He hesitated then sat back down. We sat in silence for what seemed an age and then I asked, "So you showed up. Why?"

He said he had made a promise to his mother and didn't like to let her down. He also threw in that he didn't think this was going anywhere in particular, but at least he could say he had done what he promised. This exchange was not a very positive way to begin a conversation, but I thanked him for his honesty.

I noticed the paper had arrived, so I picked it up and turned to the sports page. I had to find some kind of common ground to talk about. Perhaps he was a fan of some kind. Being a Yankee fan, I made some comment about the team finally winning it all this year, and he declared he was a Mets fan.

I said, "Sorry for your luck."

He looked at me and then just grinned. Not for long though. It was as if he remembered how angry he was supposed to be and came right back with this jibe: "At least we don't buy our championships."

This beginning led to an hour of going back and forth with "yeah, buts" and then he stood to go. But instead of moving to the stairs, he just stood there. It was as if he was waiting for me to ask him back or something. I said that I had enjoyed his point of view although I didn't agree and that if he ever wanted to come back for another round he was welcome to do that. I never thought he would, but again he surprised me.

The following week on the same day he showed up, only this time he was more prepared to do battle with me. We actually ended the day with another open-ended invitation. And again he showed up the next week. He seemed more relaxed. Perhaps he returned because I didn't ask about school or challenge him about anything. The conversations were becoming more open and wide ranging. We talked about other things besides the Yanks and the Mets.

Then I took a chance and asked him if he missed going to games without his dad to join him. He looked at me as if I had jabbed him with a sharp stick. His eyes welled up some and he tried to turn his head away. He did not want to show me how vulnerable he was. He was trying to be tough at all times. "Real men don't cry" was the message I got. I wished I hadn't asked him but, like toothpaste out of the tube, once out there is no going back in.

The silence was deafening and then he just got up and left without another word. I let him go. The next week came and went. Jacob was a no-show. I wondered if he was ill or maybe he was done with our chats. Funny thing, though, for a kid I didn't much care for I had come to appreciate him a bit more. Certainly he was hurting. Of this there was no doubt. There was something else, though.

He's a lost soul was the thought that kept creeping back to me. I felt sad for him then. He was too young to experience that every day. I was beginning to understand that he had a great deal to offer the world he lived in. He did have an interesting sense of humour. He did enjoy a lively debate and he was aware of many things. But there was much more he didn't know. There was much he would need to know if he was going to survive in this world as a man.

Was this my way of leaving my mark on the world? Could I help him understand what manhood was really about? Had I learned enough to be a guide to him, to be a mentor of sorts? Would he even be open to me playing that role?

The world is changing so fast. It has become so difficult for us men to keep up with the new rules of engagement and the expectations that are being made of us. Suddenly, at a time when MY life was supposed to be getting simpler, it was becoming much more complicated.

So Much To Learn And So Little Time

Here I am thinking about this subject matter and Jacob hasn't even returned, let alone asked for any mentoring. The likelihood is that he will just move on and not much more will come of this. But, as he has in the past and continues to do, he surprised me.

The following week he was walking past my walkway and then stopped. He looked at me sitting there and then asked if he could talk to me for a minute. When invited to do so he came up and sat down. He apologized for not showing up last week, but the question I asked he said, bothered him so much he didn't know what to do or how to respond. He was both angry with me for asking it and grateful that someone had bothered to notice his pain and anger about not having a dad. I was going to apologize myself but then something told me to shut up. I thought that the best thing to do was to say nothing at all. It struck me, however, that here sat this angry kid who really didn't seem to be connected nor did he appear to feel it necessary to be connected to anything or anyone. But he was willing to put himself out there, to take a chance, for some reason.

14

He didn't know much about me yet I felt as though he might be willing to open up just a bit perhaps because I had mentioned or noticed how he felt about not having a father. Most folks just got angry with him for who he was and what he did, but I didn't do that. He admitted how lost he feels at times. He just blew me away with his honesty. This is a kid who wants the world to believe that he is a man because of his manly behaviour yet he could easily turn the tap on and share for hours what is going on with him.

I needed to be careful not to let that happen here. He did need to talk about it – of that there was no question – and he seemed ready to do so. But I have seen people bare their souls and, after having done so, had been so ashamed and guilty and embarrassed that they shut right down again. I did not want that to happen to Jacob. I wasn't sure why I felt like that. I just did. He was on the edge of something that would either envelop him or free him. I wanted him to be free: free to learn, free to feel, free to think and free to grow into manhood and to understand his roles and responsibility as a man in the world.

Some would say it's a death sentence. I say it's a privilege.

He had taken his chances with me and now I needed to take my chances with him. I said to him, "Jacob, I have come to know a bit about you. Probably enough to know that you are not the person who wants to end up coming home in the back of a police car once a week. And I know enough to say that you love your mom and that what she thinks of you is very important to you. I also know that you are bright, intelligent and articulate although I'm not sure where you got that from. That's a joke, by the way."

He just looked at me with large eyes, so I continued. "So I have an offer to make to you. There's no need to answer right now, but if you accept my offer there are some provisions attached. If you don't honour the provisions then the deal is off. Capiche?"

He stared off down the street and then nodded for me to continue. "I will meet with you once a month for 12 months, right here. Each month we will discuss something different about being a man in the world today. For example: to understand and accept the historically expected roles that are a part of who we are and how do we exist in this world that is changing so quickly when we can barely keep up? How do we do it and maintain our dignity, our integrity, our passion for living and our compassion for our fellow planet dwellers?

"You know, Jacob, some men have begun to apologize for being a man. That's utter nonsense and that needs to stop and now. To a great number of people we are the bad guys. As men, we need to get back to feeling relevant and to celebrating and honouring our maleness. Other topics will come from these, to be sure. Ask all the questions you want or need to, and I will try to answer them if I can.

"The provisions are these: You will attend school on a regular basis, starting tomorrow. No more rides home from the local police department. There will be some work for you to do each month, so my expectations are that that will be done before you come to see me each month. I will take this very seriously, and my hope is that you will too. You can get out of this anytime you want. Just don't show up and I will know that you want out of our deal. No hard feelings on either of our parts.

"The last thing that I need you to understand is that I am, in no way, trying to be your father or to replace him in any way. That is not my intent here. You have a father and unfortunately he is not able to be with you now. Perhaps you can honour him by becoming the man he would want you to be. If you choose, I can help you along that path. That's it—that's the deal.

"Take some time to think about it. I know it's a big decision. If you decide not to do it, that's OK. I'll understand, with no hard feelings. If you decide to do it, then we can start next week. You pick a day that works for you and I'll fit it in. Now go home. I have things to do."

Let The Journey Begin

Jacob took a day or two to get back to me. When he did, he said that he had given this a great deal of thought but had decided that he knew enough already and would not be sitting with me to discuss this manhood stuff.

I said, "I can live with that, and good for you that you know all about your manhood and what it means to be a man. Perhaps you could enlighten me before you go."

He stood there and looked at me as though I had two heads. He began to stammer and sputter and then stopped.

What I realized was that he had no clue about any of this. Likely what he thought he knew to be true came from some second- or third-hand conversation he'd overheard. Most young men get their information about what it means to be a man from movies, porn flicks, some uncle who is "cool," magazine articles, ads on television and so on. They have not had the benefit of listening to the wisdom of men who have lived their lives and have found the truth through experience and observation. What I saw in Jacob's eyes was fear and embarrassment, which are two powerful emotions that drive many men to run or to cover up with bravado or a show of non-interest.

I looked at him and simply said, "It's OK. I get it. However, if you're good with this the way it is, so be it. One thing that you will need to understand is that admitting you need to know more about something before you can make a decision is a sign of strength not weakness. This is something that successful men understand and something that they do. One of the characteristics that excites us is that we are knowledge seekers. We need to know how things work and how we can do it faster or better the next time. But, hey, you already know that right?"

I left him standing there hoping he'd think about what I had said. I went in the house and when I came back out he was sitting in a chair on the porch. He looked at me and said, "When do we start?"

"I'm thinking tomorrow," I said. "Right then, I'll see you at four o'clock and don't come empty handed." He just grinned, got up and started to leave. He turned around and said, "Thanks for the first lesson." With that, he trotted down the steps and back home.

Day One

True to his word, he was on time the next day and he did not come empty handed either. In another lifetime I would invest in a coffee joint that sold donuts. He consumed his favourites during his visit, and I had the others.

We shared some light and easy conversation and then I got down to business. "I'm new at this too, but I think this is the way we need to go. I'll do the talking and you do the listening. If you have a question – and I sincerely hope you do – let me know. Don't wait till the end of the day. Just let me know, OK?" He nodded and on we went.

"The one thing that seems to get us into trouble most quickly is the words we use to express ourselves, not only as people but as men in the world. At the best of times, men and women don't speak the same language. I'm amazed sometimes that we ever make ourselves understood to each other at all. Oh, we use the same words, but the meaning attached to them is often interpreted differently. What we mean is sometimes misunderstood.

17

"I guess that's why it is so important to treat each other with respect. That way we don't take offence to what each is saying. If we respect each other, it is easier to accept the idea that we would not, deliberately, say anything to hurt or to upset the other. This comes with trust – but I am getting ahead of myself. What I am saying is our conversations are not meant to be about "us vs. them" and not about "good vs. bad" and not about "right vs. wrong.""

"Our conversations will be about what it is like to be a man in today's world. Things have changed dramatically for us as men. The changes are occurring so fast that it is difficult for us to keep up with things. The expectations that come with all of these changes are very confusing and, in many cases, go completely against who we are or what we would naturally do in response. Are we supposed to be this or are we supposed to do that? How are we supposed to act in one situation and yet exhibit a whole different set of skills or behaviours in a different setting or circumstance? Where do we fit in, or do we?

"If we, as men, are to survive and to be a part of this new world, we need to understand what the changes that have come and those that are coming will mean for us and how far we are willing to go before we say, "That's far enough."

I stopped and looked at him for a moment then said, "Are you with me so far?"

He responded by saying "Yeah, I think I get the point, but where are you going here?"

"OK," I said, "let me go at it this way."

Be Careful Of Absolutes

Have you ever heard this expression: "You can take the dog out of the hunt but you can't take the hunt out of the dog"? Jacob looked at me hesitantly, so I went on. "Some dogs have a special aptitude for hunting, tracking, herding, retrieving or swimming. When they are born, it seems as though it's second nature for them to do certain things. Over the years there have been many discussions regarding how or why this happens. The modern-day thinking is based on a question about whether or not it is nature or nurture that is responsible for shaping these characteristics in us. Are we born to do certain things or are we taught, encouraged and nurtured in a certain way and therefore we learn these things. I don't want to get into that discussion here. We can at some other time if you wish to but I don't think it's important for you to know which is which right now."

"What is important is that you understand that men and women are like that too. Men tend to exhibit qualities and characteristics like being the protector, provider, warrior, decision maker, hunter, competitor and the one who steps in front of the family to 'take the bullet.' These are roles that most men appear to assume or demonstrate naturally.

"We need to be careful here about using words that suggest absolutes. Not ALL men do this. Not ALL women are caregivers and nurturers and not ALL women are concerned with and assume the responsibility for making sure that home is what is most important to the family. His castle and her nest? I'm not completely certain. Not ALL women are great communicators and arbiters who try to ensure that there is harmony in her home, but a good number are. They seem to come by these characteristics and the associated skill sets that enable them to perform these monumental tasks naturally. Kids who need some love and care or a bandage on a cut are drawn to mom. So for the sake of our conversations let's say that these roles and characteristics have been associated with men and women since the beginning of time. Are you good with that?"

"Yeah, I'm good with that," he said, "but I still don't get why it is important. I get the bit about the dog. That makes some sense. It's the rest that leaves me confused. I mean who needs to care about that stuff anyway?"

I stopped to think this through for a moment or two before continuing. "If we have no idea of where we came from or what has changed, then how can we possibly know where we need to go or how we'll get there?"

"I suppose that's a good point," he said begrudgingly.

"Now these are simple examples – and there are many others that are much more complicated - but I hope that clears up some of what was bothering you. Hang in there because it does and will get easier to understand. Remember that most of this stuff is new information, so it will likely take some time for you to get your head around some of it.

"Let me finish this point off. Just because we demonstrate different roles and we see the world differently doesn't mean that one is better or more important than the other or should be treated differently. I have always supported and believed in the idea of equal work and equal pay, for instance. If a woman can do the job as well as or better than a man, then she should most definitely be paid the same wage. She needs to perform at the same level as her male counterpart and understand that there won't be any special consideration for her because she is female.

"We are both human beings and need to be treated that way. If any man gets upset by this, then he needs to go and get more skilled or work smarter so that he can compete for that position instead of assuming it will come to him strictly because he is male.

"Women need to have the same rights as men have in the workplace, in society and at home. There is no question about that. But my concern is that the swing from the way it was to the way folks want it to be is happening far too quickly. Men are finding it extremely difficult to understand what's expected now, let alone accept it all. We can't assimilate the new standards into our daily lives as quickly as expected.

"Let's try to remember the time-honoured roles by which we each operate. You cannot take the hunting instinct out of a dog just because you want the dog to be something else. It is what it is. You can teach it to do other things, and that training takes time, but the time granted qualities and characteristics will be there, no matter what.

I wanted to continue in this vein and tell him that today men are becoming angry and resentful. We are resisting the rate of change and the scope of the new expectations that are being thrust upon us. Young men and older men alike are standing up and are saying, "Whoa, enough! What's been going on for centuries is not going to change in a few decades. This is going to take time and dialogue if we are all to survive it."

Some men are feeling as though they have to be one thing on the inside of their homes, yet when they walk through that door to go to work they are supposed to assume other roles, those that are admittedly more natural and comfortable. On the inside of the door we are supposed to be more caring and nurturing, to assume more of the household duties and be more of a Mister Mom kind of guy.

When we go to work, we are supposed to assume the roles of provider, warrior and competitor. We are expected to work hard and climb the ladder so that our family can have more stuff, including security and opportunity, and enjoy a higher standard of living. When we return at the end of the day and walk through that two-inch door to re-enter our homes we are expected to demonstrate our feminine side and become more nurturing and care giving so that we can fit in to the new world that is emerging complete with its growing expectations of what is now appropriate.

I want him to understand that mom is becoming more like dad and dad is expected to be more like mom. Androgyny is looming just around the corner. Mom is finding it difficult not only to handle a second job but also to manage the nest at the same time.

Something has to give, and it seems as though it is supposed to be dad's natural role or roles, the socially ingrained ones that have guided men for centuries. We still want to be seen by our families as the provider, the hunter and the protector. I want my sons and daughters to know that I am the warrior and the competitor and that the buck stops at my desk.

The conditions under which our homes function – what is acceptable and what is not – can be determined through consultation and mutual respect, not power and control. But these lines are blurred and more confusing now. Men are becoming overwhelmed with the stated need to "get with it." I take that phrase to mean we need to set aside our old ways and get with the new more progressive way of doing things.

My response to that is to witness how the state of the family has deteriorated. The proof exists that this is not a particularly good way to go. Many men are struggling to preserve their inclination to lead and be held accountable for safety and respect in their family home. Now men are saying, 'Forget it. It is not going to happen, at least not this way.

I asked Jacob if any of this felt familiar. He looked shell shocked. I thought that perhaps I had overloaded him with information and ideas that went over his head, but instead he just nodded. He looked more astounded than he did anything else. It was as if he was asking me, with his eyes, how I knew what he was thinking and feeling at that exact moment.

"To be honest," he said, "I don't know how I am supposed to feel about any of this. Part of me has specific thoughts and feelings and then I hear that that is "old school" and that times have changed and I need to change with them. Girls that I know and my male friends don't talk about this kind of thing very much. Why can't things just be simple? I like you and you like me. Let's get together and have some fun. Why do there have to be all these rules about who does what to whom and why?"

That was exactly my point, I thought.

I continued on. "I was on the Internet the other night and came across this article which listed some of the seemingly double standards that often occur:

21

a. If you put a woman on a pedestal and try to protect her from the rat race you are considered to be a male chauvinist.

b. If you stay at home and do the housework, you are a pansy. If you work too hard, there is never enough time for her and the family. If you don't work hard enough, then you are seen as a good-for–nothing bum or someone who doesn't care

c. If she has a boring, repetitive job with low pay, this is exploitation. If a man has a boring repetitive job with low pay, he should get off his backside and find something better

d. If you get a job ahead of her, that is favoritism. If she gets a job ahead of you, that is equal opportunity

e. If you make a decision without consulting her, you are a chauvinist. If she makes a decision without consulting you, she is a liberated woman

f. If you ask her to do something that she doesn't enjoy, that's called domination or exploitation. If she asks you to do something that you don't enjoy, that is about doing her a favour.

g. If you buy her some nice flowers, you must have done something wrong or you want something. If you don't, then you are not thoughtful.

"Remember this is not about right or wrong. Rather, this is about how things are changing, and men are being expected to change with the times but not question or even agree that it's OK. They should just do it and move on

"Unfortunately," I continued, "there are men who are fed up and are fighting back, sometimes literally. They are becoming more violent in their resistance and more demanding and control-hungry. They want to protect the old days and ways when at least they understood what was expected of them and times were more stable and consistent. I am not saying those times were better, but I am saying the expectations were consistent and therefore easier to understand. The boundaries were clear and the expectations were clear as well.

"Some men are just giving up and are 'going along to get along.' Still others are just walking away, physically, mentally, emotionally or a combination of each. In some cases, they are abandoning their families and their homes because they find the whole business too difficult to navigate.

"This creates a whole other problem that will come up later, but it has to do with young men growing up in fatherless homes with no role models to emulate. I know that it has been difficult for you, Jacob, and I hope that our conversations will somehow make it a bit easier for you so that when your time comes to be a dad you will be better prepared."

He just nodded at me. He seemed to do that a lot.

"That's it for me. I'm tired, I said. "I can't think that you have too much more space up there for any more stuff right now. So this is what I would like you to do. Go get a blank book to write in. It will be like a diary, so don't leave it lying around. It's not for me to read, but for you to read. I hope that you will read it again and again because each time you do there will be more for you to learn. Each week I will ask you to do certain things based on the discussions that we have had. Questions to answer and such.

"My thoughts are that you will have a month to deal with them and will come to our next time together with that work done. You good with that?"

He said he was not very good about doing that kind of stuff. I explained how it is much more powerful when you write things out and for him to try it. If he didn't like doing it, then we'd do something else. Jacob likes to have that option rather than follow any orders.

"OK. This is what I would like you to do. Draw a line on the page and put the numbers from 1-10 on the line like this:

1	2	3	4	5	6	7	8	9	10

Now mark on the line how comfortable you are, right now, today, when you think about being male. Put today's date below the mark you make. Write your thoughts about the following questions – don't be shy about this – and be honest:

1. What would need to happen for you to be able to move that mark on the line up one number?
2. What would be the benefit of getting to a higher number?
3. How do you want other people to see you as a male? (point form would work)
4. What does the word 'manhood' mean to you?

"The next time we get together we will take a look at self-esteem and the vital part it plays in our happiness and our maleness. It is one of the keys to everything that will follow regarding your happiness and satisfaction with the world you live in. We can't change what is happening, but we sure can change how we respond to it and how we can keep our dignity and our self-value and still be OK with what is going on around us. Say hello to your mother for me."

SELF-ESTEEM:
The First Of The Four Cornerstones

You Are Who You Think You Are

I was actually looking forward to my next meeting with Jacob. I just didn't know if he felt the same. This whole thing had started out by chance and certainly was not by my design either, but the teaching/learning process was moving in a different direction than what I had thought it would. I was seeing Jacob differently, as well, which was a bit confusing for me. Was I feeling a bit guilty thinking that I was using him in some way for what I myself needed to get before I reached the evening of my day, so to speak? I would need to stay focused on what the real purpose of this mentoring thing was actually meant to be about.

He returned, as we had agreed. Jacob had, to date, lived up to his end of the deal. He showed me what he had done during the time between our previous visit and now. He had worked hard and I told him so. He had been diligent, and I told him I was proud of him for that too. It was apparent that some of the information I had provided had gone over his head, but for the most part he had grabbed the gist of it pretty well. I assured him that at the end of our time together it would all make sense to him. He relaxed some at that point, and soon we were ready to go at it again.

"Tell me what you know about manhood or being male?" I asked. He fed me back some description of what a man does and then gave me some of the information that I had given him last time we had been together. As I suspected he would, he had missed the part about recognizing and accepting particular qualities and roles that seem to be more natural to us than others.

"Manhood is about how we feel as men in the world, I said, "and how that shows up in our everyday behaviour and actions. It's about being true to our socially ingrained roles and the expectations of us that are attached to them. These roles and expectations are, for some, considered to be our driving force. The idea of manhood is not about power and control, but it is about feeling good concerning who we are in the world and how we are responsible to live our lives according to those very principles and ideals.

"In essence, it is about developing and maintaining a positive sense of self, of who we are, and striving to be who we want to be. But that's easier said than done.

"As men we no longer are free to be who we want to be according to our nature; rather we are becoming a composite of what others believe we should be. Our self-esteem as men is and has been under assault by other folks who would see us change into who they would like us to be so that it is easier for them to get along with us.

"We do need to change some things, no doubt, but not at the expense of who we are, meaning our social identity. We will change some things because it is in our best interests to do so, not because someone legislates change or demands change from us. It will be because we see the value to ourselves and others in doing so. Understand that change by force or mandate is doomed to fail. It has never worked and it won't in this case either.

"This is key, Jacob. Remember this point as one of the four cornerstones necessary for men to build lives filled with dignity, passion, compassion and respect. If we are to be true to ourselves and find peace and harmony in the world we live in, we must manage these four areas with dedication and determination. Without a positive sense of self everything else seems hollow and unstable. It's like building a beautiful home on a pile of sand. It looks good on the outside but falls over during the first storm.

As men in and of the world we need to accept three things:

1. We cannot change the new rules that have been implemented, nor should we put a great deal of energy into trying to change them.
2. We need to abandon the idea that we are graded as men by how much money or how many toys we have. Money cannot purchase happiness, class or peace. So the pursuit of anything other than attaining comfort in our own skin is meaningless. These statements need to be our priority. We need to manage our humanity so that we can be strong yet flexible, passionate about something without compromising our principles, and mentally and emotionally tough enough to withstand most challenges that are surely to come our way;

3. We need to look and work within ourselves for our solutions. We have the skills, assets and personal resources that are necessary for us to manage our lives successfully utilizing and understanding our qualities and at the same time being flexible enough to accept some of what is being expected of us."

Again I felt as though he was not tracking me very well. How well did I know him? How far could I or should I go here? Will he get fed up with me talking to him, and does he really even care? So I asked him if he was good with what I had said. Did he have any questions? All this time he had not asked me one question—not one.

He was either really invested or incredibly bored, but I asked myself, why would he come back if he were bored? Maybe because of Annie, his mom. Silence fell. We just looked at one another. Then he said, "I feel so stupid. I feel like I should know all this stuff and I know nothing."

I said, "First of all, you are not stupid. It has taken me a lifetime to figure some of this stuff out and I still know only parts and pieces of it all. Jacob, listen well and please don't take offence at what I am about to say. I mean no malice and I am not being smug here. You want all the privileges of being a man, yet you don't want the responsibility that goes with that.

"There are dues to pay to get into this club, my friend, and you are not willing to pay them yet. I get that. You look at yourself and who is it you see? C'mon, who do you see?"

He thought for a bit and then said, "I see a guy who bull s— who cons his way through things he doesn't understand and everyone thinks he is cool. I see someone who is terribly unsure of what he is supposed to be doing and how is he supposed to be doing it. And I see someone who is pissed off because he got short changed. That's who I see."

"Yeah, I'd be pissed off too," I said, "but at least you have a parent who loves you and wants the best for you. If you think that what she did to get us together was easy, then you are up in your sleep, my friend. So you have two choices here. You can continue to learn about being a man in this world either from me or someone else who will be straight up with you. Whoever this is will need to help you to be stronger and work smarter with confidence knowing you understand the landscape, or you can continue to feel sorry for yourself and keep coming home in the back of police cars. Pick one."

"Screw you," he said and got up to leave.

I knew that I had gone way past the point of no return and way outside our comfort zone but my Irish was running at full speed now. I said to him with a look that would have burned a hole in a two by four, "You can run now like a boy who is trapped, or you can stay and discuss what is happening for you right now, like a man would do."

I stopped him in his tracks with that one. He tried to stare me down. We stood there eye to eye and nose to nose. To anyone walking, by we would have appeared as though we were waiting for pigeons to take roost. Finally, and by good luck and no planning, we both started to speak at the same time. Both of us had kept face. It's very important to us men to keep face. Any encounter becomes a competition of sorts, and we love to compete with each other. I deferred to him. Another minute went by. It seemed like an hour and I noticed for the first time that I was tired. Physically tired. I really needed to sit down but I couldn't until he made the first move.

This was a turning point in our relationship and we both seemed to know it. He looked at me and said, "Sorry, I didn't mean to be disrespectful. I guess I haven't buried all that after all."

"All what," I asked him.

"You know, stuff with my old man."

"You mean your father? How does he figure into this?"

He looked at me with conflict in his eyes. Not a physical kind but whether he wanted to go there.

Then he said, "He used to call me out all the time. He would call me a pussy and gutless because I wouldn't stand up to him. So when you got going I decided I wouldn't let that happen to me anymore so I pushed back. I shouldn't have taken my stuff out on you."

And with that, gratefully, he sat back down. I had dodged more than a bullet here and I knew it. I couldn't risk going there again, at least not until this relationship was a great deal stronger. My respect for Jacob had grown dramatically, however, and I thanked him for staying.

He didn't realize it at the time but he had just passed the first test that would propel him toward a state of manhood. He had set aside his pride and found a way to stay with his dignity and his ego intact. He just nodded. He likes to do that. I'm guessing it's his "cool" thing.

He looked at me and asked the first question: "Seeing how we are talking about it, what do YOU see when you look at me?"

What a loaded question to ask me. Did he trust me enough to answer it, or was this just residue from the anger he had felt a few minutes ago? "I'll answer that if you truly want me to, but I have to ask you this first. Are you absolutely sure that you want me to tell you? You shouldn't ask the question if you are not prepared to hear the answer."

"I asked", he said, "so, yes, I want to hear the answer."

"OK," I said, "When I look at you, I see a boy in a man's body. I see someone who has not finished grieving the loss of his father and someone who is just realizing that he will never receive or hear the wisdom that fathers owe their sons. You are angry at him and you miss him at the same time, so that must be very confusing for you.

"I see a boy struggling with incorporating the time honoured roles that he feels but doesn't understand as yet. They are powerful and relentless and confusing. What does a provider do or a protector or a competitor or a hunter, warrior, decision maker do? What does it mean to 'take the bullet for the family'? It feels as though you are missing something but don't know what. There are spaces or gaps in your very being that are empty, and you don't know how to fill them up."

"Perhaps that's why you act out and why you are so angry and come home in the cruiser. I see someone who is still ill equipped to assimilate them because he doesn't understand their significance or their importance. I see someone who is angry at the world – and perhaps with good reason – but can't find a way to make the anger go away.

You make decisions based on sheer emotion, with little or no experience or thought given to the outcomes when other people are concerned. You don't mean to hurt anyone. You are just being you. Right? I see someone who is lost in a sea of grief, anger and fear with no one who understands what you are going through and no one you can trust to guide you.

"On the other side of this coin, I see a young man who is intelligent, strong, determined and sincere. These are all the ingredients necessary to do the work to transition into a man's world and succeed. Understand this, Jacob. You are not alone nor do you have to be. But that is your choice, as it should be. Don't let anyone ever tell you that this experience is not possible for you and do not let them tell you that this is not important. It is vital in my mind.

"So here we are again," I said. "That's the short version, but please don't be overwhelmed by it all. There are a great number of young men who are where you are right now. There are many of us who have been where you are, and we did just fine. It is one of the most miraculous learning experiences you will ever be involved in. It will be one that you will pass on to your sons as well. I envy you that."

"Does that satisfy your question?" I asked.

When I looked at him he appeared different to me somehow. I'm not sure how—just different. Perhaps he looked a little more settled because someone took the time to see him for who he was on the inside. Maybe it was because someone had identified his restlessness and made some sense of it for him.

He looked at me and said, "I have another question for you."

I replied, "I have created a monster," and we both had a laugh.

"I hear friends and my girlfriend and teachers talking about self-esteem, but no one wants to define it or explain how you get it. So where does it come from? How do you get it? How will I know when I have it?"

"I like your stubbornness," I said. Then I followed with, "That's not a bad thing to have. In this case it's a very good thing. It means that you won't quit until you get what you want. Good for you." I continued on, "As I mentioned before, self-esteem is one of the four cornerstones of a healthy and happy human being. It is primary. True inner peace is not possible without a positive sense of self. It is not a disease that you get. Self-esteem is something that is worked on and we'll talk about some things that you can do to make this happen for yourself. It is solitary work, meaning that, although others can help you with some of the work, it is up to you and only you to develop it and to maintain it. That, to me, is the good news. Once you experience a positive sense of self, and you will know when that happens, you can keep it for as long as you want or you can give it away anytime you want. The choice is yours and only yours. As valuable as it is it is relatively easy to come by.

"We, as humans, think that because a problem is complicated so must be the solution. Not so. In fact, the easiest or simplest solutions are usually the right ones. Often times we overlook or do not consider the simple solutions that show themselves to us all the time."

Making It Grow

Anything that is built needs a solid foundation in order for the thing to stand. Self-esteem is like that too. Understand that you have all the assets, resources and skills you need. They are within you. Knowledge, information, talent and determination are all there for you to have what it is you seek. You just don't recognize them and you don't know how to use them but you will.

There are three basic parts that help create this foundation:

a. a feeling of competence-that we have the skills, the talents and the assets needed to get the job done
b. a feeling of confidence-that we are able and capable to deal with life as we live it or as it comes to us, and
c. a feeling that we are worthy of and deserve happiness.

Competence comes first. If you don't feel that you have enough skill, go take a course, talk to people who can help, learn what has to be learned and then apply that learning to the task at hand. Put yourself around positive people, those whom you consider to be successful and those who have what you want. Listen for what they know. With moderate success comes great competence.

Think about the first time you did anything. It was difficult but somehow you experienced some success. The next time you did the same thing you did it better and quicker. You begin to feel as though you could handle that same problem with little or no problem. You simply learn how to do it because you continue to try.

Confidence comes from the competence you develop in your skill levels. The more success you have the easier and less stressful is the job.

Feeling worthy is a bit more of a challenge because it has to do with expelling 'old tapes" of past efforts that weren't successful and being reminded that we will never get it right. We need to dismiss anyone — ANYONE — who cannot or will not support our efforts at improving the quality of our lives. If you are not with me then you must be against me is the rule here."

"This is how you make it grow. It is simple and it is basic," I said to him

He opened his mouth to ask another question, but I had to stop him mid-sentence. He was just getting started but, unfortunately, I was spent. I felt exhausted and this lethargy concerned me some. Perhaps I was just feeling the warmth of a beautiful southern spring day. Perhaps.

"Jacob, I need to ask a favour. Could we meet every two weeks instead of once per month. At least for a while. Something has come up for me and I need to attend to it. I will admit that I really do enjoy talking with you. It has surprised the hell out of me too, to be honest. So if it's OK with you, that's great. If you can't, then I will come up with something else that we can do."

He looked over and said, "Sure".

"Good," I said and that was it.

"Here's your assignment for the next two weeks. I want you to think about how this self-esteem stuff relates to us as men in the world. How does it help us cope with change and the rate of change according to the new rules?

Next draw a line and number the line as you did last week.

1	2	3	4	5	6	7	8	9	10

"Mark on the line how comfortable you are, right now, today, when you think about your level of confidence and competence in your abilities to deal with life on life's terms. Put today's date below the mark you make. Also put a mark on the scale using today's date that would indicate where you would like to be so that you could say "if it doesn't get any better than this, that would be great."

Then I would like you to spend some time answering these questions:

1. How would people around you know that you are feeling more positive about yourself? What would they see? What would they say is different about you?
2. How will a more positive sense of self-esteem and self-worth affect the quality of your life? What are some of the benefits?
3. Was there ever a time that you can remember when your sense of self-esteem and self-worth were higher/greater than they are now? If so, what was different then from now? If you recognize your self-esteem was lower than it is now, what do you think happened that affected your sense of self-esteem and self-worth?
4. During the times when you are feeling more positive, pay attention to who is around you, what you are doing and where you are. Write your answers down in your journal."

"We good?", I asked
"Yeah we're good," he said and trotted off down the walk.

In Pursuit Of A Life

U p until now I had often daydreamed about what I would do with a million dollars or if I knew that today was my last day on the planet, how I would I spend it. Those mental exercises had seemed distant and unreal and far away. Truthfully, I hadn't spent a great deal of time thinking about them since Jacob and I cut our deal. More recently, however, they had been creeping into my conscious mind more and more. They were not overwhelming yet, but they were certainly there more often. I recognized that when I felt the walls closing in a bit, I would "run" a little faster to try to stay ahead of the issue, I guess. So when Jeff dropped by later that evening, I wasn't ready to talk about what he wanted to know.

He asked, "How are you doing, really? I mean how are you DOING?"

I knew what he wanted to know but I just didn't understand about the "why is that important to you" part. I know that he cares about me. Perhaps it has to do with his own mortality."

"How does one do?" I asked him. "What am I supposed to be doing?"

He was curious about my life and how I was coping with it all. What did I do to get through my days? I hadn't told him much about my relationship with Jacob and what that was all about. I suppose I didn't know either, other than I enjoyed and looked forward to our conversations.

Jeff is a pretty bright guy and not a great deal slides past him so he asked, "So you are going to need to talk to someone about it all, don't you think?"

"About what?", I asked back.

"You know I love you like a brother, so don't blow smoke my way. I know when you are hurting and I know when you are concerned. Right now you are both. Maybe it would be a good time to go see Leo. When was the last time you saw him anyway?" he asked with concern in his voice.

"It's been a while. In case you haven't noticed I've been a bit distracted," I snapped back, perhaps too quickly. "Sorry, I'm just a bit worn out. Thanks for the reminder. I'll call him tonight before I turn in. It would be good to see him. Thanks."

We chatted a little longer. Then off he went. I had heard somewhere that you can gauge a man's value by the number and quality of his friends. I have been truly blessed in that regard, and Jeff is a shining example of that for me. I called Leo. He was surprised and pleased to hear from me. We agreed to meet the next day for coffee, his treat. It never turned out that way, but it was a running joke we shared.

We met as agreed. It was good to see him. Leo had been and remains, I suppose, a mentor to me. Everyone needs a mentor, someone who can be trusted implicitly concerning both confidence and honesty. There aren't many around, so I was blessed to have Leo in my life.

I suddenly realized that he didn't know. He had no idea about what had happened, the news I was about to bring him. How would I tell him? What would he say? How would he respond? We made small talk and then I just put it out there for him. He just sat there studying me. There was silence of course, but he was going over the implications in his head and at light speed.

He finally said, "How can I help? What do you need from me?"

True and pure Leo. I told him things that I had only thought about but never said aloud. I told him things that I had not yet thought in any depth because I was having difficulty putting words to them. Thoughts and ideas and feelings just spilled out, and I could not turn off the tap. He just sat there taking it all in. He knew, instinctively, that this is the way it needed to be right now.

And then I got to Jacob. I told him about how we had met and how I really didn't like the kid. He had an attitude, and it rubbed me wrong. He had the world by the cajonnes and he couldn't care less. He had no idea of what he had and it didn't seem to matter.

Finally Leo looked me in the eye and with that crooked smile of his said, "Gee, this kid sounds like some snot-nose know-it-all-guy I met a few years back. You remember him, don't you?"

Ouch. "Guilty," I said. What else could I say?

I eventually went on. "I'm struggling with the fact that the closer I get to death the more alive I feel. How ironic. I see the value in this kid. I see the hurt and the confusion and the ease with which he could be channeled off into a place where there is nothing but pain and grief. It doesn't have to be like that for him. He is bright and thoughtful underneath the hurt and anger and pain. He wants to learn but is also a prideful person. There is no one to turn to or to guide him into manhood. There is no one to challenge him and to help him understand

34

that he can be the author of his own story. There are experiences yet to be lived and that he had control over how most of them turned out."

I had to stop for a minute. I was excited talking to Leo about Jacob. I wondered aloud, "Am I using him for my own purpose? Damn it, Leo, it's not supposed to be like this. So many questions! There are times when I feel that I am getting too close to this to be as objective as I need to be. I can't own his outcomes, I understand that, but I look forward to talking with him. The reality is my time is ticking by relentlessly. It is true that time stops for no man. I notice that I have less energy now than I did even a month ago. I know that I need to be careful not to let my need to do this interfere with his need to learn and his discovery experience. He will get this at his own speed and not at mine or because I need him to.

"I do lose sight sometimes of why I am doing this. My passion for this has changed, and Jacob is becoming more the son I lost to what I am still not sure."

I was almost out of breath. I was so dialed in it seemed as if I was talking to myself here. I was asking questions and answering them in the same breath.

I finally looked over at Leo and he had a grin back on his face. He doesn't say much. He subscribes to the economy of words approach when dealing with me, but what he does say is usually bang on. It's as if he can read my very soul.

Leo said, "Get your ego out of the way. You know the right questions to ask yourself and you are answering them as fast as you ask them. Use your own instincts to guide you. You'll be good with that. Trust in your own intuition to know when to step in and when to step away. These two things got you to me. That tells me that they are working just fine, just as they are supposed to."

And that was it. That is what he had to say and he was, of course, correct. I didn't need to get away. I needed to trust that I would know when it was time and when the job was done, when to let go and send Jacob on his way. It would be the same no matter who I was working with, a son or not. There comes a time when it is done and you step away so that he can go his own way. I will need to trust that I have done my job.

We spent time talking about unrelated topics and then it was time to leave. I promised to return soon and he said he always looked forward to seeing me. He was my friend and I loved him for who he was and for what he gave me in such an unselfish way.

Back To Basics

I watched Jacob walk down his sidewalk and up mine. He walked with purpose as though he was supremely focused. He came up the stairs, sat down, looked at me and said, "I did the stuff you asked me to do. When I was done I was more confused than when I started. You said that it would become more clear as we went along, but it's not."

I looked at him and then looked away and then back to him. I asked him, "What do you need to have straightened out so that this makes more sense? Don't think about it; just tell me."

He responded immediately: "This stuff about time honoured roles and whatever. I still don't get why that is important. It doesn't have anything to do with what I think we are supposed to be talking about."

"OK, thanks for clearing that up for me," I said. "Let me ask you this. If someone was giving your Mom a hard time, what do you think you would do?"

He thought briefly and said, "I'd tell him to back off and not to be treating her that way."

"Why?" I asked him.

"Because she's my mother and I'm supposed to be looking out for her."

"That's right, exactly," I said to him. "Who told you that? Who told you that is what you needed to do?"

"Nobody", he said "I just feel like I would need to do it."

"Again, you're right. It is what we do as men. We try to protect those we love and care about. It is culturally developed in us, meaning that from a very early time in our lives, as males, we know that that is what we do. We know it because we witness that behaviour in other men. We are exposed to certain expectations from other males. It doesn't matter where or when we try to protect our loved ones and it doesn't matter if they are family or friends. We are socialized to do what we can to ensure their safety and to help ensure their best interests.

"We also work to provide food and shelter for our loved ones, to hunt for our survival, to build things, to challenge and compete and to be leaders and decision makers. There are many of these qualities that are male oriented.

"Women also follow a similar process in their lives from an early age but I'm not qualified to talk about them other than to tell you that, in many cases, they are different than ours. Theirs are just as vital, just as important and certainly just as meaningful to us as human beings. We need to accept and understand them for what they are because it is together that we survive as a species. Collectively they are complimentary to us all. Neither female nor male qualities are more important than the others. That's really important.

"As for men I can say that recognizing these qualities, these characteristics, and accepting them as a part of who we are is really important as well. We need to honour our histories and ensure that we don't lose sight of what they mean to us. These qualities and characteristics are what help determine the roles that we play in our day-to-day lives, how we function and what drives our behaviour.

We have been talking about self-esteem. When we honour our roles and when we understand them and fulfill their demands we feel good about who we are in the world. When we feel good about that we tend to feel positive about who we are. Our self-esteem and our sense of self-worth are elevated. Does this help clear up some of your confusion?"

"Yeh—now that you put it that way I can see how some of the other feelings I have as a male begin to make some sense. I used to think that I was just a bit strange because I had such strong reactions to certain things, but what you have told me helps me see it differently. It also helps me understand a bit more about why I do some of the things that I do. I'm still not sure about the whole roles thing though."

I started to explain what a role was but then stopped. I asked him to consider this: "When you think about your home, what do you think about? How do you see it? What does it mean to you?"

"Well," he began, "it is a place where Mom and I can go to be safe. It is where I can put my stuff. I have privacy there. It also says something about us who live there. That's why I need to start painting the fence this week because I want people to know that we care about what we have and, besides, Mom has worked hard ever since . . ."

He stopped dead right there. Here we were, finally, face to face with the unasked question.

"We don't have to go there if you don't want to," I said, "That call is yours alone."

He looked at me with a flash of anger in his eyes. That anger was not for me but just there, and then his look softened and he continued, ". . . he left. She wants to make sure that we have a nice place to live in."

37

"A home is a man's castle," I said. "It is what he provides for his family. It is where he can be sure that his family will be safe and protected. Unfortunately some men feel the only way they will be judged is by what they have and not who they are. Money is a terrible way of keeping score or to account for a man's life, Jacob. We dare not define a man by the amount of money he has but rather what he does with it. There is no reward for the one who accumulates the most. In the end, we all die. Money can never buy class either.

"For a woman, her home is where she 'nests,' She creates the warmth and a feel for where she raises and cares for her family. She is also a protector, nurturer and a caregiver of the highest order. She needs to be sure that her family is taken care of, that there is comfort and security. Also that love and respect are demonstrated openly and that to show feelings is OK. "She is a teacher and a doctor. She is an arbitrator and a confidant. And so much more.

"There was a time not too long ago when our culturally and socially developed drivers worked in harmony to provide both of these situations: 'a castle' and 'a nest.' More recently, in the last two generations particularly, these roles and the expectations that are connected to them have come under assault.

"Different groups want them to go away or not be considered as important in the scheme of things. Some will call it social progress. I call it a disaster in the making. Is there a need to change how business is done? Absolutely. Is there a need for women to be treated more fairly and with equality concerning opportunities to be all they can be as human beings? Absolutely.

"Of this, there is no question. It is not the 'what' that is problematic; it's the 'how'. Things change too quickly and men can't keep up with the expected changes. That is the problem."

"But we've discussed this earlier. We can again, if you wish, but my hope is that you can see more clearly how and why roles remain important. I believe that it is possible to alter the behaviour connected to our historical gifts. But it takes time and negotiation and understanding and acceptance by everyone.

Unfortunately, the move currently is more toward androgyny meaning a blending of masculine and feminine roles and traits that distinguish neither gender. We are becoming more like each other. We are beginning to dress the same, look the same and talk the same. At some point one of us will become unnecessary, redundant. Our historical roles are necessary so that our behaviour and the expectation of each by the other remain defined and predictable. Let me ask you this. If I was holding a jar in each hand and held my arms straight out from my body and then you filled one of the jars with rocks and the other with feathers what do you think would happen?"

He thought for a moment and then said, "well unless you are Superman, which you aren't, your arm with the heavy stuff in the jar would begin to go lower."

"True enough," I said. "And what would be the result do you think?"

He thought again and then said, "you'd look lop-sided."

"Yes. I would look and be out of balance. That's what happens when we all become the same. There is no balance. There is nothing in the system to offset the other to keep a balance. Balance is what protects our integrity as human beings."

I was running out of gas again. I wanted to scream, NOT NOW but I continued. "I don't mean to cut off this discussion, and I will be happy to spend as much time as you want talking about this because it is important to what we are doing here. So does this make it clearer to you now?"

By his look we were getting closer but we weren't quite there yet.

"Let me summarize what I am trying to say and then if it still is not clear for you we'll try to look at it another way, OK?"

In typical fashion he just nodded and on I went. "The short of it is this: when men attempt to satisfy what we know to be the draw of our historical roles in the world we feel as though we are acting with purpose and that we are relevant. We need to feel that we measure up to the expectations others have of us, whether those expectations we feel are fair or not. When we do we feel good about ourselves, our self-esteem is fortified.

"I'll give you a typical example. Men don't like to ask for directions or take orders from others, especially our female partners. Many jokes have been told around this very topic. Simply put, we, as men, need to show that we are capable of getting us from point A to point B without any help. It shouldn't be that difficult. We are expected to know how to do that.

"Remember the fragile male ego? Well, to get lost en route to somewhere is a blow to our ego, our manhood, so to speak. Sound silly? It likely is, but when it happens we feel as though we have let our wives or family down. Some feel embarrassed; others feel inadequate. Still others feel that if they can't do something as simple as follow a map or directions, they begin to question their own ability to protect or guide their families. What does it mean if they can't get from A to B without getting lost?

"We need to be seen as competent, so that our loved ones will trust in our ability to look after them. What we, as men, need to understand is that our manhood is not measured by our ability to get us from A to B. It is measured by our ability and willingness to be flexible, to negotiate a win/win solution where possible and to help problem solve or participate in fairness without compromising our character or always feeling as though we are being challenged in the process. We don't have to give up our historical identities in order to get along in the world. We are capable of doing both."

I had to stop to regroup or, rather, to be rejuvenated. I looked at Jacob and could see that the wheels were turning. "Does that work for you? I mean, does that make any more sense to you?"

"I never realized that there was so much going on," he said. "I didn't know any of this. Why didn't I? Why don't they talk about this stuff in school? If they did, maybe more of us would stay longer. It sure is more interesting and useful than some of the crap they put out there."

"Yeah, I agree," I said, "but frankly I don't care about that right now. I just care about whether or not you get it."

"I can't say that I get it all but it makes more sense now than when I first sat down," Jacob said. "Let me sit with it for a while. I need to think about it before it sinks in. Mom says I have a head like a rock sometimes. I know when she is thinking that because she calls me 'Rocky' and we both have a laugh. So what you are saying, then, is as men we have these feelings from birth that we don't learn much about. They are just there with us, and those feelings help us to behave or do things in certain ways. It's not bad for us to have them or feel them or act on them as long as we respect other people in the process."

I grimaced. Out of the mouths of babes? Why didn't I just say it that way?

"Yes. That's what I am trying to say to you," I said. "I'd say that you got it pretty well."

Keeping What You Have

Jacob, excuse me for a minute, please. While I'm gone I would like you to write down five things that you like about yourself and I'll be right back".

40

I had to get up and move. I wanted to make sure that I could maintain my focus because this part of the journey will be important for Jacob, and I need to make sure that I get it right so that he can get it right. In some ways he is older than his years, and in others he is too vulnerable to pressure, especially from his peers. I want to ask him about his father, but I know that I can't. That needs to be in his own time, and I have to respect that.

When I returned, he hadn't moved much. "Struggling are we?" He just looked at me. I could tell he was very uncomfortable with what I had asked him to do.

"I don't know what to write." He looked at me with a lost look, as if this was a totally new thought that he had been asked to identify.

I said, "Just write the truth. There is nothing stronger than the truth."

"Well, I don't really know what the truth is in this case."

I knew he would struggle. "So here's the thing. We are not brought up to focus or dwell on our positive qualities. We are not encouraged to think about what we do well or how good a person we are. We are told by our elders and sometimes our peers that it isn't cool to brag about who we are. They think that people will see your good stuff and think what they will, but it is not up to us to brag about ourselves.

"Actually we are more often encouraged to recognize our down side, our faults, and correct them than to feel good about what we believe we do well. That's sad I, think. How will we ever know who and what we are in the world-, especially as men? How will we know what our strengths are and what we have to build on? At the very least, we need to have our thoughts about ourselves validated in some way. It is OK – no, it is imperative that we be able to express what is good about ourselves. There is a difference between bragging about oneself and acknowledging our strong qualities. Part of the confidence I spoke about earlier is based on this inner feedback so perhaps you can begin to see how this is starting to be connected and how it is up to each of us to build and maintain our own positive sense of self.

"Did you write anything down?" I said.

He looked a little embarrassed but managed to say, "Loyal."

"That's a good start. What else?" I asked.

Reluctantly, he began to write down some other words, and when he was finished he looked at the list and handed it to me.

I said, "I would rather you read them to me because they are yours, and you need to be able to identify them and believe in them".

"Good athlete, loyal, kind, intelligent, good friend," he said, almost apologetically.

"That's a pretty accurate list, I'm thinking. There are several others that I would put on that list as well, but that is a great start. Thank you. It's most important that you do this little exercise every once in a while. As men in the world, we will be under increasing pressure to give up our thoughts around our roles and how we see ourselves. We will be centered out for our selfish ways of thinking and encouraged to get with the program. We will be told that our way of thinking is outdated and that we need to change how we see our place in the world. Some will even call us Neanderthals.

"That is why it is more important than ever for us to be able to understand our own truths. We know who we are better than anyone else and no one can tell us otherwise. The question now is how we use our self-awareness to keep our historical heritage relevant and still participate in the world as it continues to forge ahead at a torrid pace."

"That's part of my question about how do I keep this once I have it?" stated Jacob.

"If I said to you, 'Everything you do either adds to you or diminishes you as a person,' how would you respond to that?"

Silence followed. It continued until finally he said, "I think what it means is everything I do has an effect on my life, one way or the other, so if I am really good, then that will have an effect on my life as well."

God bless the kid. I felt like hugging him and telling him just how bright he really was.

"Yep, you got it." I said. "That's it. Let me ask you this, then. Do we 'do' first or do we 'think' first?"

By watching him I could tell he was starting to get into this. He liked to be challenged. He enjoyed having someone ask him what he thought. He wanted to show me that he could hold his own and that he wasn't some dumb kid who had nothing going for him. I could feel myself getting drawn into his world another fraction of an inch. Whether that was a good thing or not a good thing was becoming less relevant.

Finally he said, "I'm not sure. I think that we 'do' first. At least, it feels like that sometimes. But probably it's 'think' first."

"Nice cover," I said. "You'd make a great politician with an answer like that. If we look at what just happened here, what did you do? It appears as though you had to 'think' about your answer and what you wanted to say before you delivered it. We always think about what we are going to do before we do it. The exceptions would be when we breathe and blink and when our heart beats. Those are called autonomic responses. There are others as well. Our thoughts might be in nano seconds, but we do think before we act.

"Good so far? And, yes, there is a point to this. We have established that the things we do have a bearing on our lives in one way or another. We have also determined that we think first and then we 'do.'

"So what? Next question then: What is one thing that we do every day? Most of us do this many times during the day."

He looked at me with a glimmer in his eyes. I could tell he was thinking about being a smart-ass, but instead he answered, "I don't know. What?"

"We make decisions," I said. "Some are very important and some have less significance, but they are all decisions. It is our decision-making that determines what kind of a life we will have. If we make or continue to make decisions that are not in our best interests, the quality of our lives will be lessened dramatically. If we make decisions that support our best interests, the likelihood is that we will enjoy more contented and satisfying lives, yes?"

I could see he was working quickly at connecting the dots. "Shall I continue or do you want me to stop for now?"

"No, no don't stop now. I want to know where you are going with all of this. I'm with you so far."

I was, again, becoming tired, so it was difficult to keep a focus, but on we went. I could sleep later. "OK. If our decision-making is the main thing that determines what we do, how do we make our decisions? What are they based on?"

He jumped in right away by saying, "What has happened to us in the past."

"You are partially correct," I pointed out to him, "but there is more to it than that. Our past experiences came about by a decision that was made. It is kind of like the chicken and the egg idea. Which came first?

Four main or major influencing factors fit into our decision-making process:

1. Our morals

Those principles that we choose to live by, like not stealing and not lying and not hurting other people. They form our rules for living. We all have rules by which we live our lives, things that we will or will not do in the course of our day-to-day living. They aren't always popular with the people we hang around with and it doesn't always feel good to do the 'right' thing. They are what help us make the decisions that are right for us, or at least we think they are right for us.

2. Our beliefs

Those are what we believe to be true even though there is no visual or concrete evidence that would suggest they are true. There is no way for us to prove that certain things are true, especially those things that are told to us by our parents or loved ones. We trust that they will tell us the truth about things. So we just accept things are as they are. In part, for instance, that is how prejudice gets a foot-hold. We are told from a young age that certain things are true about others and we take them as the truth, with no apparent evidence to support the claim. As children, we have the Tooth Fairy, Santa Claus and the Easter Bunny. Think how that works itself out in our young lives and the decisions we make based on those beliefs. Beliefs can be very powerful.

3. Our attitudes

These determine how we choose to go about our day-today living. If I have an attitude about how the world owes me a living, the decisions I make will reflect that. Our attitudes tend not to be in our best interests.A poor attitude will sabotage our self-esteem in a heartbeat if we are not careful. The thing with attitudes is they are pretty easy to change. We work hard sometimes to keep a bad attitude going because it feels good to us somehow. It justifies what we are feeling and thinking. Thinkabout being angry at someone and all the excuses we create in order for us to keep the negativity going.

4. Our perceptions

These explain how we choose to see the world we live in. We can see the world as a place of grief and darkness and danger or a place of beauty and light and opportunity. It really is up to us.

"If you want to make decisions that are in your best interests, you have to look hard at these four things. If you are not happy with the kinds of decisions you are making, you need to change how you think.

"Look at the four points I just outlined and go over each one carefully. Be sure to ask yourself about your own morals and values. What of your beliefs: do they make sense to you anymore? Are they still accurate when you think about your own life and what it is you want? Do your rules for living still make sense to you? Are they still relevant to your goals? Are your beliefs still valid? Do they still make sense to you given what you are seeing and hearing around you? Do your attitudes bring out the best in you or the worst in you? How is that working for you these days? Is the world as you see it just black or just white or realistically does it seem a shade of gray that makes more sense to you? We all need to evaluate and re-evaluate these influences on our decision-making processes from time to time.

There is one more thing about decision-making that is important. As human beings, we tend to be fear driven when it comes to decision-making. We tend to think more about what will happen if we don't do this or that. We tend to think the worst, make decisions based on that and then feel relieved somehow when the worst doesn't happen.

The other side of this is to make decisions that are quality based. In other words, ask yourself how will your life be enhanced if you decide to do this. Then only make decisions that are quality based instead of fear driven. If what you decide to do can't or won't end up adding quality to your life, don't do it. It's your choice.

"You had asked me a question a while ago, something about 'how does someone make us feel bad?' I'm not convinced that anyone can make us feel bad. We can certainly choose to feel bad about things that upset us or that sadden us, but unless we allow others to have control over our feelings and emotions then I don't know that others can actually make us feel bad.

"I remember reading this somewhere and I can't place it right now but it said: 'Our background and circumstances may influence who we are, but ultimately we are responsible for what we decide and who and what we become.'"

I could see it in his eyes. I could read it on his face. He knew exactly what I was alluding to. What he struggled with was 'Is now the time or not?' He decided it was not.

Instead he said, "OK, I think that I understand what you are saying about the self-esteem thing. I get what 'it' is and 'how you get it.' I think

45

I get how you keep it. I need you to connect the last dots for me. How does it connect to what is happening with the changes and with the expectations that people have of us?"

I could feel my energy waning and so I knew that I didn't have much time left for today. I began, "Let me close out today with this, and see if it answers your question.

"What is Manhood? Well, it may be easier to say what it is not. It is not about getting drunk or high whenever you want to. It is not a license to be obnoxious and disrespectful to others. It is not about treating women poorly, with no regard for their feelings or treating them like they are gum on the bottom of your shoe. It is not about using women for your own gratification and having reckless sex. Women are not toys to be used for our amusement. It is not about forcing women or coercing them to do whatever you want them to do for you with no regard for what is good for them. It is not about making babies and then not taking responsibility for what that means. If you don't understand what it means then you shouldn't be making babies. It is not about being rude and ignorant—there is absolutely no excuse at all for demonstrating bad manners and for ignoring others rights and freedoms. It just says you have no class, that's all.

"What it is about is honouring what your society and your culture has ingrained in you about your role as a man and as a human being, about honouring those feelings that we spoke about earlier that are an integral part of who you are right from birth, like knowing to protect your loved ones and to provide for your family, and so on. It's about accepting the responsibility of where those characteristics take you as a man in the world. It is about making decisions, no matter how you feel, and taking responsibility for their outcomes. It is about doing what needs to be done when you really want to do something else. It is not being influenced and not going along with the crowd, especially when you know that what they want to do just doesn't feel right. It is about standing up and showing some integrity. That has to do with your rules for living and honouring them. It's about making a decision to do something and following through after considering how that decision will impact those significant others around you. That's also part of those rules for living. It's about being a leader and not a follower. Anybody can be a follower. It doesn't take any balls to be a follower, but it takes a man to be a leader. Men show courage, wisdom and strength in the face of being unpopular.

46

"You can't possibly make the really big life decisions at 14, 15 or 16 years of age because you just plain don't know enough. Oh, it's true that you may have experienced great pain or loss in your life to date, but that doesn't qualify you for manhood. You can, however, begin to make the important decisions about how you will treat others and the level of respect that you will show them.

"Know that, in the future, if the rules change again, and they will to be sure, that the expectations others have of you and those that present themselves to you, as a man, cannot change who you are. You may need to change some behaviours and you may need to look at or re-consider some of your beliefs, but you always remain in control of what you do next because that depends on your decision-making.

"Our manhood and our self-esteem do not have to change. We remain the same human beings we have always been. Those things that are important to us as men in and of the world do not change. They are ever-present. We can manage our actions and our emotions successfully because they also depend on our decision-making. Know that your values – your qualities and your value as a person and as a man – don't change. They remain in tact. They do not disappear. So where does that leave you, Jacob?"

He looked at me with a confidence that I hadn't seen before and said, "In a different place." I was done and so was he. There was much he had to make sense of, but I think he was doing it. There was much left to say to him to make sure he "got it." I didn't have it to give him and it angered me more than I wanted to admit, but there it was.

Next! Like It Or Not Here It Comes

What I'd like you to do is go over your previous work and do the scale stuff again. See if there are any differences, considering what we spoke about today. When we get together again I'll ask you to give me a number and you let me know if that is up, down or the same. You understand?

1	2	3	4	5	6	7	8	9	10

The other thing I'd like you to think about is this:

1. How angry are you? (put a mark on the scale that would indicate your anger level)
2. About what?
3. How do you think anger interferes with the quality of your life or does it?

He nodded to me, a gesture that I have come to understand means that he is not sure how he feels about something rather than meaning it's all good. He got up and headed to the steps leading down off the porch.

"Hey, Jacob, do me a favour? I've got to be away for a day or two. Would you keep an eye out for the place?" I wanted to leave him thinking that I had more trust in him now. He needs to know that his hard work and his risking himself to me has meaning.

"No problem. When are you going?" he asked.

"I have to leave tomorrow sometime. Thanks."

UNDERSTANDING ANGER:
The Second Cornerstone

The Times They Are A Changin'

I had decided not to tell anyone where I was going. I didn't want to hear I shouldn't go and what happens if . . . and all the rest. I hadn't taken the time to travel the coastline for quite some time, and time seemed to be a major dictator now. So much to do and so little time. I wanted to do this while I still could because I really had no idea of how much time I had left. I had a fading hope that some miracle was going to happen, and this would all be a cruel or a happy memory. In my very being, however, I knew. I was running out of time.

Everywhere I went I was reminded of how important time is/was/will be. And what about Jacob? What happens to him if we only get part of the way through our meetings together because I run out of time?

I really have to stop thinking about this, I said aloud to no one. I could spend the rest of my time worrying about how little time I had left and not use very wisely whatever amount of time I had left. Around and around these thoughts went in my head, and the more they went around, the angrier I got because there was no solution to this.

There is supposed to be a solution to all dilemmas, isn't there? Finally I had to pull over and get out of the car. It's fortunate that no one was driving along past the rest stop because they would have witnessed a lunatic strutting around the parking lot talking and shouting to himself.

Eventually I ran out of the mental energy required to fuel this fire I was carrying around. I sat down to rest, only to view the most beautiful sight in the world to me. I could see down the coast for miles. White sand like snow stretched out with blue sky, almost neon, touching the water that rolled in. Waves smashed onto the outcroppings of rock. White foam sprayed everywhere. Beautiful. They had been receiving that treatment since time began and had endured.

I was reminded that the only time I have is the time left in this day and that I better decide to enjoy it in all of its splendour while I have the chance. The only difference between me and the other folks who may be looking at the same sights somewhere else is that they may have more days to spend. The sight is no more beautiful to them because they do. That understanding is as close to an epiphany as I have come in quite a while. Back in my car I felt somewhat different about the whole thing. I also recognized that, although I was still angry, I didn't let it take control of my emotions and determine how I would spend the remainder of the day.

I slept the sleep of the dead, so to speak, and woke up the next morning ready to meet with John, my physician. I drove back to town and stopped by his office right on schedule. He pushed his head out of his office door and said, "Come on in. How are you, my friend? Hey, you look good. What have you been up to?"

"Stop the BS! What's happening?" I said, with a bit of a smile. I nodded toward the file I had come to recognize as mine on his desk. They – whoever "they" are – say that hope springs eternal. I guess that's where I've been for the last while, in the "hope springs" place.

He looked me straight in my eyes and said, "There is some good and some not so good news. Which first?"

"Surprise me," I quipped. "Look, at some point I'll hear both. Right now I just want to get to it so if you could give it to me I'd appreciate it, OK?"

"The chemotherapy, to date, has slowed the growth down considerably but it is still growing. With extensive radiation – at the highest your body can handle for as long as you can handle it – we may be able to extend the diagnosis by six months. Even longer, perhaps, but you would need to start immediately."

I felt like saying "OK, but what's the good news here?" Blood rushed to my head. I felt light-headed, as though someone had vacuumed all the oxygen out of the air. I sat down. I just looked at him. Up to this point I still thought that somehow by some divine intervention I would be eventually cured of this hideous disease and that some great learning experience would transform my world into one of gratefulness to the end of my days.

John sat next to me, and said, "I know that this is much more than anyone could comprehend, let alone make a decision about, but I need to know what you want to do soon so that I can make arrangements and we can get going here." His words seemed to hit my brain but didn't register. They were like white noise to me.

"Decision, make a decision," I heard myself say. "John, I couldn't tell you what the hell I had for breakfast today. Make a decision? If I had to decide right now, I'd say the hell with it. I'm not doing that."

He looked at me stupefied, and said, "What do you mean? You have to do this. This is the only option you have."

"No, it's not the only option I have, John. I can choose to live out my days in relative comfort with most of my faculties, and the inevitable will transpire. Give me a day to think this over. I promise I will get back to you tomorrow and we'll go from there."

With that I hugged him, thanked him and told him that I appreciated him for being my friend and for his help with all of this. I walked out simply putting one foot in front of the other, not knowing where my feet were taking me.

I had walked two or three blocks in the wrong direction before I realized where I was. I found my way back to my car but just sat in it. I wasn't able to drive anywhere just yet. I began thinking about what John had said and then I thought about Jacob. He, like many others, doesn't know about any of this. What would all of this mean to him? Does he even factor into my decision-making process? Should he figure into it?

Finally, I was able to start my car with enough confidence I wouldn't kill anyone on my way back home. I accelerated out of the parking lot, onto the road, turned up the tunes, rolled down all the windows and drove the hills as a thirsty man would approach a bottle of water. I didn't know if or when I would ever see this view again and I wanted to drink it all in.

Life had changed dramatically in the last few hours, and it had taken on a new meaning for me. I also noticed a growing sadness or was it more a melancholy deep down in the depths of my being. Why now and why me? Again Jacob crept into my thinking, no matter how loud I played the radio.

By the time I got home, it was dark and late and all I could do was crawl into bed. Sleep would not come to me. Part of me never wanted to sleep again, afraid that I would not awaken. I didn't want to miss a thing. It was then I knew I had made a decision about what my life would look like for the next few months. I was at peace with it.

Sleep finally found me, it was early morning before I knew it. I rang John first thing and told him my decision. I said that I would get back to him later, but I wanted him to know it right away. It took two days for me to connect with John again, but that was plenty of time for me to wrestle with my decision and to wrestle with the emotions and feelings that came as a result of that decision.

Anger was the one emotion that continued to haunt me, and it took all the strength I could gather just to deal with it. It's not where I wanted to spend my precious resources right now. In the end I knew that the decision I had arrived at was the right thing to do but many doubts were never far away.

I explained my decision to John so we could proceed with a treatment plan of some kind. "John, my good friend I know that you only want what is best for me, but I can't do the treatment thing. Not now. If this thing has slowed down somewhat, that's good, but I can't spend time, my time, laid up somewhere throwing up everything that shouldn't be thrown up, weak and tired, angry, with stuff falling off so that I may live another six months, or may not, all with a very questionable quality to my life.

"At this point I would rather live as pain-free as possible for as long as possible and enjoy life for as long as possible before my time comes. I have much to do and very little time left to do it. I can't see myself cashing it all in now for a 'maybe' and a short 'maybe' at that. I need you to understand and I need you to work with me to help me get as much out of what time I have left with as little pain and with as much energy as I can muster. Will you help me do that, my friend?"

I thought I could hear his heart beating on the other end of the line. I knew what I was asking went against all he believed in. I knew he would find it difficult to accept my wishes on a professional level, and I also knew that he would, in the end, honour my request because we were friends, good friends. He did not disappoint.

"You know I will, you stubborn Irish bastard. When can you come by the office so we can get going on some kind of protocol? I'll need to speak to some friends in the business to find out what they suggest according to how you want this to go. Can you give me a day or two?"

"I can," I said. "And, John, thanks. You have no idea how much your support means to me. Especially now. Let me know when you want me to show up." It was done. There was no time to waste.

One of the things that I had decided to do was not to sleep in anymore. I needed to sleep well enough to maintain an energy level that would sustain me. I would see more sunsets and sunrises and a lot less TV. I would listen to more of my favourite music and not be concerned about singing out loud on my front porch. I have a terrible voice but, hey, if you don't like it, don't listen or come and join me, 'cause you're welcome to.'

I was pleasantly surprised when I found Annie sitting on my porch early the next day. I first thought that something was wrong. Was it Jacob? Was it Annie? Was she all right? When I asked, she said she could not thank me enough for what I had done.

"I'm not sure I follow you, Annie. What are you talking about?"

She continued, "There has been such a difference in Jacob in the last weeks, and I can't think of anything that has happened other than he has been spending time with you. You can't tell him that we had this chat, though. He's at school right now, but he'll be home later. You know he has only missed two days of school since you first spoke with him, and they were legitimate misses. There are no more rides home with the locals, either. He doesn't seem to have the same interests in hanging out with the people he used to see before. He speaks to me and to others with a little more respect now although he still has a ways to go there. I don't know what to think about it all, so I just wanted you to know that it must be you and what you have said to him."

"I doubt it has much to do with what I have said. It likely has more to do with his just being able to hear that he isn't the screw-up everyone thinks he is and that he has a great deal to offer the world he lives in. He's a good kid Annie. I think he needed to hear that from another male in his life. You are his mother, so you are supposed to tell him that stuff. But another man says it and it means something different. Not more important, just different. So if he is looking at the world from a different perspective, that's on him not me, but thanks for the thought."

Jacob and I weren't scheduled to connect until later this week. I had much to do before then but I knew one thing for sure. The topic of anger and its toll on our well-being was certainly the next area to look at. I had an inkling of that when we last saw each other, but now I understood the connection unresolved anger would have on any of Jacob's future relationships or his ability to parent his children, indeed on his very manhood. And I knew, too, what the topic needed to be and where we needed to go first.

Ready? Can We Ever Really Be Ready?

I watched him as he approached my porch. He walked with a confidence that had not been not there before. He carried himself with more height. He looked as though he had less of the world to carry on his shoulders or at least knew what part of it to carry and what part to leave behind for now. He came right up, sat down, looked over at me and said, "Hi." That was it, just "Hi."

So I said "Hi" back. That was it for me. Then we just looked at each other, and we both started to laugh. There was a playful side to him I hadn't seen before. He always showed me something new each time we met. Was he becoming more comfortable around and with me? Perhaps we shared the same inkling I did the last time we met, and this was his way of telling me that he didn't want to go there.

"Well, how have you been'" I asked. "You look different somehow."

"I suppose I am. I'd be lying if I told you I bought into everything you said to me the last time, but the questions and the scale thing got me questioning some stuff. I did see parts of what I have been doing as not good for me and decided to change some things around a bit. Then there were other things that I recognized I was doing that were just plain stupid. They couldn't possibly get me where I think I want to be."

Wow! Again he was showing me something that he hadn't until now. I saw a humility and a common sense without as much of the arrogance, or an edge. I needed to be careful that my ego didn't get in the way of my own common sense. After all, he is the one that is doing the processing here.

"Speaking of the scales, where do you see yourself now? I'm thinking about the anger scale."

He began, "About the self-esteem scale, I'd say that one jumped up pretty good, up maybe two from where it was. I just feel better about who I am and I see my chances of becoming the person I want to be as pretty good. I understand that I have more to say about who I become than others have to say by trying to discourage me from becoming how I'd like to be seen. Does that make sense?"

I could barely contain myself. I wanted to get up and do a jig around the porch. He got it! He knows that he can be whoever he wants to be and that it's in his capacity to make that happen. He no longer has to be dependent upon the thoughts of others, whether that is a group or a single person, for his sense of self. He may not know how to mobilize those skills yet or those talents, but he knows he has them and right now that's important for him. The rest will come.

"Yeah, I know what you mean and, yes, it makes perfect sense to me. I'm glad it makes sense for you, though. That is what is truly important here. So where do you stand on the anger scale?" I persisted.

His face clouded over instantly, but I had decided there really was no easy way into this topic. Lets just wade right in and see what happens.

His face had transformed from buoyant and excited to wary and sullen.

"You really want to go there, don't you? Why? Why is it so important?" he demanded.

"I can assure you of this, Jacob. I take no great pleasure in bringing it up. It gives me no joy to see you pained by memories, but the whole issue of anger is vitally important to your well-being and your happiness. You will never be at peace until you learn to deal with those things that create pain, discomfort or uncertainty in your life.

"You cannot have a meaningful and loving, caring relationship with anyone else until you can face your demons, until you take away their mystery and their strength and power. Anger is, in my mind, the most powerful and potentially destructive of all of our emotions. The results of our demonstrations of anger can destroy a lifetime in an instant. We can be so blinded by our anger that we can lose complete control of our actions.

"Have you ever heard the phrase 'white rage'?" It means that it is possible for us to go from mild upset to searing destructive rage in a heartbeat and back again and not be aware of what happened to us. Call it a white-out if you like. We can use anger like a rapier to slash at people verbally. Verbal and emotional abuse can be just as damaging (many would argue more damaging) as any physical abuse.

"Anger can also be the most powerful and potentially beneficial and useful of all our emotions. It really does depend on what we do with it, how we respond to the situation that stirs anger within us. We must realize that we can and do have the choice as to how we will respond. Our response depends upon our ability to manage ourselves and not let our emotions manage us.

"Is anger a bad thing? No, it is not. Do we need to get angry sometimes? Yes, we do. Is it OK to get angry? It sure is. Is it OK for men to get angry? Absolutely. The last time I checked men were about 50 per cent of the population of planet Earth. Anger helps to mobilize us—to spur us on to bettering ourselves and to protect ourselves or others who, for whatever reasons, may not be able to look after themselves. Anger is not the issue. Our expression of it is. Learn to use it as a strength.

"Anger is as natural a response as breathing or blinking. It is not something to fear. It helps us to know when something is wrong and that we need to be prepared to deal with whatever it is."

I stopped here for a moment to see his reaction, but it seemed that he was content to let me carry on.

"If we trust that our angry responses or feelings are simply indicators of other issues and not an opportunity to lash out, our feelings of anger can help us identify what the underlying issues are when we consider the source of our anger. For instance, you like to play varsity football. Tryouts come up and you have worked out most of the off-season. You feel as though you are in pretty good shape and are ready to compete. The coaches' son and you try out for the same position and he, the kid, gets the nod. Of course you get upset because the coach obviously picked his son over you. It didn't matter what you did or how good you were, he was going to pick his kid.

"All your buddies said you should have won the spot, so it is not only disappointing to you that you didn't make the first string position but you also feel embarrassed. Then you find out that the son spent most of his off-season at a pro football rookie tryout camp and had the good fortune to be coached by some of the local pros.

"Begrudgingly you have to admit that he was in better shape than you and that that gave him the edge he needed. You can either go around pissed off and feeling sorry for yourself or you can work harder at being in better shape so that when your opportunity comes to prove yourself you'll be ready. You could ask one of the assistant coaches what you have to do to make a difference in their assessment of you as a player. You can use your anger as the fuel to improve. The same logic works in other areas of our lives as well. So what are you so pissed off about?"

I could tell he wanted to speak, but at the same time there was a reservation that stopped him.

"Are you concerned that if you take the top off the bottle you won't be able to put it back on again?" I asked.

"Something like that," he mumbled.

I took a deep breath and said, "I won't let that happen, Jacob. I won't ask you to trust me, but I will ask that you trust you. You will only put out what you can handle. Look, you have been living with this thing for years now and, although it has eaten away at you, you have also survived it. What we are talking about here is whether or not you want to do more than just survive what and how you are feeling about it all.

"You have given 'it' a great deal of power. You have to decide if you want to take some of that power back. I held up a piece of paper and said to him, "I read this on the Internet the other day and I saved it for you to hear. I thought it may come in handy so here it is."

I read slowly. "It is called 'The Two Wolves' and we don't know who wrote it.

"One evening an old Cherokee man told his grandson about a battle that goes on inside people. He said, "My son, the battle is between two wolves inside us all. One is Evil. It is anger, envy, jealousy, sorrow, regret, greed, arrogance, guilt, resentment, inferiority, lies, false pride, superiority, and ego. The other is Good. It is joy, peace, love, hope, serenity, humility, kindness, benevolence, empathy, generosity, truth, compassion, and faith." The grandson thought for a moment and then asked his grandfather, "Which one wins?"

"The old Cherokee man simply replied, "The one you feed."

Jacob quickly looked at me and then the floor and then the ceiling and any other place he could, as long as he didn't have to look at me again. But when he did finally meet my eyes, tears ran down his face. He didn't try to hide them from me now.

There were no words for a long time and then he started to speak. At first he proceeded carefully, but as his anger grew and grew so did the difficulty he had trying to control his emotions. Finally there was nothing but invective raging forth. It was as if a dam had burst and it was running wild with little chance of control. I let him go to it. And he did. For what seemed several minutes he ranted and raged and swore and cursed. Then he began to slow down. Then he just stopped as suddenly as he had started. Frankly, it took me by surprise. I thought he had just shut down.

He looked at me again and said quite calmly, "I can't think of any other words to use. I can't say that I feel a whole lot better right at this moment, but there it is. Now you know."

He was trying to show his bravado to hide his outburst. I didn't want him to run away and hide, so I said, "Hell, I thought you would never shut up. You'd have made a truck driver blush."

We both started to howl, and we laughed for a long time. Tears came to our eyes at one point. Slowly our laughter subsided and I said, "I can only guess at how difficult that was for you to do. I want to thank you for trusting me enough that you could do what you really needed to do."

And then he did the predictable. He looked at me and just nodded. I said, "I'm not sure if you can understand or if you can see how anger, unresolved and denied anger, can interfere with or at least influence the possibility of enjoying any quality experiences in your life right now, but I suspect you will."

"I have so many questions about what my dad did and why he did it," he said. "I hate him for hurting my mom and for just crawling away in the night like a worm. I doubt I could ever trust him, and I know that I wouldn't respect him either. And despite everything he did, he is still my father and I still would like to know him. It is very confusing. I get angry as much about being confused and not knowing how I should feel half the time. I see and watch my Mom and how brave and tough she is. What about her? What happens to her and how does she feel about it all?"

"I know," I said. My response felt inadequate but there was little else to say right now. Sometimes saying nothing says it all. I just let him sit with it and then after a few minutes I said, "My hope is that some of these questions will get answered for you or by you during the next few times we get together. That is, if you still want to do that?"

"Well, why wouldn't I? Unless you are looking for a way out of this," he said, looking hard into my face.

"No, not at all, Jacob. This is as important to me as it is to you. I just didn't want to assume anything."

"Do you mind if I slip home for about an hour? Mom will be coming home soon and there is something that I need to ask her. I want to be there when she gets there," he said, backing off the porch.

"Not at all. I'll be waiting for you when you want to return." The truth was I was grateful for the break. I was feeling too many emotions myself and needed some time to sort them out before we continued.

Forty-five minutes later he returned looking a bit more relaxed than when he left. I asked him if everything was all right and he assured me it was all good at home. We sat down with the intention of picking up where we left off. I was about to ask him something when he says, "So how does anger happen? Where does it come from?"

"Before I answer that," I said, "I would like you to tell me where you think it comes from. What happens to anger you?"

"That's not fair. I asked you first," he complained.

"Life isn't always fair, and you'll find that out soon enough if you haven't already." I grinned at him as I said, "So just answer the question."

He thought for a minute and then began, "I think it happens because someone does something that I don't like or they know I don't like it and do it anyway. Most of the time it is stupid stuff, but sometimes it's serious stuff and so I have to stand up and be counted. Show any weakness and you get hammered for it, so you can't let that pass. Someone gets at you, maybe embarrasses you, especially in front of your friends or worse in front of your lady. Then you have to get back at him right away. Definitely can't let that pass.

"There are times when I just don't want to be around people or at least certain people, so I show them a little anger and they tend to leave me alone. I get upset when people keep telling me how to live my life as though they always know the best way to do everything. Sometimes they tell me it's for my own good. What do they know about what is good for me? I'll be the judge of that. I'm not a little kid anymore. I get really pissed at people who always have an opinion about everything and they are always right, or so they think. They want you to hear their words, but they won't hang around long enough to hear the other side. Most of these guys just run their mouths because they like to hear themselves talk. Sometimes they are trying to impress the ladies in the crowd. Either way, I get angry about that. You want me to keep going?"

"You go as long as you want. I don't have a problem letting you do the talking for a change," I said.

So he did. "I don't like waiting for people and I don't like it when the tough guys pick on the little guys. I hate bullies. That really sets me going. People that jump in line ahead of me, especially after I have been standing there for 10 or 15 minutes, stir me up. I burn when people stick their nose into my business like they have a right to do that.

"I guess the thing that angers me most of all is when someone doesn't live up to the promises they make. They don't do what they say they are going to do. Liars really piss me off too. They make excuses and blame other people for their failures."

With that, silence fell upon us. We both knew where those emotions came from and I saw no need to go to the source of them right now. I found myself staring off down the street after I had gauged the hurt on his face and I could see the white knuckles on his hands as he squeezed the sawdust out of the arms of my favourite porch chair. "Well? It's your turn," he said as his voice brought me back to real time.

"You touched on quite a bit of it, Jacob. Before I give you what I think, I'd like to clear up a couple of things. Misconceptions, I guess, would be the best word. Don't let people tell you that anger is wrong or bad. Don't let them take away your decided response to situations that are upsetting or that are a must to deal with. As men we are challenge oriented and we are competitors. Our first response might be to jump in and face the challenge. As we talked about before, anger is not a bad thing. We need to step back from it long enough so that we can decide how we will deal with it that's all. Remember that we are also protectors and providers. We need to continue in these roles and to honour these roles, if for no other reason than to help other men accept the call as well and to understand that it is OK to do so.

"Sometimes our anger is the only thing that can or will keep us safe. We need to learn how to use our anger to our advantage. Most of the time this is difficult to do, I admit that. But I also know that it can be done.

"If you look at some of the great social movements of the time like Greenpeace, Wild Life Federations, MADD, environmental groups and Amnesty International, to name a few, they came into existence because angry people with something to say recognized that to ban together and pool their energy was much more dynamic and powerful than individuals acting alone. My point here is that anger can motivate change for the better as well. It's always up to us and not up to 'them'.

"You asked me to speak to where I think anger comes from. The greatest source, in my mind, is injustice. I believe more folks get upset, get angry, because they feel a sense of injustice. Injustice is about having someone do or say something that hurts someone we care about, someone who is important to us in some way. It doesn't always have to be family. It can be a good friend or it can be the underdog or the little guy, as you had said. Think about your need to be the protector. I'm not sure where that comes from. You said you find it difficult to watch as the underdog gets pushed around. You feel anger begin to grow in you. You feel the need to jump in and protect him or her. It is natural for us to do that - to help somebody out that has difficulty doing that alone.

"Dreams not met are another source, in my mind. I see so many people who look angry and act in a threatening way. It is a way of life for them. Others see it and comment on it. 'Oh that's, just the way he/she is.' We are not born angry. Rather, it's an acquired behaviour. Dreams not met are especially hard to deal with because we place so much importance on them and, when they don't come true, we tend to give up on them and ourselves. I'm not trying to pick the scab off what we just talked about, but if you look at the dreams you had that were not and may not ever be fulfilled, think about how angry that makes you feel."

Jacob began to say something and I cut him off. "I know you want to jump in here, but I'm on a roll now so hold those thoughts. So we walk around believing that we are not worthy like others seem to be. We begin to feel inferior and take on an edge. Fear, loneliness and grief are also major sources of anger, but anger is complicated and tricky. It comes dressed up like some of these other feelings and emotions.

Look at this list I have of emotions that anger resembles:

- abandonment or being ignored
- betrayal
- blame
- judgement
- boredom
- being cheated
- condemnation
- confusion
- domination or intimidation
- frustration
- embarrassment
- jealousy or envy
- rejection or isolation
- emptiness or exhaustion

"These are just a few of the faces or masks that anger wears. So when you ask where does anger come from, think of some of these."

Still holding the list, he looked up at me. "I'm getting where it comes from, but I'm still not clear about what it IS. Why is it so powerful and why does it get us, me, into so much trouble?"

What Anger Is

Where to start? "Well, it is not easy to pinpoint exactly what it is. It is easier to talk about what anger look's like but that wouldn't answer your question. I guess the best way to describe what anger is that it's a combination of an emotion and a feeling that crash together at the same time. We experience it because something has happened or someone has done something that we don't like or we can't change. So far so good?

Jacob nodded and then said, "That makes sense so far, but why does it get so many people into trouble?"

I continued, "When we consider what anger is, we need to understand that there is a big difference between feeling angry and expressing anger. Also, many people mistakenly identify aggression as anger. They are not the same thing either. It is certainly possible for someone to be aggressive without being angry. Aggression is more about attitude and learned behaviour than it is about physical arousal or wanting to smash someone in the face.

Is it OK to feel it? Sure it is. OK to express it? Not if it hurts you or anyone else. But we do need to learn how to manage it so that it doesn't manage us."

What Anger Isn't

Anger is not an opportunity to blame other people for how we feel or for what has happened to us. If we give up our responsibility to look after ourselves or to make our own decisions, we must accept the outcomes of that choice. It is not an excuse to hurt other living things, human or otherwise. You need to be aware that words can hurt as much as a punch in the mouth. Sometimes more so.

"When we haven't learned how to use our anger to our advantage it can grow inside us until we become blinded and often directed by the sheer volatility we feel inside. The result is that we often hurt other people.

"It's not an emotion for us to use to take advantage of others who may not be as strong as we are. We must not use it for revenge against other people or attack their vulnerabilities. Punishing others and 'teaching them to never do that again' is not a useful way to spend our time. It's a 'no-quality' type decision. It keeps us stuck in a negative state of mind. Our anger is not for manipulating or controlling other people so that we can get what we want.

Using our anger to vent our negative feelings on other people is not only unhealthy but can be dangerous for all concerned. You've seen it and you've heard about it."

"About what? Seen and heard what? he said. I'm not following you here." His tone gave away his frustration. Maybe I'd hit close to home with that one.

"Revenge," I said. And then I said it again. "Revenge. How sweet it feels though, doesn't it? The trouble is when we just shoot off at the lip, we often hurt those who are closest to us or who are the ones we love the most. You asked me before how anger gets you into so much trouble. Any clearer now?

He looked at me with a hard stare as if he wanted me to shut up, so I did. He got up without a word and left the porch. I figured he was gone for the day so I went inside to lie down. I had just dozed off when the knock at the screen door dragged me back into the day. It was Jacob.

"You're pretty good at getting under my skin. Do you stay up at night trying to figure out how to do it, or does it just come naturally to you?" he asked.

"With you," I said, with a touch of laughter, "it's too darn easy. It doesn't take a lot of thought."

I didn't really know how he would respond to that, but I had decided a while ago that I needed to move this along a bit more quickly than I might have had I been healthy. I really believed I had no choice. Feeling the crunch of time and knowing what we had yet to do was driving some of my decisions now.

Perhaps this was more self-oriented than I would have admitted otherwise. Perhaps I didn't have Jacob's sole interest at heart here but it was what it was and I didn't believe any harm would come from it. I had to believe that. I would also have to be more diligent about my motives from here on in or the purpose for being involved in this would be lost or at best distorted.

If I could have seen the potential train wreck that was coming in the very near future I would have been grateful for the risk I had just taken.

As it turned out, Jacob seemed to be pushing the boundaries of our relationship as well. He looked at me and then began to shake his head from side to side. "Why do I do this? I don't know," he answered himself, "but thanks." No other explanation followed.

He walked back out through the door, sat down in his chair and waited for me to join him. I don't think he identified or realized the importance of the moment but he had just climbed another step on his journey to the land of manhood.

There Are Other Benefits Of Anger

As I sat down, he asked me. "How do you know? How do you know which buttons to push, how hard to push them and when is a good time to push them?"

I responded with a hint of sarcasm in my voice, "Just lucky, I guess."

"So what now? Where to from here?" he said.

"What's left for you to get?" I said.

"You keep telling me that there are some good things about my anger that I could use to my advantage. That sounds like an oxomoron to me."

I could feel my eyes brows come together in thought and then realized that he meant "oxymoron." "Do you mean 'oxymoron'?"

Quickly, he said, "I was just checking to see if you were paying attention." His familiar grin followed then he said, "Oh, excuse me, please. Let's not mess with little details, OK?"

I felt as though I had caught a second wind. I said, "Feeling angry toward someone or something can motivate us to assert our wants and needs, so we can tell people what it is we would like. It can help us clarify how someone's behaviour affects us when that person may not be aware of it.

"Anger can be a positive force in our development of self-esteem. It can help us establish boundaries for what is acceptable and what is not, for how we would like people to treat us.

"Expressing anger appropriately can be of enormous benefit to our health. Instead of spending a huge amount of energy and time trying to suppress our anger,– causing us to be stressed, tired, miserable, edgy, nervous, irritable or confused – we can learn to express it and let it go. We can only tell people how we feel and what we want. We can't force them to change their behaviour or how they do business.

"Oh, it's true that we could try to force them to do things differently, but remember force doesn't cause lasting change in people.

They just get angrier themselves and look for revenge somewhere along the way. How do you feel when someone tells you that you had better change something about what you are doing or else? How do feel when someone asks you to change something because it hurts them in some way. You are more likely to change something being asked of you than you would if you were being told. If we do this right it can actually help to make our relationships stronger, instead of destroying them. Those around us will know that they have nothing to fear from us when we use self-management skills and don't let our anger manage us. They can trust that we will not hurt them somehow when we are angry."

The More I Hear The Less I Know

Finally Jacob said, "The more I hear you, the more questions I have and sometimes when I leave here my head hurts. Sometimes I feel embarrassed by how little I know. What I REALLY need to know now is why are you doing this? Why do you want to help me understand this stuff? What's that all about for you?"

I could only look at him and say nothing. I couldn't REALLY tell him, and certainly not right now. "Let me think about that so that when we meet again I'll be able to explain it to you in a way that I hope you will understand. I'm not trying to side-step you here but, it could take longer than we have right now."

"I have to go soon anyway. I'm meeting up with a few of the guys I haven't seen for a while to see what's happening with them, "he said.

I said to him, "You sure that's a good idea?"

"Yeah, why not?"

I changed the subject quickly. "So, where are you on the anger scale now? We didn't have a chance to talk about it before."

"You know, you are like a friggin' dog on a bone. You just don't give up, do you?" He thought for a moment and then said, "About a seven. Oh, by the way, before when I said that I didn't feel any better after blowing off some dirt, that wasn't exactly the whole truth. I did feel better just putting it out there, but it also brought up some other stuff that didn't feel good. So it was like a trade-off."

As he got up to leave, I said, "No, it wasn't. It is the beginning of you facing your demons. That's what men do. They face their demons head on and manage them, sort them out. Doing that takes away their strength, so they are less hurtful and frightening. Good for you."

"Yeah, good for me," he said with a smile.

With that he was off. With that I was exhausted. I went in the house, had a bite to eat, laid down on the couch for a break and woke up around one in the morning to the sound of a car pulling up next door.

I looked out the window and saw a familiar sight: Jacob getting out of a police cruiser. I didn't know whether to rush out and grab him and shake the living life out of him or deal with it the next time we met. I wondered if he would tell me or if I would have to bring it up. I decided the best thing to do would be to see if he were honest enough to tell me.

"Let it be," I said to no one.

The next few days passed by quietly. They were warm and sunny and filled with thoughts. Oddly the thoughts were not the morbid type but rather a reflection of some of the highlights of earlier times. It was good.

I just sat on my front porch and watched the world parade by as if the show was just for me. Once I got up and stood on the top step, which got the early afternoon sun. I turned my face to the sky, closed my eyes and took in the sounds of children playing with abandon and smelled the fresh blooms from neighbourhood gardens and basked in the bone-seeking warmth of the sun. I had forgotten the wonder of the simplest of gifts that Mother Nature had to offer us, the ones we usually take for granted.

The lesson for that day was that I would never, again, take anything for granted. Once more I was stuck by the irony: the closer my day comes, the more I want to live so that I can celebrate all that which I had once thought would last forever.

And The Truth Shall Set You Free

It wasn't long before Jacob was at my home sitting on my front porch eager to begin. Actually he was there before I got there. I couldn't help but wonder how this day would end.

He began, "I have more questions, so I hope you're ready. But we left off at my question to you, and I need an answer to that one before we go anywhere else. Why are you doing this and what's that all about for you?"

"I can see where that would be important for you to understand," I said, "so I will do my best to explain it to you. I'll begin by giving you a little background to this. It may not seem to pertain to you, but I can assure you it does.

"I was at the mall awhile back, just sitting there watching people go by and I was struck by the kids that I was watching. That's how I learn. I watch. I don't stare. Actually, I observe. For the longest time I have known, or at least thought, that the last two generations of young men are lost.

"Remember I said that we have to be careful we don't speak in absolutes? Well, that remains important today as well. This is not about ALL young men, but certainly some. When I say 'lost' I mean that many young men don't have any sense of dignity about them. They are slobs, they are overweight, they are rude. They have little or no self-respect. Many are violent, senselessly violent.

"That is borne out by the number and the strength of street gangs. Gangs these days have taken the place of family. The members have little or no respect for others or other peoples' property. The less they actually care about themselves, the higher up in the gang they go. They don't want to go to school, so many don't get a decent education. They want to work but only if they can start off at $60K per year and have six weeks' vacation paid. They act like consequences have no importance in the world they live in, so they are untouchable.

"Things that matter to others mean little to them. They demonstrate an attitude of entitlement that makes me gag. They truly believe that society owes them something and they aren't getting it. The body piercings and the tattoos are over the top. Everything is in the extreme. I certainly understand that people strive to be different, but in this case everyone who is striving to be different is the same.

"I don't think that the last two generations of young men have any idea who they are or who they can be. It is as if they have given up on themselves and the world they live in. The violence indicates they are bored and angry and see little or no hope that things will be any different.

"So I ask myself, 'What happened? How did things get to this point? Why is there such hopelessness? What is more important, what can be done to turn this around?'

"We spoke earlier about how our society and culture often dictate certain behavioural responses from us and the importance for us to honour our maleness. As men we need to appreciate and accept the male roles that are now ingrained in us and have been for a long time. It is not a bad thing to feel as though we need to protect, challenge, provide, conquer, 'take the bullet', compete and all the other roles that are a part of who we are as men. Many men and young men have been told by various parts of society that we need to give up these roles and move on. Much pressure has been brought to bear on men, albeit subtly at first, to give up our 'Neanderthal' ways and move into the twenty-first century. Androgyny is fast coming and it is coming at the expense of our beliefs and values and our maleness.

As I have said before, it is possible for we men to retain our time honoured gifts and still be more caring, loving and nurturing. You can take the hound out of the hunt but you can't take the hunt out of the hound. We will remain who we are with our strengths and faults in tack.

I go back to the work place for example. There is no reason why we cannot work toward creating an equal playing field for all people who want to better themselves. Equality should not be based on gender or cultural differences. If you are good enough you get the job, the position or the opportunity. Period. Now I understand that this is an over simplification of the issues but the point remains. We can achieve these things through negotiation, discussion and agreement. It is possible to live with a sense of harmony and peace if we stop long enough for each of us to try to understand the 'other guy' and what drives them. We will not achieve them if we do it by coercion and threat or sanction. We men do not have to give up anything of ourselves in order for this to happen. The goals are not mutually exclusive. It will take time and it will take some common desire but it can happen.

Unfortunately, to date at least, society doesn't get that men cannot be expected to give up their particular identities and not be dramatically affected. So men in general have become angry--some have given up. The last two generations of young men are the product of having no male role models, either in their homes or in public forums, to learn from. There is a great deal of confusion in our homes and work places about who we are supposed to be, how we are supposed to act and what that is supposed to look like. They don't know how to be men, what that means and the responsibilities that come with that—no idea at all. THEY ARE LOST. Instead of planning their lives and living their days one day at a time in pursuit of their goals they live their lives from day to day just existing. They have no dreams, no goals and no hope that anything will change for them. They have no sense of direction and no drive to find any. I know that we talked about some of this before but it is so important I wanted to go over it again to refresh our thinking. We'll probably talk about it again later on too because it ties in with so much of what goes on presently in our world."

"I got you so far", he said, "But you still haven't answered my previous question and I'm interested in knowing the answer."

"OK," I said. "I have to admit that the first time I saw you and then met you I was not impressed. I know that you won't lose any sleep over that revelation but that's the truth of it. You know that your Mom spoke to me and asked if I would meet with you just to talk to you about 'things.' Obviously you agreed. To be perfectly honest I did not think you would entertain the idea of talking to me about anything so when you did I was taken by surprise and concerned a bit. I didn't have a clue what we would talk about and how that would go. I had no idea of where the boundaries were. But my word is my word so we met.

"After our first meeting I have to say that my opinion of you changed quite a bit. I still thought you were an ass with a poor attitude but you had something that I didn't expect to see. There was a vulnerability and a sadness about you. I could see it in your eyes and on your face. Now I have come to know you as a fine young man. I would be proud to say you are my friend. I also see there is a want for you to know more about who you are. I think you have a need to hear about how to be a man in this world. Not to pick at that scab again but that's the job of a father and you don't have one and I can't take his place. I know that--but I can share with you what I have come to know and understand on my own journey and maybe some of it will make sense to you and some will stick.

"My hope is that you will learn enough that when your time comes to be a father you will be able to help your sons and your daughters know and understand what it means to be a man in the world--what a privilege it is to carry that banner and to perpetuate those ingrained roles into the next generation. We are who we were created to be. I don't see how changing that is going to make us a better society. Look at how violence and fear and all the emotions that come with those situations have dramatically increased. We can see how we have become a society of people who have replaced the Lord's Prayer in our schools with 'political correctness' and now wonder what has gone so wrong with our children. Political correctness, with it's best intention, has become a tool used to distort the truth, our reality and, indeed, our integrity. I understand it to be myopic and judgmental to the point where it is and has been eroding our sense of self as men for some time. A great deal of what is happening in our world today is due to young men and women who have no direction and no understanding of what their roles are. I think that comes from having no fathers in the home— absentee parents meaning not having two parents to fulfill the responsibility of teaching and guiding the next generation so that the world truly is in better shape when they, the parents, leave it than when they came into it. I am by no means being critical of your Mom, Jacob, or any of the other single parents who are women. I accept that most do the absolute best they can but only a man can tell another man what he needs to know. Just as it is with women and their daughters."

"So to sum up my answer to your question: My desire and my hope is that you will trust me enough to be that guide for you in the absence of your father so that you stand a decent chance of having a fulfilling life—a life with some peace and harmony in it. Hopefully you will decide to carry on the responsibility of rearing your children so they treat other people with respect, with dignity, and are able to understand and honour their roles as men."

Then I stopped. I looked briefly at him but said nothing more. The thought occurred that perhaps I had gone too far too fast. He was quiet for a moment and then he said, "Ya but how do you really feel about it all." Then he laughed and I started to laugh with him. We laughed for what seemed a long time. The laughter was sincere but it also broke the tensions of the moment just passed.

Then I said, "Sorry I got all serious on you but I feel strongly about what is happening to us."

"Really! See now that part, where you get all serious on me, went right by me," he said loaded with sarcasm. Seriously. If you feel it's that important then maybe there is something for me to learn."

"Does that do it for you?" I asked.

"It's a lot to take in all at once but yeah it fills in most of the gaps. Almost. I still think there is something you are holding back but I'll respect your choice to do that." Again I was dumfounded. That he would have such insight at such a young age was utterly amazing to me. I had truly underestimated him.

"So now it is my turn to ask a question", I said. "How did your big night out work for you?"

He looked straight at me and said, "Not bad. There was lots of stuff going on and it was good to see some of the old crew." I tried to mask my disappointment. He wasn't going to mention anything about coming home in the cruiser. How would I deal with that now? I felt as though we had developed a trust of sorts and that we would be open to taking

70

some risks with each other but I had, apparently, misjudged or misunderstood that part of our relationship. I could feel the anger growing in me and I needed to be so very careful about what came out of my mouth next.

Before I had a chance to say anything more, however, Jacob said, "I learned a great deal about me and a great deal about them. I don't think that I can spend a lot of time around them anymore. What got me the most was how little ambition they have to do anything important. Its all about just 'being' and not thinking about things that affect us. Other people for instance. They talk trash most of the time. The biggest decision made that night was where we were going to go to get high and then what we were going to do to create some grief somewhere. They are bored with every day stuff so they create another reality of sorts. It's like they find little or no joy in living on the planet—they are just doing time. How sad is that? If they talk about something serious it's all negative—hopeless almost. I just didn't find it very exciting I guess. I don't want to spend my life being or feeling useless and hopeless. So I made my excuses and said I would catch up with them later. Problem was I had no wheels. Just at that moment, as if magical, I flagged down my buddy Officer O'Hanagan and talked him into giving me a lift home. Of course he wanted to know what I had done now etc. etc. It took me a bit to convince him that I was innocent of all charges--that I just needed a ride home if he didn't mind. So he did. I'm glad I went that night. I needed to see what I was missing and now I know. Time to get going--to move in another direction. That's what I was talking about with Mom. Good to see I put a smile on her face."

Needless to say I felt like an ass. Here I had the kid drawn and quartered because I had leaped to a conclusion before he had a chance to explain what had happened. So I learned that one is never too old to learn something new again. What could I say now?

"I'm glad it all worked out for the best for you. I have to admit I wondered and was a bit concerned about how it would work out but it sounds as though it went just fine. Thanks for letting me know."

"So tell me how you deal with anger," I asked him. "How do you make it go away?"

He thought for a moment and then said, "I guess like most of the people I know. If someone gets in my face I back him off. If he doesn't back off then I back him off either physically or verbally, which usually ends with a physical thing happening. He gets in--I get closer. A few beers seems to work to make it go away. It changes things for sure. I calm down most of the time. Smoke a joint, maybe do a line or two. But I find that I often take it out on good people around me—those I don't mean to hurt. Things get said and feelings get hurt. Why does it feel good, at least at the time, to yell or scream at someone or hit something or smash something? What's that about?"

"Keep that question close by but let's do this first."

He continued," That's about it. Time usually takes care of things."

"So what I'm hearing is that you tend to medicate the 'symptoms' of anger—the emotions and the feelings. Does that work for you or do you find yourself getting angry about the same things over and over? Do the same people or the same situations or the same topics keep repeating and do you keep trying to make them 'go away' doing the same things with little success? Hey, I don't doubt you can make them go away. The problem is they keep coming back."

"Mostly", he said. "I also know that I am tired of being angry all the time."

"Have you thought about a different approach? Maybe there is another way to deal with this stuff without using a drug of some kind to change your mood. What you're doing now doesn't seem to be working too well for you so why keep doing it? You asked me earlier what I thought about anger and where it came from. One of the things that I said was injustice. This is a big one. IF you want to be more successful managing your anger you need to do something different—a different approach. Anger is not bad. You can manage it and not have it manage you. It takes work—hard work. The first thing you need to do is separate your self esteem and your 'manliness' from your immediate response to anger. This whole idea that you need to 'man-up' has been grossly misunderstood and misrepresented. I'd be interested in what you feel about this idea of 'manning-up' later."

"To get back to where I was--you may have to back away yourself rather than act on the need to 'one up' the other guy. You are not less a man if you back away for a moment. I think that manning-up is about showing some maturity as a man and not having to resort to violence every time something or someone gets in your face. Violence is seldom the answer to anything. Violence usually begets violence. If we are talking about injustice here we need to remember that we often get overly protective of our close friends or loved ones and we want to protect them in some way. What we need to do is ask ourselves some basic questions about what is happening and to do that we need to give ourselves a moment or two to assess what is going on so that we can decide how we want to proceed. If the first or immediate response is to get in there and hit someone or punish someone in some way you will usually find yourself in where you can't get out. So-you need to ask yourself how much of what is happening is up to you to fix or is it about someone else and what they need to do to deal with what is happening? How much of what is happening is about your stuff? Are you owning something that has nothing to do with you? There is a difference between helping someone--supporting them—evening up the sides so to speak and taking on their battles as an excuse to work out your own anger stuff.

Alcohol and drug use doesn't work well either. Think about it. Let's say that you smash your finger. You take a pain killer to deal with the discomfort. Pretty soon the pain is gone-or at least you don't feel it anymore and that feels good. What happens when the effects of the pain killer wear off?" I continued to look at him.

He finally said, "I guess the pain would return."

"That's right", I said, "The pain would return. The source of the pain is still there telling you that something is wrong—your finger is damaged. The pain killer didn't fix the finger; it just made the pain go away. It made it easier to tolerate the damage but the source is still there. It's the same thing with anger and alcohol and drugs. Getting high or loaded doesn't make the source of the anger go away; it just makes the feelings from the source go away. When the affects of the alcohol or drugs have worn off the 'emotional pain' is back. It hasn't gone anywhere. So if you want it to go away again then you have to use to do it. The substance you use medicates the emotional distress; that's all that happens there. It doesn't produce a good long lasting solution to the problem. And you can't learn any new skills if you are cognitively impaired—high--either. I think that you already know that you can't deal with what you can't feel. Enough said about that one."

"How are you doin'—had enough?"

"I'm good if you are," he said

I carried on. "Attitude is part of the new approach. We need to do an attitude check regularly. It helps us govern the course of our lives from day to day. Enter each day with a bad attitude and you can imagine how your day is going to go. Attitude plays as big a role in the management of our emotions as anything and the good news is it is something that we can control ourselves. I asked you the question awhile ago—do we think first and then 'do' or do we 'do' first and then think. We settled on the idea that we think first. Is your glass half empty or half full? Attitude helps us decide how we are going to travel in the world we live in. In other words will we decide to see the world as a place of opportunity or of failure and defeat; will we participate in the world seeing it as a place of freedom or of oppression; will see try to see the good in others or will we always look for their faults? If we do that we will always, and I mean always, find them. Do I go through life with a feeling of entitlement—like the world and everybody in it owes me a favor and cut me a break or do I understand that if I want something I have to work for it? You never get something for nothing. Nothing worthwhile at least. Attitude is huge so YOU decide how you want to travel through this life experience. You decide how you want your sons to see the world they live in and where their place is. You help them to decide what that will look like for them. How will you help them accept their role in life as a man?"

"Do people get depressed and then the wheels fall off for them or do the wheels fall off for them and then they get depressed? I'm thinking that it happens all at once and that one doesn't necessarily lead to the other although it certainly can. There are things that we do here, too, that can help us stay focused on the 'up' side of our day to day life experience. We all need to decide who our 'travelling' companions will be each day. Who are we going to have in our lives each day? Do they enrich our lives? What do they contribute to the quality of our lives and what do I contribute to the quality of their lives? We need to surround ourselves with positive people. They would be those who see similar beauty and possibilities in the world around us; those who hold the same values as we do; those who cherish the same personal freedoms as we do; and those who can laugh at the same things as we do. Laughter is one of the great healers. It is more difficult to be down, sad or angry if you are laughing more than you are not. Understand this, Jacob. You have control over all of this that I have spoken about today. You can give it up or exchange it for misery anytime you want but it is yours to own and to have for as long as you want it to be a part of how you do your business each day. You learned that the other night when you went out with your friends. Think about how you were influenced just in that short period of time. Imagine what it would be like to be around that for a lifetime. What would you have to pass on to your sons and daughters? What could you tell them?"

I needed to stop. I really enjoy spending time with Jacob. He is truly invested in wanting to make something different happen for himself. I am convinced of this. But I was running down in a hurry and I didn't want him to see me going through that. I knew it would happen more often as we went along and I knew that I would have to tell him what was going on with me but not now—no, not now.

"Jacob, I need to make some phone calls and I'm not sure how long it will take so I'm going to need to call it for today. Before we go, though, I want to get back to your question about why it feels so good to smash things and hit things when you are angry and how you often feel justified when you do. See I do remember these things." I wanted to lighten it up some before I sent him on his way. "Think of yourself as a pressure cooker and the heat is turned up all the way. At some point you are not going to be able to handle any more heat or 'pressure'. So your top blows and all the pressure inside is released. Now you can go back to taking more heat until you get full up again and the pattern repeats itself. So it goes with anger. It builds up—needs a release—you give it that when you hit, smash, scream, or any of the other things that are physical in nature. You take the pain and the discomfort from the 'inside' and put it on the 'outside'. Smash something or someone and the pain is in your hand now-on the outside. It's the release of emotional and mental energy—getting rid of the build up--that feels good. But before it blows you are walking around looking for what it will take—'just give me a reason'--to blow the top off. It is not hard to find something or someone who will accommodate your search."

"Make sense?" I asked.

"Put that way-yeah it does"

"Good. Here's what I'd like you to think about before we see each other again: Using the scale thing put a mark on there that would indicate where you believe you are when you think about how stressed you are most days. Be sure to put a date with your mark.

1	2	3	4	5	6	7	8	9	10

1. How would people around you know that you were stressed out? What would they notice or see?
2. What could you change that would help lessen/lower your stress levels?
3. How will people around you describe you when you are less stressed?

By the way—I haven't forgotten the other question on the table either. Give some thought to the 'manning-up' question. I'm interested to know what you hear when someone says to you that you have to 'man-up'—OK?"

He got up from his chair and began to make his way to the stairs. He stopped and glanced over at me. Then he gave me the look and the nod but added a shrug. Ah, he was giving me something new. Then he said, "Sure". He took a step down and then stopped and said, "Thanks for caring." As he took another step I said, "You're welcome—you're worth it. And Jacob, I want to apologize to you for underestimating you. That won't happen again—I promise you that." With that he was away and I went into the house and literally passed out on the couch. Note to self before oblivion hit--call doc in the morning and get him to prescribe some stronger vitamins and supplements. I knew I needed to increase my staying power somehow.

The next few days went by with little disruption. I noticed how low keyed I was. I also noticed that it was taking longer for me to build up strength and momentum for my visits with Jacob. I heard myself say "Please let me do this—let me finish what has been started here." Other things began to become more apparent to me. Things like losing my focus—I would day dream of things that I hadn't thought about for quite some time. When I slept I would dream of past things that got mixed in with other happenings until they became one jumbled vision. I would stare off into the distance at nothing in particular allowing my hearing to be more discerning. I felt like I could hear a pin drop at the end of the street. Remarkable how all the senses were becoming more acute. I don't know what any of that meant but it was fascinating how my body was beginning to prepare itself for the time when my physical self would begin to falter. All the same a very solemn thought process.

Then I went back to thinking about Jacob. Was I rambling with him? So much to tell him and so little time it seems. I need to help him see and understand the importance of connecting the culturally ingrained characteristics he recognizes with living in this ever changing world. He needs to understand that it is not only possible to do this but is mandatory he find a way to do this and not forfeit his unique identity in the process. He still has to live in a world that expects much of him but does not want him to rely anymore on those qualities that have shaped men for ions. How do I help him accept that he has value to the world not only as a human being but as a man? Does he know or will he know that from acceptance of his true value comes a belief in his 'true purpose'? Part of that purpose is to protect his social and cultural inheritance. He will need to do this in an atmosphere of great external pressure to change how we, as men, do our business. He will need to thwart any attempt to move him toward a gender neutral society by living his life true to his emotional, mental and cultural identity and to believe in those qualities to provide him with all that he seeks. He will need to do this all the while learning how to negotiate and accept the valid needs of those around him. How did we get to a place that seems so convoluted? It must be very confusing and stressful for a young man like Jacob.

We are told that we need to be more caring but tough, compassionate but unshakable, nurturing but consistent. There are times when we just need to scream, "Hey, will you folks make up your freakin' minds please." Sometimes it is so easy to understand why men have taken to using more alcohol, drugs and medication as a coping strategy in a very uncertain world, not that that is a good way to deal with things—it's not, and that violence has been increasing at an alarming rate—also unacceptable. We are expected to live with all this and move on—be tough BUT not too tough.

I had to get up and move around—I went outside, down the stairs, decided to go right and began to walk at a comfortable pace.

Thinking was becoming my sole source of entertainment. I was thinking about how hard it is to stop thinking because even when you are thinking about not thinking, you are thinking. I stopped trying not to think about things anymore.

My conversations with Jacob had become an obsession, but in a good way. They were what occupied my mind almost entirely these days. I'm grateful for those conversations because I would otherwise obsess about my health and what I will never get to do and why I put off things for another' day. I always thought I would have another day. How naïve was I? There was a spiritual component attached to our conversations that I couldn't articulate but I knew that it was growing in strength. I tried not to question it, but I understood that it had great value.

I wouldn't know until some time later just how much value it had for Jacob and for me.

As I got closer to the house, I could see someone on the front porch next door. It was Annie. I just caught the tail end of her going through the front door waving something and shaking her head, a phone I guessed. As I sat down in my favourite porch chair I heard the phone ring next door and then the loud voice and the cursing that followed. Within seconds the door had flown open and out came an object that made it to the sidewalk before ending its unscheduled flight.

My first thought was to go see what was happening, but then again it really was none of my business, so I sat still. It was very strange nonetheless. Soon I would hear what I didn't want to know.

Stress/An Emotional Cancer

Calm had been restored by the time Annie came out of her house. She looked over toward me and asked, "Can I have a minute?"

"Certainly," I said, knowing full well that this was not going to be a minute conversation but, hey, where was I going?

I watched her approach and then sit down on the only other chair on the porch. She was trembling, as if she had just gotten back from the Arctic. I was very much concerned for her but let her proceed at her own speed.

"Can I offer you something?" I asked.

"A glass of water would be nice, thanks." Her voice was so quiet I could hardly hear her.

When I returned she had stopped shaking and actually looked quite peaceful. She had either retreated or recovered.

She began, "I really don't have anyone else to talk to about this stuff, and I know that you have been such an enormous help to and influence on Jacob. I don't want to burden you with anything more. And Jacob, he speaks about you all the time. Jim this and Jim that. I feel as though I have gotten to know you better just by listening to him go on. Maybe I shouldn't . . ."

I stopped her before she had a chance to go any further. "Annie," I said to her with all sincerity, "it must be clear to you by now that Jacob has become very important to me and by extension so have you, so let's not worry about intruding or whatever, OK?

"What's going on? I saw you earlier going into your house. Then I heard you and then you gave flight to the phone. Something has happened that has upset you. Care to tell me what it is?"

She looked at me and then started to cry. She cried the tears of frustration and then of anger and fear. I didn't interrupt again. Finally she looked at me again and said, "He's back."

That was it? Just "He's back"?

"Who is back? What do you mean?" And then it hit me, as if someone had punched me in the stomach. The air seemed to disappear around me. I knew who she meant.

"Jacob's father. I gag at the thought that I ever let that pig near me. Jacob was the only thing – and I mean the ONLY thing – that had any good attached to that horrible excuse for a man. He gives men a bad name. After four friggin' years that low-life bastard has returned like a horrible smell and just wants to waltz back into our lives as if nothing happened.

"He wants to take up where he left off: being Jacobs' father. That would suggest that he had been a father at one time, which he never was. He says he has his right and knows that Jacob needs him. I asked him how he knew anything about Jacob and what he needs. He said he has seen him a few times. He said he followed him around for the last day or two, just watching him. It's really creepy to me.

"You know that Jacob has a birthday coming up soon. He will be 18. I had planned to have a few people over just to mark the occasion because Jacob doesn't want a big deal of any kind. No party, but just his favourite ice cream and cake. He is going to ask you if you would come over for some when he sees you later today. Before you say anything to that, I have to tell you something and I don't blame you if you get upset with me. I don't know why I did this but I did and that's that.

"Harlan – that's the idiot's name – always knew how to push my buttons, and he still remembers, I guess. He wants to come to the house on Saturday for cake and ice cream to meet with Jacob as sort of a re-introduction/get- together at the same time. I said no and he got upset with this. So he tried some of the usual stuff: threats, guilt, accusations and finally said that he would just show up then, and the chips would fall where they may.

"Then he said that he might as well bring a few things with him so that he could stay for a bit until he got on his feet. I'd rather burn the house to the ground then have that scum sucker anywhere near us, let alone stay here.

"So I told him…"Her voice drifted off momentarily, she looked away and then she looked me straight in the eye and said, "And then I told him about you and that you had filled the father role for Jacob and that Jacob really liked you. I also told him that you would be at the lunch for Jacob on Saturday and that if he showed up that he would have to deal with you and that Jacob would truly be mortified. So if he had ANY decency left in him, he would not show up but rather just slink away the way he did before and leave us alone."

She paused, gathered some air and continued. "He just laughed and said he would see ALL of us on Saturday and hung up. That's when I threw the phone out the front door. I'm so sorry, Jim. I didn't mean to get you involved in this. This isn't your affair to concern yourself with. I just didn't know what else to say. It was out before I knew it. I wanted him to stay away and thought that, if he knew other people were going to be here, he would back off."

My heart was pounding in my chest. It was a familiar feeling. I recognized it as primitive, in that it had always been with me. The "protector," the one who stood in front of his family to "take the bullet. It was all the stuff that Jacob and I had been talking about these past months. It rushed back to the surface as if queued.

How could I not be involved now? Did I look forward to it? No. Thirty years ago I might have. Would I be involved in some way? Yes. I also realized and admitted that I saw Annie and Jacob as a sort of family. That thought was, in some ways, more frightening than the idea of facing a man who had the potential to destroy or take away everything that was now very important to me.

As well, I was not in any way physically ready or able to do anything about what Saturday may turn into, so I would have to be sure it didn't get there somehow. It was interesting that Jacob and I would likely be talking about stress and how it affects our lives from day to day.

You just never know what a day has in store for you until the sun rises and you are in it.

The only thing that I had to say to Annie was "Are you planning to tell Jacob about his father wanting to be in his life and, if so, when are you going to tell him? And what about Saturday?"

It wasn't difficult to see she was stressed to the max. Perhaps overwhelmed would be a better description. She stammered out a response but I couldn't tell what she was trying to say.

"Annie, sit down and take a sip of water. Just go easy. I'm not angry with you although I am a bit surprised. You did what you felt you needed to do, and he's a bully. I think what we need to do is move the gathering to my place so that he may think twice about barging in here. I'm more concerned about how you are going to tell Jacob, and that discussion needs to be between just the two of you. I can't be a part of that. You need to do that as soon as he gets home from school, OK?"

She nodded to me. That appears to be a trait that got passed on to Jacob. Now I knew where he'd got it. After some debate with her, she finally relented and agreed to have the get-together at my place, but only if she paid for everything and did all the work.

That was not the least of it. She still had to figure out how to break the news to him. I finally said, "Look, Jacob is not a kid anymore. He is bordering on being an adult, so perhaps you just sit him down. Talk to him as an adult would. Tell him the truth without the colourful descriptions of how you feel about Harlan, and let him do what he does with that.

"He is supposed to come over later, so perhaps I can help him with it as well. He'll let me know what he needs to do, I'm sure. There is no easy way. But if you try to influence him against his father, if you try to manipulate this in any way, like prevent him from seeing him or talking to him, you will drive him closer to him. You have to let him make his own decision about this. I suspect he will want to see him if for no other reason that to satisfy himself about what and how he thinks about his father. He may want the opportunity to tell him to get lost and never darken your doorway again. He has a great deal to say to Harlan, most of which I don't think Harlan is going to want to hear. It is part of Jacob's healing process, and he has to learn how to deal with this kind of adversity. He'll be good with it. That's my guess.

"I know you're right," she said, "but I hate the thought of that piece of crap even drawing the same air as Jacob."

A little later I watched as Jacob stepped up the walkway to his house and went in. I was inside my place out of sight because I didn't want him to see me and come straight to my porch. Ten minutes, 20 minutes and then half an hour went by. I didn't know if he was going to pass on our meeting today or not. Finally, after 40 minutes he came out and turned toward my house. It was good to see Jacob, as always. His confidence continued to show itself—he seemed more sure of who he was. His stride had more purpose now. He took the stairs two at a time and threw himself into the chair.

"So how goes it", I said.

"Mom said you know—right?"

"Yeah, I know," I said to him. "How are you doing with it?"

"How the f--- am I supposed to feel about any of it? Sorry. What am I supposed to think? Does he think that I will just run into his open arms like some puppy dog? I'd like to smash him in the face and tell him to lose our address and phone number.

81

I begin to feel good about being in my own skin—some really good things are beginning to happen to me and for me—I met some new people who actually like being on the planet--who like me just because of who I am and then this shit happens." He caught his breath and then continued in this staccato fashion, "Maybe I'm not supposed to get ahead—maybe this is the cosmos saying to me 'Hey, don't get used to this cause it ain't staying and either are you.' I don't know about anything here except I got no use for the prick. On the other side I always wanted the chance to tell him what I thought about him and what he did to my Mom. I could never stand up for her against him because he gets mean and I was afraid of him. We are probably about the same size now. It would be a different story for sure. Might even be fun."

There was a momentary silence.

"Then there is the part of me who always wanted to know why he took off—why he did what he did. Were we so bad to live with? Why didn't he love us? Why was he so angry? It would be good to have those answers, but then another part of me feels as though I couldn't care less now.

"Our time has come and gone, and I can't trust him. If I can't trust him, he's got nothing for me. He was supposed to be with me and help me learn stuff. He was supposed to teach me things. He was supposed to take me to the park and play – show me how to fly a kite – take me to a ball game and help me learn how to catch. He promised me that he would do that, but he never did and then he didn't have time and then he just took off. I don't have anything for him either. Just a lot of questions."

Then he focuses on me and asked, "What do you think I should do?"

"Two things come to mind immediately," I responded. "First off, it isn't my decision to be a part of and, secondly, this is a good time to think about some of the things that we have discussed and make your own decision. You can do that. I know you can. Trust your instincts. They will help you know what to do as well. All you need to do is separate out your emotions as best you can and think about what would be in your best interests here.

"Also, your mom figures in here, but only indirectly. You cannot decide for her and she doesn't need you to think for her or to speak for her. But true enough, your decision will have an affect on her as well. Remember we talked about not making emotional decisions in emotional states of mind. This is one of those times when it is important you don't do that. So the question is this: what do you need to do, right now, that would help you get your emotions and feelings under control?' That's your first priority."

"I'm going to take a walk," he said.

"Then I'll see you in a bit," I said as I started to get up. With that he was gone too.

As I went in the house I remembered that I had a call to make and I was not sure how to ask for what I needed. I just knew that it had to be done.

Later, I went over to see how Annie was doing. As I gently knocked on the screen door, I could hear her blowing her nose. She came to the door, smiled and said, "Hi. Could I get you some lemonade or something?"

"Sure. That would be fine."

She pushed open the door and we sat outside to sip our drinks. She was quiet and I was too. Then we both started to speak. This time I nodded to her. She smiled again and said, "He's a remarkable kid. I just hope he doesn't feel like he needs to protect me or defend me in some way and get carried away."

"He'll do what he needs to do and I think he'll do it well. I'm not sure I would want to be Harlan at the end of the day, though," I said.

We made small talk until we saw Jacob come back down the street toward us. He had been gone for an hour or so but he seemed to be more together than when he left.

As he walked toward us he said, "Are we still going to meet today? I really need to do that."

"Yeah, sure," I said. I tried to keep the tiredness out of my voice.

I handed my glass to Annie and Jacob and I headed for my porch. When we got there, we sat down and then he said, "I've decided I'm going to talk to him, but not alone. I would appreciate it if you would sit in. I don't want you to talk for me, but I need to have someone – you – there to help me stay on top and not let him get to me.

"I know what I want to say. I'll even try to be respectful but I want him to hear what I have to say. Knowing him, I don't think he'll be happy 'cause he likes to be in control. Not Saturday, though. Saturday is my day."

"If that's what you want that's good by me," I said.

"That's how I would like to handle this. Thanks." That was all he said.

"Well, today would be a good day to find out where you are on the stress scale." I chuckled a bit when I asked him.

With a smirk that was warm and friendly, he said, "Now? About a seventeen, and about a six to a seven before the bomb hit today," he said. "I'm not sure about how to reduce it without having a couple of beers or a toke or two. How I would look if I were less stressed? I don't know. I guess I would be more relaxed and less sarcastic—more patient and less serious."

"Good insights there, and good information for you. It's like a baseline to work from, if you get what I'm saying?"

"Something to compare with, you mean," he asked

"Yes, that's it. So where do you think all the stress comes from? I mean, how do we get so stressed? And why don't we know it sometimes?

"Well days like today sure cause it. Things come at me right out of nowhere, you know? I don't expect them. Sitting in traffic jams can also do it for me. When things don't go my way, I get stressed out. Also people that piss me off or the things that they do. I guess it's like anger too. The things that anger me also stress me out."

I tried to clarify what I was asking him to consider. "I know you mentioned a couple of things just now, but what about beyond that? How would you know that you were stressed? If you can't identify what the stressors are, how do you go about trying to change things so that they aren't stressors anymore?"

"I'll help you out with this one," I continued, making sure that he was still with me. "Some of what we need to pay attention to are things like our mental signs, meaning do we have difficulty making decisions, do we just 'blank out' periodically, do we have trouble with remembering things, even simple things. There are also emotional signs like not being able to see or find the humour in things where we used to, so we're irritable most of the time, nervous and anxious most of the time and feeling angry a lot of the time."

He looked a little lost here, so I said to him, "Hang in there with me. There is a point to all this. If we experience frequent headaches, sleep problems, fatigue and allergy problems, our physical condition is being affected.

"Last of all, our behaviour changes. We miss appointments, increase our use of mood-altering substances, have low energy levels so we are less active doing the things we like to do and we may overeat sometimes. All of this stuff indicates that we are carrying around stress that is becoming more than we can handle."

"Yeah, I know what you mean here," said Jacob. "I didn't know that's what was happening, just that I felt some of those things that you just talked about. I remember feeling really tired, but I wasn't sleeping well. I thought that I was tired from lack of sleep. I also remember being really edgy and sketchy. I wouldn't have known this was all due to stress."

"So how does this fit in with what we have been talking about regarding male roles and how we respond to certain things?" I asked him. "There are many who want us to change what we do and how we do them. I have said this before. We are told we need to set aside those qualities that describe our social and cultural upbringing-the lessons and values that we heard about early on. Many of the signs that I just mentioned come from our struggles to keep our masculine identities yet be more 21st century men. We hear 'quit your whining and get on with things.' Whiners are wimps. We think we should never show weakness and admitting that we are stressed out is a weakness, certainly to some, anyway.

"I don't agree with that statement, but that is how it is in many places with many people. Perhaps that is part of what your father was carrying around with him. Maybe he had had enough and just needed to leave. Who knows? I'm not defending him in any way, but considering what made him walk is important to understand. Many men carry it around. It begins to eat away at us on the inside while we smile on the outside. However, we tend to act out our stress and eventually it goes from internal to external. Road rage is a good example of what I'm talking about. There is a saying about this: deal with your stress and hurt others less.

"Again we go back to the rapid changes being made in the rules that men are expected to live by today and the wide range of expectations that we are asked to adhere to. Many of us are finding it difficult to make that leap. Oh, I do believe that some stress is necessary in our lives. I agree with that for sure. It does help to keep us focused and aware of what is happening to us and around us. I'm not sure, though, that this is the kind of stress that we need to be dealing with. Many men agree. They just go about dealing with it in ways that are not healthy or helpful to the rest of us."

"I can't remember all this stuff," he complained. "Trying to do that would stress me out. I'd be stressed trying to remember how to figure out if I'm stressed of not."

"You're right. That's true enough," I chuckled, "but you don't have to remember all this stuff. What is important for you to know here is that all this stuff can happen and often does. If you can recognize that something is out of whack and you see that you are tired all the time and can't remember simple things, for instance, it will help you say, 'Whoa, something is happening and I need to check this out.' Once the stressors are identified, the solutions come easier. We'll talk about that too.

"Imagine yourself as a high-performance racing car and you have a full tank of gas. There is a road in front of you that is perfectly long and straight and goes on for miles. Someone starts you up, points you in the right direction and lays a brick on your gas pedal. You are going flat out in no time and continue to do that until when?"

"I guess until I run out of gas," he says, a bit unsure of himself.

"And then what do you think happens?" I asked.

"It stops running," he answers a bit more aware of where I am going here.

"Precisely. You stop running. Actually you have been running at a peak performance level for so long that that level of action has become normal for you. But with no gas to fuel your energy needs, you stop. You can't carry the momentum any further and you just stop. So it is with us and our stress. We carry a certain level of it for so long that it becomes normal to us until we run out of gas and then we stop functioning.

"That is why it is important for us to check every once in a while to see how we are doing. It's important for us to question any changes that others see in us or that we see in ourselves. Please believe me when I tell you that high levels of stress that go unchallenged are the equivalent of emotional cancer. It will eat you alive from the inside of you out, and you won't know it is happening until you just stop one day. Some call it having a meltdown. Call it what you like, but it is not pretty and some don't do well afterward.

"The really interesting thing to me is that we are primarily responsible for about 90 percent of the stress that we experience in our lives. If we are responsible for it, then we can deal with it. Think about it for a minute: how many of us leave ourselves 20 minutes to drive to an appointment that we know is 30 minutes away? Think about your own situation each day. Hell, think about today and what happened. So where does it come from, this stress? Where does it come from?" I repeated.

He was really working this one over in his mind and then said, "I know that when someone wants me to do something and I don't want to do it I go around feeling a bit nervous because I know that they are expecting me to do it. So I have to come up with some excuse about why I didn't and I don't like doing that."

"That's a great example and is so true," I said. "Actually that is part of the one major source of most of our stress: Expectations. There are three different kinds of expectations.

First, we have expectations of ourselves. We expect that as men we are supposed to face all problems and have a solution for each one. We are problem solvers and fixers. That is our job, right?

The next is that we are supposed to know how to fix the lamp or the toaster. We are expected to know how to build the tree house. When the car stops, we are supposed to know what the problem is and how to repair it and get the car going again. It's almost like we pop out of the womb with a toolbox and instructions strapped to our backsides ready to go. So we not only have expectations of what we are supposed to be able to do, but other people – our partners, our children, our neighbours and the communities we live in – have expectations of us as well. How can we live up to all those expectations?

"The last one, is about our having expectations of other people and how they treat us. Say, for instance, that I do someone a favour and then I need one back. I expect that because I did this guy a favour and he owes me that he will pay up when I need it. But he doesn't. So I get gnarly. I get upset and angry perhaps because I expected him to respond differently than he did. As we know, being angry and working to keep our anger alive, especially when we feel a right to our anger, is very stressful and it takes a great deal of our energy.

"If we do something for someone, that's about our giving that person a gift. It should not have strings attached to it. If we see our good deed as something that he owes us for, then our gift is not a gift at all but rather a bribe. In essence, we are saying, 'I'll do this for you now, but you will have to do something for me in the future.' If you can't give a gift to someone, then don't do it. When we help someone out of a jam, do we hope that they will do the same for us if they can? Sure we do! Do I expect that he will. I hope not. And if he doesn't help me out, what happens to me then? Do I get angry? Do I feel disappointed or let down? Usually that's what happens when we are expecting a payback.

"I wanted to talk about some of that today so that you will have some things to use tomorrow. It's a big day for you tomorrow, in many ways. I have no doubt that you will handle it well. I'll see you around two, I guess. I spoke with your mom earlier and she seemed to think that would be a good time. I understand a few other folks will be coming around as well. That's good. No homework today. Happy birthday."

"Thanks again," he said and he was off.

I got done what needed to be done and decided that I would just take it easy and watch the ballgame on TV. Saturday would come soon enough. I felt energized and tired at the same time. I wondered how Jacob would handle himself. It will be a real barometer of where he is with his own comfort level. Will he want his father to see that he is a man too and not to mess with him? Will he be able to express what he feels and what he thinks without resorting to violence or threats? Would he be able to rely on his instincts to guide him? Does he understand that being a man in the world is about knowing who you are and where your place in the world is according to what is happening on the inside, by trusting your instincts and your intuition and not feeling as though you have something to prove in order to be seen as a man?

"Being men in the world is about accepting the roles we recognize from the inside and not needing to prove who we are on the outside. It is not by behaviour as much as it is by demeanor that we are measured as men, especially by other men. I know that Jacob is not there yet, but he will show where he is by how he articulates his needs. As much as he didn't admit it, he must feel a great deal of stress with everyone watching and wondering what he will do and how he will handle himself.

Manhood: One Giant Step Forward

Friday seemed to evaporate and Saturday came all too soon. All those invited to be at Jacobs' celebration were present. I placed myself on the porch while the others were inside and in the back yard. I could hear the laughter from where I sat. It was a good sound, one that I hadn't heard in quite some time, emanating from my house. It's usually as quiet in there. I need to do something about that.

I could see the taxi coming down the street and knew that it was Harlan. It stopped in front of Annie's house, and Harlan stumbled a bit getting out of the back seat. He lifted a suitcase out of the back as well, as though he indeed planned to move in. He paid the driver and off the taxi went. Harlan just stood there looking at the house and then began to walk up the sidewalk with his luggage in hand. I caught his attention from where I was sitting to explain that no one was there.

"Well, where are they? She knew I was coming and I want to see Jacob to wish him a happy birthday and all."

"They're all here at my house. Inside actually," I said.

"Oh." He started to make his move toward my place and then thought better of bringing his luggage with him, so he left it in the middle of the walk.

"OK. Call him and tell him I'm here to see him."

I hesitated just long enough for him to understand that that was the last order I would hear from him. I leaned back in my chair and called for Jacob through the screen. I made it a point not to invite Harlan onto my property, knowing that he would come anyway.

Jacob came to the door, and looked out to see his father standing on the walk in front. Then he came through the door and stood at the top of the stairs but did not move further to see him closer.

Harlan appeared to be confused by Jacob's action, so he came up my walkway to position himself at the bottom of the stairs. Then he said, "Come on down and give your Dad a hug, boy."

Jacob stood his ground and said, "Nah, this is OK for what I've got to say."

Harlan's expression changed. It was clear that he was very uncomfortable with how this was going. He was, indeed, used to having his way, of being in control. He tried to laugh off Jacob's stand but it did little to ease the tension that had quickly developed between them.

"I thought we'd go down to the pub now that you're the big 18 and celebrate your coming of age. You're a man now, so what do you say? I always thought this is the way father and son should be. It'll give us a chance to catch up and clear some of the air."

Jacob turned slightly to catch me in his vision and then turned back to face his father head on.

He began by saying, "First of all, the legal age is 19 not 18 so that's out. I guess the next point would be I'm not doing that whether I could have or not. Do you think you can just blow in here and pick up where you think you left off? If I didn't know better, I'd say you've already had a head start on me anyway. Liquid courage to face the music, sort of?

"You know, there was a part of me – a small part – that was looking forward to seeing you today. I had lots of questions I needed to ask you. I wanted you to be able to explain what happened four years ago that made you run off. Why? Did you have a better offer somewhere else? Some little bar-fly that caught your fancy maybe, someone you could order around to make you feel important?"

Harlan's face turned red and he made a move to come up the stairs. I could feel Jacob steel himself for the pending confrontation. "You watch your mouth, boy. You don't get to talk to me like that. I'm still your father and … "

Jacob cut him off mid-sentence with an abrupt. "No, you're not. You gave up that right when you took off. I don't have a father now, at least not a blood father."

Again he turned a bit to the side to glance at me and quickly turned back to face Harlan. Now there was an audience standing at the door on the inside looking out at the situation. I remained seated but moved closer to the edge of my chair.

Harlan edged up one more stair. He was two below Jacob now. I could see that they would be about the same height if they were on level ground. Jacob might have given away 20 pounds, if that. He was also in much better shape physically than was Harlan. It would be a good tussle if it came to that, and I must admit that part of me wished it would, but that wouldn't do what was important for Jacob to do right now.

When Harlan stopped, Jacob challenged him. "I'm not sure that would be a good idea now. I'm not some little kid who you can scare the shit out of anymore. You were a bully then and you are just a bully now. You or nothing else has changed.

"Actually I'd like to thank you for that. You helped us realize that we really didn't need you to survive. More to the point, Mom and I don't need or want you around us now. We can do just fine on our own. I thought you might have something to teach me – I hoped that this would turn out differently – and I wanted you to be different, but you're not. I can see that there is nothing you have to offer that I want or need from you. I think the best move for all of us would be for you to leave now and don't forget your bag over there. And lose our address and phone number."

It all happened at light speed. Harlan was up the remaining two steps and had reached out to grab Jacob by his shirtfront. I was up off my chair to grab hold of Jacob's arm, which had been drawn back to hit Harlan. Officer O'Hanagan came through the door in time to dislodge Harlan's hand from the front of Jacob before anything more damaging happened.

O'Hanagan said, in very official Irish police-type language, "Well, now let's see what we got here then. We got a trespassing violation, along with assault and battery, and … "He sniffed the air around Harlan. "Perhaps even a wee bit intoxicated in a public place. Am I to believe that you are on probation right now as well?

Harlan began to sputter, completely off guard, "I'm just here to celebrate my son's birthday. I wasn't looking for any grief."

With that he took a step or two backward, no doubt hoping that he could walk away if he just left now.

Jacob had taken a step backward now, so O'Hanagan had replaced him at the top of the stairs. "Is that a fact? I don't recall you being invited onto this man's property and I don't recall this young man inviting you to grab him by the shirtfront either."

A police cruiser came to a halt in front of the house, and another officer got out. Harlan knew he was screwed but was not going to go quietly. He looked at Jacob and said, "F--- you anyway. You were always a pain in the ass to have around. You want to know why I dumped you? Because you weren't worth me stickin' around for. You and your dumb ass mother were nothin' but boat anchors to me. Good riddance to all of you," he screamed.

"Officer O'Hanagan had him by the back of his neck now, opened the rear door of the cruiser and tossed him inside with a bit more enthusiasm than was necessary. He turned to us and said that we would need to come down a bit later and sign the complaint. With that he was off and it was all over in minutes. It seemed longer but that was it.

We all gathered in my back yard to continue celebrating Jacob's day, a recognition of his birth day. I knew that it would be difficult to carry on without going over what happened, so I asked Jacob for a minute. We found a quiet spot at the end of the yard.

"Are you OK?" I asked.

He got a bit bleary eyed and he shook as though he'd just been hit with an electrical shock, but kept it together. "Yeah, it's just so disappointing. I have waited for so long to speak to him and to ask him 'why?' and this is the way it ends. This isn't the way it was supposed to go. The things he said at the end stung some, but I have to consider where that came from and who delivered the message. He's just an ass

91

who doesn't know what he is giving up. Mom and I are better off without him.

"It just feels strange, as if he never existed. It was over so quick and yet I wanted him to just go away. I guess he held more magic for me in my head than in reality. Anyway, it's done and I admit that I feel much better for it that way."

The anger that I thought would be left over didn't show up. I believed that he really didn't want to concern himself with his father and those unanswered questions anymore.

"For what it's worth, I thought you handled yourself pretty well." I said. "You said what you needed to say and you said it from the heart. Good for you. It looked like you gave a lot of thought to what we have talked about and prepared yourself well. I've got to admit that when he made his move up the stairs, a small part of me was hoping that you'd nail him because he deserved it. But I'm glad you didn't because that would have created a whole different situation.

"This way you can come out of it with a sense of having done it right, and I think that you went a long way to helping Officer O'Hanagan see you in a different light. That's not a bad thing either. So what now?"

He thought for a minute and then said, smiling, "Cake and ice cream sounds good to me, I'm buying."

Then he did the unexpected. He held out his hand and said, "Thank you."

There was a sincerity in his voice that was different somehow. I thought back to his statement on the porch and the look he flashed me when he told his father that he didn't have a blood father anymore. Just for a moment I felt I had been adopted. I took his hand and we exchanged a solemn handshake. Two shakes and a look straight into each other's eyes.

"I have a question for you," I said, "but it can wait. Go ahead. I'll be right there."

As I watched him walk away toward his mother and the rest of the group, I realized that he had taken another giant step toward that illusive state of manhood. He had conducted himself in a way that would make any father proud. He had handled himself well, faced his fears and risked a great deal by dragging his secrets into the light of day. He had taken away their power over him. He had honoured his character and done the deed with purpose.

A good number of young men his age would have either discounted the importance of what they felt, feeling their feelings aren't important anyway, buried them under a blanket of anger or drugs and alcohol, struck out in a violent way, or just tried to ignore them and hope they would go away. Jacob felt strong enough and important enough to know what needed to be said and so he said it.

I needed a moment to gather myself. I hadn't signed on for this, I thought to myself. I didn't regret a moment of it either.

Suddenly I heard Leo's voice in the back chambers of my mind. His words were clear, however, and, as usual, comforting and honest. "Trust your instincts," he is saying, "Let your conscience be your guide. You will do it right because you know who you are and why this is important. Jacob has to grow at his own speed, and you will need to take your directions from him."

I moved into the room with the others and listened to them discuss Harlan and what had just transpired. They were all supportive of Jacob. Annie blushed with a mixture of pride and concern. Her son was growing into manhood and she knew it. It saddened her as well, I'm sure, because Jacob was changing and she knew she was limited in terms of what she could teach him. He was going to need her less and less, but she also understood that this was as it is meant to be.

The gathering broke up a short while later. I caught Jacob's eye and motioned to the front porch. We each took a seat.

"A great deal has happened here today," I began. "Interesting things were said. What I need to know is were they said in the heat of battle? Were they said as a mistake? Were they said as a slip of the tongue? Were they said with anger in your heart and were they meant to hurt Harlan? Were they said with honesty and truth?"

I waited for him to speak.

When he did, he asked me a question in return. "Before I answer that I have a question of you. I'll ask you, but you need to know that there is no disrespect meant. I don't know how else to ask you, so I'll just put it out there. What gives you the right to tell me what I need to do? How do I even know that you know what you're talking about? How did you get so smart?"

Well. I'll give him this. He is concise. He doesn't beat around the bush. The questions are ones that I anticipated would come up at some point. I guess today's the day. How much do I tell him? How much can I tell him?

"Do you want all that at once?" I asked.

"If you want your question answered today," he replied, "then the answer would be yes."

"First of all, I have no intention of telling you how to live your life and what you need to do. The best I can do is suggest possible solutions for you to consider. I can explain the reason certain things go down the way they do. I can help you see a side of something that is uncomfortable for you or that you don't want to consider for whatever your reasons. I can provide you with accurate information, so that when you decide to decide, you will, at least, have good information to work with and not some half-baked thinking from somebody out there who has their own agenda at play.

"I will never try to manipulate you into doing something I think you should do. It is your life to live and not mine. You have to learn by your own decision-making process. You know how that works because we have talked about it and you get it. I know you do. However, that doesn't mean that you will always make the right choice, but you will have what you need to, at least, make a choice.

"You will have options. Without options happiness is not possible. In the end, you will decide things for yourself based on your beliefs around right and wrong. These, your beliefs, will be governed, to a large degree, by the things you have seen and heard since you were young.

"You had asked me before why I am doing this, and I provided an answer to that. I said that I wanted to be part of your process and to help you journey toward manhood. I believe that I can help you understand more about the socially and culturally ingrained character traits that have helped and will continue to help how you shape your life and how you make your decisions.

"You asked me what was in it for me, and I believe that I gave you an answer to that as well. I said what I said, knowing that you were interested in learning more about how to assume the role of a man in the world. Being a part of this is a privilege for me, Jacob. It's about one male helping another to become the man he is destined to be. Knowing that you will pass this on to your sons is a great gift for me. I didn't use those exact words, but that was the short form.

"Now you want to know what gives me the right to tell you anything. YOU give me the right. You do that by coming back to talk to me on the porch here week after week. Your body language says that you are interested. and your questions ask for more information and knowledge. You have taken great risks to show me another side of you that few people get to witness, and that is important to me.

"When you sit here and we talk you have energy in your eyes and on your face. If you didn't want this you would not and could not fake what I see and hear in your voice. But you can stop anytime you want, Jacob, with no hard feelings on my part. As long as you keep coming, I will do my best to give you straight answers and explanations to your questions. I will also give you what I believe is important for you to hear so that you can proceed in this world a strong, resilient, educated, knowledgeable and capable man. The things we discuss – the words I choose to use will be those of a mentor, if you like, and of someone who cares about the messages you receive.

I needed to make reference to the mentor aspect because I needed to draw the line to be sure I didn't encroach upon the sanctity of fatherhood. If Jacob wanted it to be different, it would be up to him to state his intentions and his wishes.

"What qualifies me?" I said. "I think that is really what you want to know. Good question. My age and experience; the mentorship of another man I respect immensely and one that I trust implicitly; learning by my mistakes and not repeating them; the pain and the joy caused by my own hand; witnessing the damage of my anger and learning how to deal with it so that I don't hurt anyone on purpose; making my amends to those I hurt; trial and error or figuring what works and what doesn't work and paying attention to what is going on around me.

"We cannot continue to operate our lives with old information because we will continue to make the same mistakes; understanding, or at least trying to understand, that relationships are about much more than getting laid and feeling good; that to truly communicate with others on the planet I need to shut up more and listen more.

"The big one for me was to learn how to parent my children. Yes, I do have them and, no, I don't want to talk about them. At least not right now. Perhaps some day I will, but this isn't about them. It is about the fact that you know I have two children, a son and a daughter. I am proud of them and I love them dearly. In my opinion they have become fine human beings who seem to understand the value of respect, not only for themselves but for those they are around and with.

"So I believe all these things qualify me to exchange ideas with you and to talk openly about what the world is about. It is important to learn how to deal with it on its terms because to do otherwise is folly. If our conversations help you to identify, understand, utilize, embrace and appreciate your gifts as a man and to use those gifts wisely with compassion, acceptance, tolerance and equity, my hope, then, is that you will be a better man for it. Your sons will be fortunate to have you as a father."

"Now it's your turn."

"What is it you want to know?" he said.

"I believe you know what I need to have clarified," I said. "But to help your recall, there were two specific instances, while you were telling your father how you were feeling about everything, where you looked sideways to me and then back at your father. I need to know what was meant by those glances toward me. Your father. . . "

Jacob jumped in, "I meant what I said. I don't have a father anymore, at least not a blood father."

"You still have a father. You may not like him. You may not want him. He is still your father. Whether you give him any time or credence is up to you, of course, but you cannot just replace him."

Jacob looked at me and said, "You have been more a father to me than he ever was or did."

He began to tear up as he continued, "I want you to be my father. As much as I trust anyone, I trust you to help me. I trust my Mom too, but I also see that she can only help me with certain things. She does other things for me that only Moms can do, but you have been where I am going."

He wasn't supposed to get under my skin like this. I didn't even like the kid a few months ago and look at what is happening now. I was choked up as well. Although I knew that this could happen and I had questioned my motives, I thought I had it sorted out in my mind. He had become more than just the kid next door so what happened next would change our relationship forever.

"This I can say to you, Jacob. I cannot be your father. It would be a privilege and an honour to be your friend and to be a mentor in any way you would like me to be. That's the best I can do. I hope that it is enough. You are a remarkable young man with a great deal to learn. I think that I can be helpful to you in this regard. But your father is your father, and as a man I cannot take his place without his permission and he is not likely to give me that.

"So we are at a place where you have to define the type of relationship that we will enjoy. I will leave you with that and hope to see you next week. We can talk more about what that looks like to you and decide how and where we will pick this up."

Without any fanfare, he walked up to me, gave me a quick hug and said, "That works for me. See you then, and thanks again for the day and everything else."

Annie stopped by my chair a while later. True to her word, she had cleaned up everything. You would never have known we'd had a gathering in my home. She sat down and said, "I can't thank you enough for this day and what it meant to Jacob. He has finally had a chance to face some of the ghosts he has been living with for a long time. I noticed that my son is not a little kid anymore."

"One thing that I hope Jacob will learn," I said to her, "is that he will get back what he gives the world he lives in. I believe that it was the Dalai Lama who said that. If he gets that, and if he lives that, he will be on his way to having riches in his life that far exceed any amount of money he can accumulate. I have to find a way to help him see that for himself and not just because I told him so.

"You are right, Annie. He is no longer a kid. He is growing into a fine young man for you to be very proud of. But there are things that will be difficult for you to teach him and for you to help him understand. There will be days when you will become frustrated both with yourself and with him about issues and thoughts and beliefs that you think are important for him to know but that he will not see.

"Some of these things that you cannot help him with will make your heart ache. If any situations should arise, please feel free to come to me and talk to me about it. I can, perhaps, help you understand what he may be dealing with. I will help in any way I can, but much of what is left for him to know and to understand about manhood and who we are in the world he will have to learn on his own. He will have to slay his own dragon before he will feel as though he has a place in this world as a man.

"There is a transition that will take him from boyhood to manhood. He has taken a few giant steps along that road. He took one today. I know that sounds a bit melodramatic, but I assure you it isn't. It is the way of our world, and that is why one man needs to help another along the path that lies ahead.

"I need to find out from Jacob what the world looks like to him, through his eyes. When he looks at the world, what does he see? Where does he see himself and doing what? and why? None of us can tell him how it should look. None of us can tell him how he should act in it or be in it or what is important in it. These are all things that he needs to determine for himself. It will help him later in his life to define his purpose and we, as men, need to have and know our purpose. It helps to give our lives meaning.

"Anyway, I don't expect you to understand much of this. I get on my soapbox and rattle on sometimes. Just know that if I can help with any of this, I would be most pleased to do that."

I know her well enough to know when she has something on her mind or something that she wants or needs to say. Again I say to her, "If you have something to say, just say it, Annie. We are long past the being a nice neighbour stage, don't you think? You two are certainly more than my neighbours."

She measured her words and then said, "I fear for Jacob. He is growing and changing so fast that I can't keep up with who he is becoming. Oh, please, don't hear me wrong, Jim. It's amazing the changes, for the better, that he has made. I am so very proud of him as a son and as a young man. But I feel like he is moving away from me too quickly and I don't know how to slow that down without slowing him down or holding him back from what is happening for him."

"Pardon the question, Annie, but are you sure this is about Jacob or is this about you? I said. "It sounds to me that you are concerned he is moving away from you too quickly and you are not prepared for that."

She glared at me for just a second. Then her eyes softened and she said, "I am afraid. I'm afraid that somehow I will get left behind here. I want to know more about him. I want to know more about what he believes and what that means to him. I need to know that he still needs me because I am still his mom. I'm afraid that he will soon get to the point where he will not need me anymore and I couldn't handle that. I love him so much it hurts. Just the thought of him not being around anymore and that he has moved on to the next part of his life! I know that this will happen, but just not now. Not so soon. I feel that, in some ways, I don't know him at all. I spent most of my time just trying to survive and keep him safe that I didn't have time enough to know him. Does that make sense? Am I being selfish here?"

This was so typical of Annie. She is always concerned that the other guy is OK. She always concerns herself about what else she can do to make the others' lives better. She puts herself last in the pecking order too often and doesn't know how not to do that. That's just who she is. She is kind and thoughtful, a fighter and a great person who just wants to love the world and have it love her back sometimes.

I had been so caught up in my own little world that I hadn't stopped to think about how Annie is seeing the world she lives in, especially where Jacob is concerned.

I let what I said settle on her and then added, "I don't mean to overwhelm you but I want to assure you that you are not alone in this world. And no, you are not selfish and, yes, what you are saying makes perfect sense. You need to remember that you have those of us who care about what happens next. You are not alone nor will you be. The very things that you are concerned about are not likely to happen because Jacob is learning about family and commitment and the importance of taking care of his own. He will not abandon you, as Harlan did. It is not in him to do that.

"In days not so long ago, local communities or neighbourhoods used to take on the responsibility for raising and preparing the village children, especially the males, for the next stage of their lives. The young men would hunt or fish or build things together with the village men. They would be taught how to do certain things that would add to their capabilities and lead to independence. The children felt connected or attached to the community, so they felt as though they had a place in that society.

"It is vitally important that Jacob feels as though he belongs here and that people have an interest in his well-being and that he is responsible, not only to you, but to all who are vested in him.

"This experience was especially true for the kids of families who had lost a parent somehow. The villagers stepped up to fill the void. Nature hates a void, I am told. That seems to be the case here concerning Jacob. When I talk to him I hear that he is moving rapidly toward this idea. I sense a strong need in him to feel he belongs and that he is valued by the adults around him.

"He is more man than boy, but is not in either camp right now. It's like being in a no-mans-land. He's too inexperienced for manhood and too aware for adolescence. I will try to help him through the confusion concerning his manhood and those things connected to that. He asked me, today, to be his father, but I explained why I couldn't do that. He understands why not.

"You will need to help him with some of the other things. Respect for women for one thing. This is the next frontier for him. If I haven't missed my guess, it will happen soon, if it hasn't already. I think he knows that he is loved and cared for. He knows that he has a solid foundation underneath him. You have done a fine job of showing him that. I'm sure he feels he is ready to build other attachments and connections that have more to do with his own decision-making processes.

"The tough part for you will be allowing him to do that without withdrawing from him. You will need to encourage him and support him to do the very things that enable him to move away from you.

"Welcome to parenthood. As I mentioned to Jacob earlier, I can speak to you about this with some experience behind me. We raise our children and prepare them to leave us and venture out into the world. It is our job. Men do this by teaching their sons skills so they can satisfy the social and cultural gifts they have been exposed to. Women do this by showing their sons that emotions and feelings are integral to their complete survival. A well-adjusted male does both well."

"How can I support him? Annie asked, her eyes searching mine. "Can you help me understand what he is going through when I can't see it or understand it? I'm still having difficulty thinking about the time when he will be on his own and making his own decisions. I'm angry that he is doing all this wonderful stuff and I don't have a part, a real part to play in much of it. I already miss him and he hasn't left yet!

"I just want to have some time with him when there is nothing else going on. Just the two of us, together, so that I can watch him and talk with him and appreciate him without worrying about him. I want to enjoy who he is, just for a while.

"I can help you understand," I said, "but I think the answers lie with you already. And you support him by allowing him to live this process at its own speed and, what is most important, by letting him know how proud you are of him and that you love him unconditionally. If you want to know what he is going through, ask him. If he can't explain it so that you get it, come and we'll chat, OK?"

Annie smiled and looked down. She raised her eyes and said, "You make it sound all so simple. It's not. I have to learn so that I can understand what he has learned and what there is left to learn. Look. I know that this is part of my learning journey as well. I get that. I just get angry that time has picked up speed it seems and I'm falling behind no matter how hard I try to keep up.

"Thank you for listening, though, and thank you, again, for being a part of our lives." She got up to leave. . .

I couldn't go on anymore, and I don't think she could either. I was exhausted, and I don't think Annie felt much better. I guess today was the day that hugs were meant to come my way. I must admit that it felt great to be hugged by people who were genuine with their behaviour and their feelings. She hugged me with a little extra squeeze and went down the stairs to her home.

I disappeared into my house but felt restless and couldn't settle. Some Moody Blues eased my edginess, but sleep escaped me. I couldn't stop thinking about how much time I had left and what there was to tell Jacob. Would there be enough time? Other than being tired a bit more, I felt no different today than I did six months ago. "That's good," I kept saying in my head. "That's good."

Sunday morning came and I decided to go to church. I got dressed in something other than jeans and off I went. There is an energy that exists for me at church that I don't always find otherwise. I think it's the music, the choir especially. I luxuriated in the old hymns, and before I knew it I was thanking the pastor for his time and the message.

It's odd how you get what you need sometimes from the most unexpected places. Today I was going to get a double hit of that.

Before I went home, I stopped at the park and just walked awhile. Parks are great places to visit because people seem to be able to put aside the week's business and just enjoy the beauty. It is good to see that play itself out. Dads were flying kites or playing catch with their sons. Moms were watching their family play, with no worries for the time.

It's the way it should be more often. Why don't people make the effort to care for themselves more, to take the time to do the things that really matter most?

As I turned into my drive I could see someone sitting on the porch. At first I thought it was Jacob, but upon closer inspection I could see it wasn't. Then I said to myself, "What is he doing here?"

I got out of my car and stepped carefully up the stairs. "What are you doing here? Is everything all right? Are you all right?"

"Gee, nice to see you too." the man said. "I feel all warm and fuzzy inside. Kinda makes a man feel really appreciated. I can see now why no woman could stand to have you around for more than month or so at a time," said Leo.

"Hey, sorry about that," I said. "I didn't mean for that to come out that way. I'm just surprised to see you and thought that maybe something bad has happened. But what brings you? Want a coffee or something? Hungry?

"Relax," said Leo in that calm, soothing voice of his. "I just thought it had been awhile since we chatted and, seeing how you don't stay in touch as you said you would, I would come by, unannounced, so that you couldn't duck me, and we can get caught up."

"How is it you always seem to know when I need to sort things out?" I asked. "You are a sight to be appreciated though, and much has happened. It is all going too fast, Leo, and I can't slow it down. My life is winding up, yet I can't take the time to contemplate what that means because there is so much to do in such a short period of time. I get panicky sometimes and don't know how to handle it all.

"That's when you seem to pop in and I get to unload and you go away and I say 'Hey, what about you?' I don't take the time to ask about your life. What's going on for you?"

"Whoa, whoa, whoa," he said, "You're rambling on like some ole freight train. I didn't come here for that. I'm just interested in how you are doing, that's all. So? How are you doing?"

"Let's go inside for a bit. Tea? coffee?"

"Tea would be good."

"Tea it is. Come on," I said, and he followed me through the door.

"I'm not sure, even, where to begin," I said. "The world has changed in the last while. There are times when I feel that I am just barely hanging on to my place in it. Rightly or not, I have given little thought to what is coming and whatever implications there are connected to that. My affairs are in order. Should something happen to me today everything is done. But I spend little time thinking about 'IT.' I don't think I am in denial about it. I'm not sure that I fear it, but I just haven't spent or don't spend much time thinking about it. There's time for that later, I guess."

"Well, then tell me what you ARE thinking about," he said.

"How my life would have been different if my father had taken the time to know me, to actually want to know what was going on in my world," I replied. "He had no clue and, from what I could see, he had no desire to know. As you know, he was a good man. He did all the right things, like providing for us. But he just didn't have any emotional interest in who I was.

"If he had, how different would my life decisions have been? Would I have chosen to follow the same path, to travel the journey? I guess it's like trying to summarize it all, I don't know.

"My life has taken on a different meaning now. That's good. I get upset when I look at what could be and sometimes that's not so good only because of the time factor. Because you live in my head, I hear you tell me to do the best I can with the time I have left and be grateful for it and to focus on what I can do, as opposed to what I can't do."

"How's it going with Jacob?" he asks me. "I assume that he is where your energy is going these days. I hope he understands, at some point, just how lucky he is to have you as a neighbour."

"He is well aware of his gifts," I said, "and he is seeing the impact they can have on his life, how they play out. He's a bright kid. He's a quick study, too, like a sponge. Did I mention that he asked me to be his father? I told him no, that I couldn't do that, but if he wanted a mentor of sorts, I could do that.

"I was reading an interview that the Dalai Lama gave the other day and he said, 'Being happy is not a matter of destiny. It is a matter of options.' How do I help him understand that?

"That's one of the things that you helped me to understand. How did you do that? How do I help him understand that his pursuits should be focused on being more compassionate and accepting of others, sensible, loving, and not just concerning people, but places and life itself, acting more as a humanitarian. I want him to understand that doing things for others with no desire in your heart to be paid back at some point, that being responsible is a gift you give the world, not something that takes away excitement and that sharing and living by our ethical and moral standards is a good thing.

"This is the way to peace in our world. This is how men live their lives. This is what enables us to negotiate an acceptance of who we are and our place in the world, instead of the crap we are being fed about 'political correctness,' 'getting with the program' and living in the 'new era.' All that means is there are some who are not interested in understanding or caring about the importance of what guides us as men. Trying to have us behave in a way that is not our natural way is making us sick.

"But Jacob still sees the almighty dollar as God. I forget, sometimes, he is only 18 years old and these concepts are seldom understood or even considered by kids that age. But I have to try because I will not be around when he grows into these ideas. It's not that I want him to get all serious and not enjoy the energy of being a kid. He needs to make his mistakes to learn by. But he also needs to be aware that life as it is now and as it will be are very different animals."

He looked at me as he does and said, "Why do you worry about what you have no say in. You can only let him know what you are thinking and allow him to take from that what he will. You cannot

103

create a carbon copy of yourself, and you can't make him your lost son. I know how important this is to you. You are basically exchanging the remainder of your life for this opportunity to help this kid. It's a hell of a risk, but worth it. I agree, on so many levels.

"So don't worry about facts and information. Just talk to him from the heart. Remember how you like to ask people about thinking versus doing. To me that is what this whole thing is about. This is about teaching him how to think as a man and not do as a man. If he thinks first, his instincts – those ingrained gifts you speak about – will kick in and he will be guided by them. Have faith in that.

"This is about honesty and truth, and that is why it is so difficult to grasp. That's why it is such a great achievement and that is why he will be strong at the end of this journey. No one can take his maleness from him if he follows this path.

"Your challenge is to help him follow the path, not direct his life as you would have him live it. Being a man is a way of travelling in this world, remember. Trust in the fact that he learns from you and how you live your life. He watches and he puts things together. You are not going to know all that he learns and where he learns it from. It is you, my friend, it is you who have taken the time to care about him. That's where he learns from and not by what you say, but by what you do and how you do it."

The old saying goes "You can't see the forest for the trees. I was taking on the outcome of my efforts with Jacob and forgetting that I can only provide and guide. The outcome is not my responsibility nor my right to determine.

Leo and I spent the next hour or so catching up on the stuff that good friends have fun discussing, like sports and politics. He has such a fine mind, and I enjoy his company and consider myself fortunate to be able to call him my friend. I would see him again, I knew, but I will also miss him desperately when my time comes.

It rained for the next three days, a blessing of sorts. I could lie down and relax without feeling guilty about not being outside or doing some of the yard work that was becoming more of a challenge than a joy. I used to like sprucing the place up and having it neat and tidy. I took pride in my place, but now I had relegated some of the chores to others to do for me for a small fee. I had learned that money is just a tool to use for our comfort and not something to hoard or worry about.

Men Have Rules Too!

aybe it's wishful thinking, but every time I see Jacob he just looks more grown up, more assured, more excited about moving ahead with his life. So it was that day as he sat down on the porch.

He started right in, "I've given a great deal of thought to the things we spoke about the last time. I think I understand why you can't be my father, but does that mean you won't be someone who I can talk to and check things out with?

"I decided before, when I stopped hanging around with my friends, that I wanted more than what I was going to get with them. They were good guys, but not for me. I admit that I felt sad when I decided not be around them nearly as much, but I want more than what they can give me. I hope that's not arrogant but that's how it is.

"So what I need is for you to help me understand what this manhood thing is about and how to live my life differently than I was. You keep talking about those social and cultural gifts and most of the time I get it, but sometimes I don't and I want to get it all the time. I don't know why I feel the way I do sometimes, but I know that it is not a bad thing, just something I don't always get. There are some things that I feel I don't even think about. It's almost automatic—something happens and I feel as if I have to respond in a certain way, without thinking. I know it's the right thing to do. That's strange to me but I'm getting used to more of it.

"When Harlan showed up, I immediately looked at Mom and I knew that if he came near her or said anything to hurt her, I would've stepped in and backed him off. It wouldn't have been about anger. It would have been about taking care of someone I care about. No one is more important to me than she is. I want to understand what these gifts are and what they mean to me. I need you to tell me what you know, what you have learned. So what does that make you, a mentor? Is that the right name? Is that something that you can or want to do?"

And so there it was. It's all out on the table now. I felt excited and anxious and sad all in the same heartbeat. What an awesome responsibility. And this is what he wants from me.

"OK," I said to him, "but as with anything else, there are rules."

"I knew there was a catch," he said. "There is always a catch when something seems too good to be true." He was ticked a bit.

"One of the rules is that you let me finish before you make a judgment about what was said," I began. "If you ask a question and I give you an answer you don't like you don't get pissed at me about it. If you ask, I'll tell you what I think is true. Also remember I don't have all the answers to all the questions. The last rule is that you always make up your own mind about what is right for you and not because I say so. I'm not going to be around forever and you need to become confident within yourself to make the tough decisions. It's your life and not your mother's or mine or anyone else's. If you're good with that, then let's go."

"Where are you going?" he asked.

"What do you mean?" I asked him.

"You said you weren't going to be around forever. That usually means that something is up. One of MY rules here is that I need to know I can trust you to be completely honest. I don't need any more games and excuses. I want none of that shit."

I needed to be careful. I suspect that he is afraid to be abandoned yet again. I don't want to lie to him but I can't tell him the whole truth yet either, so I said, "I'll be gone from this planet long before you will be, Jacob. That's all. And yes, you can expect the truth with honesty. Just remember it may not always be what you want to hear."

"I can deal with that."

"Good," I said. "I need to clear up something about my deciding that I can't be your father. Let me start by saying that you do have a right to throw your father to the curb and move on. If you don't want to have anything to do with him, that's cool, but don't decide out of anger and hurt. Understand that not all fathers run away or leave without reason. They usually have lots of reasons why they take off.

"I'm not saying that Harlan was justified or made a hard choice. It appears he just wasn't cut out to be a father. That doesn't make him a bad guy. I understand that sons need to have their fathers in their lives, to be their teachers and their examples and to help them become men and to learn what men do and how they do it. Sons want to feel attached and connected to their fathers. This is not to say that we don't love our mothers. That's for another discussion. But there is a special bond that exists or needs to exist between fathers and sons and, if that is not present, the son usually ends up feeling abandoned and detached, disconnected, from his place in the world and his family unit. As well, he usually goes on to feel angry and begins his learning process in all the

106

wrong places with little or no guidance because there are no checks and balances, no voice of reason.

"You may decide that, at some point in the future, you want to give him another shot. He may change how he goes about his business and would like to know you as a son. I don't know, but if the door is open, at least, that is a possibility. If the door is closed, it could never happen, regardless of who did what. All I am saying is think about leaving the door open just a crack. You never know. This way you can move on with your life and not invest any more emotional energy into hating him or trying to forget who he represents to you. The next move is his, and you are free to move on. That's why I didn't want to assume that role in your life, but it is an honour to be thought of in that way. Thank you, again."

I caught my breath and continued, "About wanting to 'get it' all of the time? That likely is not going to happen to you. I'm not sure many of us 'get it' all the time. The more you accept those gifts as being a part of who you are, the more likely you are to understand why you feel as you do. You still need to make good decisions when you are being challenged, but at least you can now be true to who you are.

"We all need to live with the consequences of what we choose to do at any time. This is where your instincts and intuition come into play. You need to be able to trust them in times when confusion reigns or you are being challenged to respond a certain way."

I had thought hard about the next thing and said to him, "Next, I was thinking that perhaps the best way for us to continue is for me to just extend to you an open-door policy. What I mean by that is you are welcome to come over at any time and talk about whatever is happening at the time, instead of meeting once a week or every other week. That way, if something is going on for you that you are not clear about or sure of, you don't have to wait to discuss it. Just knock on the door. What do you think?"

Quickly he said, "Yeah. I was thinking it would be good to do something like that because there are times when I get so full of stuff and get frustrated that I might forget something important. I just didn't know if you'd be good with that. Thanks for bringing it up. Sure, that sounds good. But, hey, I'm sure there are rules attached, right?" He said it with a grin on his face.

"You betcha," I said, with as straight a face as I could conjure up. A moment passed and then I said, "The only one would be don't show up at three in the morning and expect me to be Mister Nice Guy. As a matter of fact, don't show up at three o'clock, Period." He agreed.

"Did you think I had forgotten about the scale thing? I asked you, on a scale of one to ten, where would you say you are with regard to your stress levels now. Lots has happened in a short period of time. It appears as though you have handled it all pretty well."

He thought for a moment and then said, "I thought it would have been much more difficult, more crazy making, than it was. It's all I have been thinking about the last day or two. I've been going over the scene with Harlan and how Mom was and how she handled things. She kept it together pretty well, I thought. The whole birthday thing and being 18 now made me understand looming manhood. I don't feel older and yet it seems as though I am older. It's hard to explain. People expect more from me now.

"I remember when you talked about expectations and how they can be stressful. I can see that. Even some of the people who were here said, 'Well you're not a kid anymore, so it's time to get serious and, oh yeah, now that you're a man what are you going to do with yourself?'

"How the hell do I know? What's that all about anyway? I've been thinking about you and what to do with that. It feels like a lot of time has gone by since I played with old friends, yet it's just been a few months. I've been out a few times just because I needed to blow off some stink, but that was different from how I used to do it.

"Did I mention to you I have met some new people? Probably not. A couple of them I really connected with. I met them through some other people at school. I didn't see that coming, let me tell you. A couple are snotty bastards. A bit too uppity for me. Good for a laugh, though. One caught my attention, however.

"School has been OK. I used to hate going but now, since I'm more on top of what's happening, it's not as boring. Actually it's been no problem at all. All things considered, it's been tough, but nothing I couldn't or can't handle. Seven."

"Seven," I said

"Yeah, seven."

"So what's the story on this 'other one who caught your attention'? You blew by that one pretty fast. What's the deal?"

Hanging his head in mock embarrassment, he said, "Man, I thought you might have missed that one. That slipped out before I could stop it," he complained. "I knew you'd be all over that and I don't want to talk about it because I'm not sure about what it is."

"That's OK, No problem," I backed off for now.

"Maybe when its time comes," he said.

"Sure, that would work."

Balance: Accept No Substitute

"Getting back to what you said before about being at a seven. You rattled off about five or six things that you have been dealing with all at once, but said you were OK with it. I always found that when I got to that same point I needed to slow my inside world down to counter the increased speed of my outside world. You ever feel like that?"

"I guess," he said. "Sure, more so now that I know what to look for. I knew things were spinning and if I wanted to deal with them right away I had to slow down and deal with them one by one. That's worked well for me the last while. What also helped was doing simple things. Spending time at the beach and lots of pine time." When I looked at him, confused, he said, "Walks in the woods." I just nodded. Briefly the roles had changed, so I was nodding to him instead of him to me.

I took advantage of the teachable moment. "It's called finding a balance. Balance in all things is very important. It's what keeps us sane and helps us remain connected to the world around us. Lots of 'pine time' appears to be working well for you. It's those who struggle to find or keep a balance, those we see as homeless or those who self-medicate using alcohol or drugs to excess who are troubled. They believe they are balanced when they are high. Not so, and not even close. I think of those who are angry or those who are feeling out of balance with the world they live in. When you think back to your old days, how balanced were you?"

"Not at all," he said quickly.

"One day I would like you to meet Leo. Leo is my dearest friend and he is my mentor. He would not be offended, if he were here, and I said to you that he was a simple man, certainly not concerning his mind but in his approach to living life. He keeps it simple.

"I can remember when I first met Leo he said to me that if I wanted to find any kind of peace in this world that there were some simple things I could do to make that happen: Don't spend a lot of time on things that either don't concern you or that you have no control over because that just takes away from the time and energy you can spend on the things that do matter to you and those things that you do have some control over; make sure that you stand up for something, so find something you are passionate about and go for it; and really feel connected to what you do in all things. I think he meant that we need to be energized and invested and dedicated regarding how we choose to spend our time— we need to have a purpose and be counted amongst those who care for something. His last point was to not give negativity a chance to rob you of your dreams. In other words, hope that good things will happen. Don't plan for when not so good things happen. By doing that you, have already opened the door to being unsuccessful.

"Keep these things in your heart and in your head," I said, "and stress will seldom be a problem for you to deal with. He also says to me whenever I need to hear it that happiness is an ATTITUDE, not an occasion.

Oh yeah, I read this the other day and thought you'd find it interesting. It was a quote from a great man whose name was John Wooden. Is that name familiar to you?"

Jacob shook his head. "Who's John Wooden?"

With some exasperation in my voice I carried on, "You kids don't have any idea of the great leaders of our time. He was a teacher, philosopher, writer and many other things. He coached basketball at UCLA for years and taught his players how to be men and how to harness their energy. He taught them much more than how to play the game.

"Anyway, he said this: 'Be more concerned with your character than your reputation because your character is what you really are, while your reputation is merely what others think you are.'

"What I would like you to do is think about his quote and think about how it may fit into your life now that you're 18. No scale stuff today. And by the way, what's her name, at least?"

"Who?" he asked.

"What do you mean 'who'? The one that caught your eye, that's who."

Playfully he said, "Oh, that 'who.' You said that you weren't going to bug me about it right now. What's that about?"

"Asking her name is hardly bugging you. I'm not asking about any great details. How am I supposed to know you are talking about her if I don't even know her name?"

He looked at me and said, "Good point. All I will tell you is that she's got the whole package, man."

With that he was up with a grin and off down the stairs. Isn't young love a wonderful thing! He was feeling excited about his future for the first time in a very long time was my guess and he would do whatever he needed to keep that feeling alive for as long as he could. It would turn out to be his greatest challenge to date and he would need to call on all the things he has learned in the last months and some things that he hasn't learned yet in order to survive it.

LIVING IN RELATIONSHIPS:
The Third Cornerstone

It's Often All Or Nothing

For many of us (and young folks are certainly in this mix), relationships are an all-or-nothing prospect. We use them for all the wrong reasons and then marvel at the fact that they never work out for us. We don't want to stop and think that perhaps we participate in them for all the wrong reasons and we are seeking all the wrong things. They are not about securing a future. Rather, they need to be about developing and building a future that both agree would be best.

I have certainly been accused of being overly simplistic in my thinking at times, but I believe that we should commit to a relationship because we happen to care for the other person and who that person is and what that person stands for and what that person brings to the relationship table and not based solely on this feeling in us that is not easy to describe at the best of times.

This feeling is so powerful and all consuming in the beginning that it drives us to do crazy things that we would not likely do when we are thinking rationally. But such is the wonder of love, as we can best describe that condition, so we go for it and hope for the best, but it is not a great plan for success.

I know from working in the human services business for 20 plus years that there is no other situation or condition that commands and consumes most of our emotional energy quite like a brand-new relationship. There are few other situations that can nearly destroy us as quickly and as thoroughly as a relationship that has gone bad.

I've worked with those who get involved in one right after ending one. They are called relationship junkies. They use relationships, and by extension, people, to fuel solutions to their own shortcomings, like loneliness, grief, resentment, anger, fear and especially power and control issues. For others it's about ownership – ownership of some other person's mind and thoughts – so they tell the other person how to think and what to think.

This is different from power and control issues in that in this instance they actually believe that they are right and they want to pass on their wisdom to the person that they care about. Their intent is not to harm them but to enlighten them. This wind blows both ways, though. Many ladies have their own ways of manipulating their partners once the ring is on.

It takes commitment and patience and discipline to make a relationship work. And a lot of luck, too. When they are good, they are very good. Fortunately, I have friends who have that in their lives today. They are inspiring as well as exceptional people.

The other thing I know to be true is this: If you don't have your emotional work done before you commit to a relationship, your chances of being successful in that relationship diminish dramatically. How many get into relationships thinking that they will find a partner that needs to be fixed and go to work to save him/her because they couldn't save a loved one previously? When I think about how many try to work out their abuse issues, their trauma issues, their addiction issues – whether it is to food, drugs, alcohol or sex – by using a partner or, worse, their children, it is easy to understand why the divorce rates are so high and why some men just walk away from their families and their sons. Toss in the efforts some make to alter our social and cultural identities and our characters as individual human beings and we have quite a mess going on.

So when I think about Jacob and I know that we are going to talk about this very topic, how do I help him when I know where he could be headed? I stand to risk OUR relationship because the likelihood is that if I go against anything that he wants or thinks he has a chance of getting he will dump me like yesterday's leftovers.

The last day or two reminded me why I wanted to go day by day with Jacob instead of by week by week. Now we can meet more often for shorter periods of time. I am finding that, although I still feel pretty good, my energy levels get depleted more quickly now and I need to be able to stay on top of what we talk about. I need to stay focused and alert enough to give him what he expects from me. I also want to know that I have done right by him. That's what he signed on for, and I don't want to disappoint him, not now. Admittedly, when my time comes, I want to know that I left my mark, that my time and place here stood for something important.

Jacob and I hadn't agreed on a specific time or day to meet again, so I didn't concern myself when he didn't show up right away. It was good to be reminded that he had a life of his own and that I was just a player, albeit an important one to him, I was sure, but nonetheless just a player. If I guessed right, he had jumped headlong into this relationship with his new love interest and was otherwise occupied. I knew that he would show up, and so he did.

Are You Sure You're Thinking With The Right Body Part?

Saturday morning came, warm and sunny, and I thought that this would be a great day to string my hammock on the front porch and do some navel gazing. Just as I went to dig out my gear, a familiar rap came to the door.

"Hey, are you in there?"

"Who wants to know?" I asked.

"It's me. Remember me?"

"The voice sounds familiar but I am having difficulty putting a face to it," I said.

"OK, I know. I've been out and around the last few days. Sorry I didn't let you know."

"Something happen to your right index finger, boy?" I looked at him through the screen door making sure he could see the slight grin on my face. "Look. You don't owe me an explanation of where you are, who you are with and what you are doing. It's your life, your time and you don't have to check in with me. I was just concerned about you and wondered if you were OK. That's all. I'm glad to see that you are all right. Have a seat, I'll be right out."

"Cool," he said and plunked himself down. I joined him shortly with a cold drink for him in my hand. As I sat down, I said, "Well, how have you been?"

He recounted the first couple of days – school, tests, starting to wind up classes and the stuff that goes with parting for the summer holidays. He also said he had been looking for a summer job with little success but would keep looking. He was sure that something would pop up.

Then he mentioned the young lady that had caught his eye. It was no secret that there was much more to it than that, of course. He was obviously struggling about what to say next, so I decided I would not make it easier for him. I let him take his time and start wherever he wanted.

Finally he said, "The other day you asked me her name. Her name is Sharna. What else do you want to know about her?"

"Whatever you are comfortable sharing with me. As I said, it's your life, and you decide what you want me to know, if anything."

I knew he wanted to tell me all about her, but I suspect he didn't know how to do that. He wasn't used to being open with all things personal although we certainly had peeled away a few layers. This was different for him. That other stuff was painful or came from bad memories. He needed to drag those things into the light of day to take away their mystery and their strength. This was new stuff. Perhaps he was afraid that if he got really excited about it all, something would happen to take it away from him. I also knew that if I let him go at his own speed he would eventually put it out there to see how I would respond. His next words were very revealing.

He started by saying, "I know that I am supposed to know all about this relationship stuff by now and that I was supposed to have learned it from my parents and my father. We know how well that went down. Dear old dad was MIA. I feel like a rookie here, that I am out of my league. Whenever I was involved with other girls I always knew how to do things. They were so easy to deal with. The motto was 'aim to please so please aim,' if you get my meaning here."

Now I might be a bit further over the top of the mountain than some, but his meaning was crystal clear. He continued.

"I pay attention to this social cultural stuff you talk about, but I don't get how some of it is attached to what I want or need to know. How do I use it to get what I want here? It's as if I'm flying in the dark. It's frustrating because I don't know if I'm doing it right or not and I don't want to blow it with Sharna. I mean I learned some things from watching Mom and how she handled what Harlan did to her. I don't know if she would ever be involved with anyone ever again, but she doesn't pass that on to me. I will never treat my wife like he did. I guess that's one lesson learned from him—what NOT to do."

"First of all," I said, "you don't have to become someone else in order to have any kind of relationship with Sharna. If you have to change who you are, then she is not for you, my friend. She obviously saw you and liked what she saw before you ever said a word to her. She wanted to know more." I stopped briefly and then continued,

"Let me ask you this then. This goes back to what we said before about mentoring and so on. We agreed that in order for this to work, we needed to trust one another. I trust you; do you trust me?

"No need to answer that right now. There are other questions that we need to ask and answer before this goes anywhere. I need to know if there are any topics that are off limits for you and me to discuss? How do you want to proceed here? What do you want from me? Are you sure that you can hear what I am saying to you and not be angry or judgmental? I don't care if you don't agree with what I am saying but you will need to do it with respect. I will respect you as well. If we can't do that then we need to walk away from this. I know that we have discussed this before but I need you to know and you need to know that nothing has changed regarding this."

"You want it all at once?"

"That would be fine. You talk and I will try to shut up," I replied.

"You and Mom are the only two people in this world that I can trust, so that should take care of your first question. I can't think of anything right now that I wouldn't want to talk about, but there may be some things that I'm not used to talking about with anyone else so it may no be all that easy. Shit, I have no idea where this could go, so how can I say one way or the other? What about if I just say I don't want to talk about 'that' right now. Would that work?"

I nodded my head and he carried on.

"This is all new to me, so I don't know what to say about how to proceed. I guess the best way is to just start talking about how all this came about and you ask me or let me know what you think I need to be thinking about. That sounds sort of lame, but I don't know what else to say. If I believe that you are doing the best by me and you are really trying to help, I can deal with the anger part. I need you to tell me that you won't lie to me or tell me things that you don't believe in. I know about the trust thing and how that's supposed to work, but I need to hear you tell me that."

"I looked him in the eye, held his gaze and said, "You have my word on that, Jacob, from one guy to another."

Now it was his turn to nod and say, "And you have my word as well, one guy to another."

If there had been some doubt about the type of relationship that we shared, that doubt had been erased and our bond had been established. For the first time in a long time, my chest felt full of energy and excitement and kinship. There was also some sadness in there, but that was my stuff to deal with and had nothing to do with Jacob and the moment.

"What do I want from you? Honesty, truth, and commitment. I guess that's what I would want from you if you were my father too," he said slowly.

I was just able to squeeze out a few shaky words, "I think I can manage that."

We were both quiet for a moment and then I broke the silence by changing the subject. "Tell me about her. Where did you meet her, how did you meet her, family stuff. You know the drill."

"Well," he said, "she is 21 years old. That should interest you. You know, the older woman going for the younger guy. We met through some people I had met at school. She was there visiting with some friends of hers and we just saw each other. I thought she was gorgeous. As I said, the whole package."

I guess I had a curious look on my face because he followed up explaining just what that whole package was.

"She is really good looking. She's got these legs that just don't quit, if you know what I mean."

"I'm older, not dead," I said. "Yeah, I know what you mean."

Grinning, he continued. "Her parents are East Indian and European. Her father is East Indian. He has an import business so he travels all the time. She might see him a couple of days a month sometimes. I've not met him yet, but Sharna says he's pretty quiet and he's very smart, and a hardworking guy. Her mom is from Spain and is tall, attractive, athletic and very busy in the community they live in. I guess they are well off because they live in this big house across the bay with hired help to look after everything. They have this great pool and some tennis courts out back of the guest house. I've been hangin' out around there for the last week—great spot. I met her Mom the other day. She seems really nice."

"Getting back to Sharna . . . ?" I said, trying to get him back in focus.

"Oh yeah. Well, as I said, she's really good looking. She has long black hair, big dark eyes and she sure looks as though she is pretty fit. Wherever we go, heads are turning. She's really easy on the eyes. She is smart, doesn't smoke, doesn't drink much – a glass of wine maybe – and not into drugs or anything like that. Actually she is pretty serious about who she is and what she wants and how she is going to get there. She mentioned today that she is going to university in the fall but she is just not sure where yet. Great lips too. We talk about all kinds of things like what I want to do when I graduate and interests I have. It's great to talk to someone who is actually interested in something beyond where to score and who is partying where.

"Something else is interesting, no, different. With the group of people I used to hang with, getting some sex was never an issue. If you wanted it, there was always somebody who would keep you busy for a while. They see oral sex and hand jobs as being no big deal. They don't see that as having 'real' sex. Not that that makes them tramps or anything. That's just how they all connect. They play games with each other, each trying to outdo the other with no concern for the consequences. It was all about the outrageous. Sometimes, though, I think it's just about the boredom. Sometimes I think it's all about feeling a part of what was happening at the time—you know, belonging, having a place.

"With Sharna it's a different deal altogether. She doesn't put out like the other girls I used to be around. I have to admit the challenge is there though, no doubt."

"Sounds like you are all in here, as if you're thinking about this as more than just a casual thing."

"I don't know about that," he said. "I just know that she is really different from what I have been used to and it feels good. It's exciting. I also know that I don't want to blow this thing and that I can't treat her the same as I have treated other girls I have been around. I'm not sure what to do here. Any great ideas?"

He asked this half-heartedly, but I knew he was serious about hearing my response.

"Are you asking me for some advice? I said. "If you are, I've got to say I don't give advice. The trouble with advice is that too often people take it and then whatever happens, especially if whatever happens goes bad, the fallout lands on the giver. In this case, that would be me. I can tell you what I think or what I know, but you have to make your own decisions about what you do or how you proceed from here."

"That's cool. I get that." He sat back in his chair.

I looked at him sitting there so full of excitement and curiosity. He really was concerned about how to behave around her. He really was interested in understanding how to do this. Young love is such a powerful and sometimes all encompassing thing. Everything is at risk because they tend to be all or nothing encounters. Emotions are given with little thought behind the giving. For males, testosterone is partially responsible for granting different parts of our anatomy to do our thinking for us and generally excludes the use of our brains. Trust is often given based on impulse that is connected to feeling and not earned by time and experience.

This was our first conversation about this topic, and I didn't want to come across as if I knew all there was to know about the subject. I don't think any man can make the claim that he has his female companions figured out. There were, however, some things I thought I could speak to him about and do so with a modicum of confidence. This chat needs to be safe and simple, basic. I thought that including some information he had already become familiar with might be a good way of opening some doors. I also knew that – no, not knew, felt – I felt that there was more to this than just a wee fling of sorts.

Not knowing Sharna or having met her, I was uncertain about what was in this for her, but I couldn't concern myself with that right now.

Jacob is a good kid. I can see and understand what a relationship like this was all about for him. This will be the first time that he is emotionally connected to someone who exists outside the only world he knows anything about. He will be travelling in uncharted waters, so to speak, and is feeling uncertain. He is not one to feel confident when he is uncertain about the rules he is expected to play by. I'm sure that's the way it is for most of us.

"Well," I said, "I think the first thing you need to consider is what do you want from this relationship? Can you even call it a relationship or is she just a casual acquaintance at the moment? How serious do you want to get here? Once you decide that then you will need to determine if Sharna wants the same thing. If you want one thing and she wants another, then it's not likely going to be a very good experience for either of you. You'll each spend more of your time trying to change the other's point of view. I'm not saying that you come right out and ask her although that would be one way of doing it. Just pay attention to the signs, such as the things she says. You're a bright guy. You'll put it together pretty quick.

"You wondered how to do this? Just be yourself. Don't try to be what you're not because it will come across as phony, and if you want to drive her away quickly, then just start acting as someone other than who you are. She wants to learn more about you because of what she saw or heard. She wants to hang around together because there is something about you that interests her. If she didn't enjoy being around you she wouldn't hang around.

"Just as you get something from being with her, so she also gets something from being around you. Change you and you change that. This social cultural stuff, as you put it, is not meant to be 'used to get stuff' but rather to help us, as men, follow our instincts and our intuition about the life we choose to lead. Recognizing and honouring our gifts helps show others what we stand for and helps us describe who we are. When you ask about doing 'it' right, I'm not sure about what 'it' is you want to know. You are who you are. Just be Jacob, as I said a minute ago. There is no doing 'it' right. You are not a performing seal.

"One thing I will mention, and it is the closest thing you'll get from me concerning advice and that is this: As men we recognize that one of the driving forces for us is the need to engage in the chase, the hunt, so to speak. Remember, we are conquerors. We like the challenge and the excitement of the game. And we are competitors.

"One of our great challenges, as men, is to satisfy our need to conquer our female partner, to be involved sexually, and obviously consensually, with them. Most of us are not good at waiting for this to happen. Most of us believe that once she commits to giving us this 'gift' that only she can give, then she is serious about the relationship and we become more comfortable with where things are. We like to be comfortable here as soon as possible. We feel that we have become special to her and that we have faced the challenge successfully.

I cannot place enough emphasis on this point and I believe it to be true, at least in theory. She takes the greatest of risks here because this experience is the most important and the most personal thing that she can give to anyone and she has chosen you to receive it from her. It really is the ultimate level of mutual human intimacy.

"I don't believe that many kids in their teens are really capable of grasping the meaning of sex. Don't abuse the privilege and never take what is not yours to have."

I stopped at this point because I didn't want it to sound like a sermon. But I did want him to understand that this is a topic that he needs to understand and take very seriously.

"Any thoughts?" I asked.

I didn't know how comfortable Jacob would be with this, but he moved into talking about it easily. "Yeah, I think that most guys – and the girls too for that matter – don't see what the big deal is. Sex is sex. I think for some they do, but for the most it's nothing special. It's more a game, or something that they do when they are bored or have nothing better to do. Sometimes getting laid is a way of blowing off some stink, you know. Getting with someone else is a way of getting over some anger thing or being pissed off at the world in general. For some it's the only way to show they still have some control over something.

"They put it out for whoever they decide, so it's their choice. They decide where and when. I hear some talk about having sex as being one of the only things that parents can't stop them from doing and that's what makes it important. There isn't a great deal of concern about diseases because most don't believe anything bad will happen to them. That's why there are kids having kids. It won't happen to me. Half of the girls wish it would happen to them. Having a kid, I mean. I think that's the only way some think their life has any meaning to it, if there is something/someone around that depends on them or that they are important to something or for something.

"Girls use sex and being sexual as a way of connecting with a guy early on so that he won't go anywhere else. She 'puts out' as a way of holding on to someone or at least staying close by.

"They also use it to control the person they are interested in. That often depends on what a girl is willing to do that the other girls aren't. But there is also an unwritten code that kids out there live by. Can't get too weird or they will toss you out. They think it's cool to be involved in some kind of sexual action right away though, so it's no big deal. They think oral sex isn't really sex anyway, right? Yeah sure. Most of the people I know or knew didn't understand that you could pick up something without laying someone down. I think it's more about insecurity and the fear of not being a part of the group they are with. And if the guy isn't getting what he wants right away, he won't hang around too long or he won't keep her around for long. Guys know how to play that pressure card too. The 'hunt' or the 'chase' continues. I'm not saying that it's this way for all kids. There are those who understand this, but many more who don't."

I could see by the look on Jacob's face that this was beginning to get challenging for him. He wasn't sure how much further he wanted to go with this. One thing struck me for sure and that was how much he had thought about this and what he didn't want to be a part of. Perhaps he had decided a while ago to accept certain thoughts and situations as 'that's the way it is,' but just not for him.

I decided to finish up with this: "Reputations are not what they used to be. It seems if you have a questionable reputation today, that's a good thing. Perhaps that means acceptance. The news flash here is that boys don't bring a 'questionable reputation' home to meet Mom and the girls certainly don't bring 'the bad boy' home to meet good old dad.

"Reputations don't have the same meaning or value today as before. It really is amazing when you stop to think that women have been fighting for fairness and equality for quite a while now, but the very thing that they want is the exact thing they have given away. In far too many instances, young girls have become mere toys and objects to be used, abused and tossed aside when their usefulness has been exhausted. It's like dumping the car when the ashtrays are full."

"Well, you didn't leave anything in the back room today, that's for sure," Jacob said. "I thought this would be a kind of easy conversation between us guys. I hear what you are saying, but things don't work quite this way in my world. I mean, our worlds are different in many ways. I think that in some ways I like how it was in your world, but it's seems too slow. It's too much like painting by numbers. First you do this and then you do this and you don't do that until you do this. I think I like the idea of just getting at it, you know?"

"Sure, I know," I said. "People today are more about instant gratification. That's what the computer world provides for you and text messaging and cell phones, etc. etc. But because it was a certain way doesn't make it not right anymore. Ultimately you are the one who has to decide, based on what you feel is the right way for you to go about your business. And besides, you asked and I gave you what I believe to be true. That was our agreement, right?"

"Right."

I wanted to put a bow on this so that there would be some reason we got here, so I said, "The one thing that hasn't changed much over the years are some of the values that women share with us. There are things that they like and don't like, just like us. For instance, they like being treated with dignity and respect and not being used or taken advantage of, being appreciated for their intelligence and their diplomacy, being recognized for their ability to nurture and to care of others and not to be seen or treated as just good for making meals and mopping floors. They won't sign on for or buy into a life of servitude. Using a relationship as an excuse to be a pig is just not going to be acceptable to any woman with any sense of self-worth either. But hey, you will find all this out and so much more as you go along.

"At least now you can't say that you didn't know. Give some thought to what you want from the world as a man. Recognize what a man does and does not do and know what's expected from a man in today's world. We'll see where you are with all of that when we gather up the next time you are by.

"And Jacob, it's always good to see you. Catch you later."

As he was going down the stairs, I added, "Are you going to bring her by some time? I'd like to meet her."

"Yeah, maybe I will," he said over his shoulder.

123

A few days went by and I had not heard from him. Something was up, but I had to trust that he would surface when he was ready. He had had a great deal to take in and process in the last while, what with his father showing up, his decision to let me into his life as a mentor, his new-found life outside his usual social circle, passing on his old crew and now this new relationship with a woman he knew little about.

I decided to check in with Leo since I hadn't chatted with him for a bit and catch up. I needed to get away from the house for a while, too. Claustrophobia was settling in, and I knew I would be seeing a lot more of these walls soon enough.

Just as I was getting into my car, I noticed Annie trying to get my attention. The sight of her filled me with pleasure and concern. I have always been a sucker for a beautiful damsel in distress. She said that Jacob had been a bit down the last day or two, not sad but distracted but didn't want to talk about it when she asked. It was sounding as though he had retreated to the privacy of his own mind and isolated himself. That's what we do when we are challenged and not sure of what is to come next. We need to sort through things and put the information together. I had a strong feeling I knew what was up but I didn't say anything. It really wasn't for me to say anyway.

"I'm sure when he decides to show up on the porch he will share his concerns with me. Don't worry. He'll be OK. How are you by the way? We should do tea soon and you can tell me how life is going post-Harlan."

"I'd like that," she said. She could see that I was preparing to leave so she excused herself and off she went.

The smell of the water and the warm, fresh breezes in my face were a wonderful tonic. Being on my way to visit with a friend who I could be myself with and have a conversation about things and not other people was exciting. It's the everyday things that count, especially for me these days. Just for a moment or two I actually felt blessed. I had called Leo ahead of time to be sure that he was at home. As Leo does, he made me feel welcome even on the phone.

He came to the door dressed in his usual attire. He reminded me of a younger Jimmy Buffett, but with "a cuppa joe" in his hand. "Tea is brewing for you. It'll be a minute." The band America was playing on his tape deck. He'd never got rid of that old deck because he said it was perfectly fine and played as well as any of the new technology available, so why bother. He'd never got caught up in the hype of new.

I really did love this man. I quickly flashed back to Jacob and if I could have told him that he could do no better than to fashion himself after Leo in his quest for manhood I would go to my grave feeling good about what I had done. I was still off somewhere in the far reaches of my mind, when Leo handed me a cup of tea and said, "So?"

What do you mean, so? I can't come for a visit with an old friend on a beautiful day without my motives coming into question? You are getting cynical and crotchety in your old age, my friend," I said.

The banter continued back and forth for another moment or two before he said, "How are you, Jim? What's happening for you? I'm always glad to see you, and you know that, but are you OK?"

This was different for Leo. He was not one to carry his concerns and his feelings about things on his outside like this. Usually he let me carry the conversation to him. He would join me wherever I went in terms of the topic. I could see the care and concern on his face now and I could see love in his eyes. He was catching up to what was happening to me and that he could do nothing to stop the process. I saw sadness in his eyes as well.

"I'm OK, Leo. Really, I'm OK. I don't have any pain. I don't have as much energy as I would like so I have to plan how I will spend it carefully. The vitamins and the meds John has set me up with and the regimen are all working well, so the quality of life right now is good. What I would really like to do is go for a walk on the warm sand in my bare feet. I really don't have anything that is weighing on me. I just wanted to spend some time with you and talk about whatever comes along. You are probably the only one I can spend time with, not say anything and feel like the day was well spent. So if you can spare the time. Let's go eat on the beach somewhere. Oh, and it's your turn to buy, you cheap . . . "

"Yeah, yeah. OK," he said, "but I pick the spot. I'm not shelling out a whack of dough on some fancy place where you get two crumbs and a stick of celery. I want quantity if we're doing this."

I shrugged and said, "Lead the way, my friend. I can't wait to eat your money."

Off we went with, at least temporarily, not a care in the world. Halfway through our lunch, I confessed that I did have something' that I wanted to run by him and of course he was all ears.

"Leo," I began, "Not to get all messy on you because I know how much you love that stuff, but I need to say a few things and need you to listen. Good so far?"

He looked at me with a wary eye but nodded he was.

"I have thought about our relationship and wondered how I would approach this, but of course you were in my head saying 'just say it.

So I will just say it. I have appreciated you for all these years more than you could know. I would not have become the person I am today without your guidance, your patience, your fellowship and your amazing counsel. You are a true friend and a good man.

"If the truth be known, you are the only person on the planet that understands who I am and what I stand for. You know my weaknesses and my strengths. You understand what motivates me and what discourages me. And you know what is in my heart as much as anyone could. You learned all that because I trusted you, and you made that easy for me to do when I never thought that would happen with anyone.

"Now I find myself staring at the end of my days, and there is an urgency I feel that is unmatched to anything else I have ever experienced or known. I guess what I am blubbering to say is that for the time that is left I want to see you and consider you my friend and not my sponsor or my mentor or anything else. Just my friend. I don't have a good or best friend in this world aside from you. John and I have a good relationship but it's not like ours. And I hope that didn't come out wrong and me sounding ungrateful for all you are and have been to me. I would like to see you as someone that I share with and someone who would honour me by trusting me and sharing back.

"I would like to know more about you. I always bring my stuff to you, dump it and move on. I haven't asked or tried to find out who you are and what makes you tick or how you feel about certain social issues or how you learned what you taught me. I would like to know who you are. I guess I'm talking about an egalitarian relationship. Do you think that this is possible? Is this something that we could do? Is it something that you would feel good about? If you want to keep it as it is, I'd understand that too and we'll carry on just as it is."

There. I had said what I wanted to say and, frankly, I was at a loss for any further words. Leo, I did know, was a man who used few words, but when he spoke he stated volumes. He was also long on honesty. So I left it at that and let the silence grow.

Finally he looked at me straight in the eye and asked me to pass the ketchup. Then he started to laugh and so did I. The silence settled on us again. I think that I had truly unnerved him. I had never seen that reaction from him before.

"It would be my honour, Jim."

And that was that. That was all the conversation that was required because we both knew what each other wanted and meant by what we had said. Such was the nature of what we had.

The next morning was an adventure, to be sure. I knew I would pay for the big, greasy lunch we'd had, but I wouldn't have traded it for the best meal money could buy anywhere. After a couple of antacids and some tonic water, things settled down and I was free to reflect on some of our random thoughts.

It had been a great day, all in all. Leo asked about Jacob and I told him what had happened. I also said that this thing with him and how he was responding to our chats was more about good luck and good timing than good management. He disagreed but seemed quite interested in what was going on. This, too, was a bit different for Leo. He was not one to wander into someone else's domain. I tucked that bit of information away for future consideration.

Paradise Lost Or Just In Danger?

Another three days passed before Jacob walked back up my walk to his chair on the porch. I was sitting out enjoying a warm mid-afternoon when he came by. He didn't have the recent spring to his step. He looked confused or perhaps unsettled.

"If you don't mind me saying this, you present yourself a little differently from the last time I saw you. What's happened, or do you prefer not to talk about it right now?"

He blew out a breath, looked at the ceiling and then said, "I thought that things were going along really well. We talk about all kinds of things and the time flies by when we are together. And then one day last week she says to me that her father is coming home this week and would like to meet me. Obviously he has been told that I am in his daughters' picture. I understand that, no problem. But she says . . ."

I interrupt, "Who is 'she'?"

With some exasperation in his tone, he says, "Sharna. Who do you think I meant?"

"She has a name," I said. "Even if Sharna is not here, we need to show her some respect. And if you want me to listen, I have to keep the players straight. I know that you are pissed about something, but yapping at me isn't going to help that."

"You're right. Sorry about that. I just thought that I had this figured and now I'm not so sure."

"Do you mean that you thought you had Sharna figured, the relationship or both?"

He thought about that and then said, "Both. I guess it's both things that I thought were pretty clear, and now I'm not sure of either one."

"So what do you want? How can I be of help to you? Or do you just want to vent, to blow off steam?"

"I don't know what to do. I want to understand what is going on. The more I think about it the more pissed off and angry I get."

"OK, "I said. "A couple of things here that might be helpful. You haven't known her long enough to come close to figuring her out. Until you see the worst Sharna has to offer you, you can't make any assumptions about who she is. Sharna has shown you nothing but her good side. She's likely been on her best behaviour. I suspect you have been doing the same. (He nods.) It's pretty natural to do that, for both of you. Each of you wants to show the other that you've made a wise choice. But people can only hide their true identity for so long before realistic thoughts and feelings begin to slip out sideways. Judging by the amount of time that you have spent with each other, that time has about run out. This is not a bad thing, but it does bring reality to the front pretty quickly. Relationships have their trials, and until you have shared some of those, you will never know just how well suited you are together.

"The other thing is this, and this is something that you need to understand about females and males. I talked about this when you and I were first getting to know each other a bit. Judging by some of what you have said about what has happened lately, you are hearing now what was mentioned then.

We, meaning males and females, do NOT speak the same language or use language for the same purpose a good part of the time. Yes, it is true that we both use English, but there are many words or phrases that we each use that come out having different meanings or are interpreted differently. I have no idea why this happens, but I can tell you that it does. Perhaps it has something to do with perception posing as reality. We also tend to hear what we want to hear. There is no blame to be placed here by the way. It is not our fault or their fault. It is simply the way we do our business.

"Consider phone conversations, for instance. Men, for the most part, use an economy of words. In other words, we say what needs to be said and save the rest for when we meet. Women will talk for hours on the phone and then go over it all again when they meet. Our conversations last seconds and women's last for multi-minutes, if not longer.

"Also, if we want something, we tend to just ask for it. Women often use subtle hints and, if that doesn't get our attention, they use obvious hints. If that doesn't work, they think we are either not paying attention or we are being negative or difficult.

"The point is don't ever make the mistake of thinking that you know women or you have them figured out. You don't and you won't. I came across this the other day and I can't give credit to who wrote it because there was no name attached to it. So it will just go as Anonymous."

I retrieved the page from inside the house, came out, sat down and began to read: "This is called 'One Wish.' A man was riding his Harley beside a Sydney beach when suddenly the sky clouded above his head and in a booming voice, the Lord said, 'Because you have TRIED to be faithful to me in all ways, I will grant you one wish'." The biker pulled over and said, 'Build a bridge to New Zealand so I can ride over anytime I want.' The Lord said, 'Your request is materialistic. Think of the enormous challenges for that kind of undertaking, the supports required to reach the bottom of the Pacific and the concrete and steel it would take! It will nearly exhaust several natural resources. I can do it, but it is hard for me to justify your desire for worldly things. Take a little more time and think of something that could possibly help mankind.'

"The biker thought hard about it for a long time. Finally, he said, 'Lord, I wish that I and all men could understand our wives. I want to know how she feels inside, what she's thinking when she gives me the silent treatment, why she cries, what she means when she says nothing's wrong, and how can I make a woman truly happy.

"The Lord replied, 'You want two lanes or four on that bridge?' "

I think Jacob was a bit confused. He looked at me and I could see that he was trying not to laugh but in the end he just let it out. I guess he thought that I was being dead serious and he wanted to be respectful of my effort to make the point.

I started to laugh as well and when the laughter subsided I said, "So, good luck trying to figure it all out. We are sharing the planet with other people who view it in a completely different way than we men see it. As I have said before, there is no right or wrong way here. This is just the way it is for us. We can't and won't change any of this, so what is more important is the question of how do we get along so that we can each have and get what we need from each other and at the same time enjoy some peace and serenity in our day-to-day interactions with each other?

"And how do we remain true to who we are as individual human beings? There are times when we know what our partners need but many more when we don't have a clue. The best we can hope for is to ask a straightforward question and hope that we get a straight forward answer. If not, guess and duck."

I asked him again, "So are you going to tell me what's been happening?"

"As I said, Sharna's father is coming home this week." He began. "We had talked about what he is like and how to act around him. She wants me to make an impression, I guess. I'm thinking that I should just be me. What's wrong with me as I am that I can't show him that? Well she – sorry, Sharna –says that he is pretty particular. So Sharna wants me to clean up a little. You know, get a haircut, be sure to shave that day, be careful of the language I use around him and be sure to not be bold and talk about my opinions. Apparently he has enough opinions for us both. Sharna said for me not to be surprised if he grills me about my future and what my plans are, etc. Hey, I'm just looking at having some fun with his daughter and seeing what comes from that. The list was a little longer, but you can see where I'm coming from, I'm sure. All of a sudden I'm feeling like I'm not good enough to be there or that Sharna is embarrassed by me."

"You feel threatened? misunderstood? or what?" I asked. "Are you afraid you won't cut it with the dad? You know that if you don't, the relationship is going to come to a halt in a hurry. It may or may not be fair, but fairness doesn't enter into this situation. The world isn't always fair.

"You said you just want to have some fun with HIS daughter. Maybe that's the point. He's a father first. You need to understand and respect that. If I don't miss my guess here, there is a very strong cultural bias that lives in their home and his daughter will live by it. The rules and expectations are very different from ours.

"Look, Sharna has given you a heads-up here. What do you want to do with it? You can't live your life according to how others want or think you should live it. If you do, you will never become the man you were born to be. You can take into consideration what Sharna has told you and asked of you, but in the end you need to show up at her house as Jacob. Be true to who you are.

"If you were in the father's shoes, would you be interested in who your daughter has been running with while you have been away? It's a question that every father asks himself, especially about his daughter. When you become a parent, you'll understand that daughters are treated differently than sons. Right or wrong, that's the way it is.

"It goes back to what we have talked about before, about our male characteristics and what we know to be our social and cultural standards. Fathers believe that their sons are capable of looking after themselves but they worry about their daughters being taken advantage of somehow or hurt in some way, that they need to be protected from the unpredictability of the world they live in.

"This is about a parent – a father – wanting to protect his family. He assumes the responsibility of being the leader of his family. I would think that the buck stops right at his desk. In this case, he will have the final say about his daughter and who it is she sees.

"If Sharna is an only child, that will add another dimension to the deal. Dad will definitely assert himself as the dominant male here. This is true, especially where the cultural expectations have a strong base.

"So if you show up and be Jacob – the real and honest Jacob – and that doesn't sit well with Sharna's father, it would be better to know that now, don't you think?

"The other side of this is that he will like you and will see the good in you. He is likely to appreciate your honesty and see it as an important human value. He will also want this for his daughter because he will see that you will protect her as well, that you will take care of her while she is with you and that you will not harm her in any way or put her at risk. You have to decide who you want to present to him when you meet. Who will show up? Jacob or some other guy?"

There is still something here that is tugging at me, but I can't say anything to Jacob about it, at least not right now. Sharna could be playing Jacob against Dad in order to get something she wants. It sounds as though Mom doesn't have a great deal of power in this family or doesn't have the time to be involved and with Dad on the road a great deal, this could be Sharna's way of saying to one or the other or both that they need to pay more attention to her. If they don't, then it's as if she is saying, "See what I might do."

It certainly isn't fair to make any judgments of her or her motives without first meeting her. I am concerned about Jacob more than anything. This is his first go at a more mature relationship and I wouldn't want to see it hit the skids so quickly. I just can't see anything serious developing. She has already said that she is going away to university in the fall, so this is a summertime thing at best.

"How did you leave it with Sharna?" I asked. Did you agree to do all this stuff?"

"No, I didn't agree to anything. I just said that I heard what she said and I would think about it. So what do I do?"

"As I said you weigh it all out and decide what is true to you. The likelihood is you would go to meet him cleaned up anyway, right? So there's no big issue there. The part that is challenging is that you may have to compromise who you are in order to show him you are not someone he has to concern himself with, as far as power goes. He has it and you don't. That's the way it is. And that isn't you.

"Can you be honest and straightforward without being rude or pushy? You know how to do that, I know you do. If he asks you a clear question, can you provide him with a clear answer, one that comes from your heart? I think that is when you are at your best, when you speak from your heart. Can you be true to who you are as a person and as a young man and accept the outcome of the visit regardless of how it goes?

"It is not important if I believe that you can, but it is important for you to know that you can and that you will survive the experience with class and understanding. If you decide that you can, there really isn't a problem here at all. You just be you.

"Oh yeah, you were going to tell me what you thought a real man does and how he behaves, what he is all about. Care to elaborate?"

"Well, I think I know what you want me to say," he said, "but I'm not sure about it all yet. I can say that I'm beginning to understand how it fits with who I am and how I feel about certain things, though. I get the protector part for sure. I can see that one being a part of me and who I am and how I see the world. That was evident with Harlan.

"I have felt like that in other situations as well. I get the provider part too. It's important to carry a big part of the load. I've got to step up sometimes and take on the tough stuff. It's important to work hard for those around you who matter to you. Again, Mom comes to mind here. A couple of my aunts reach out every once in a while and it feels good to help them with stuff they can't do themselves.

"I have a feeling that I'm going to learn a tough lesson soon and that's going to be interesting how that all goes down. I'm not sure how the manhood thing comes into play on that one."

"The manhood thing is about accepting those times when you will hear or see something that you don't want to hear or see," I said. "It's about understanding, accepting and deciding that others have a right to their way of doing things, just as you do, and not getting all snotty and angry because you couldn't have your own way.

"We all do things primarily to satisfy our own needs. You do that, I do that, and most of us do that. And most people decide to do things, not to piss us off or to do us harm in any way, but rather and simply to get their own needs met. Let's not personalize their decisions. If we can do that, we will be a lot less angry a lot more of the time.

"Besides, you are not entitled to whatever you think you deserve. As men, we cannot go around blaming others for what happens to us. We need to take some responsibility for what happens to us. If we do that, then we can keep some control over the solutions that will be needed. We cannot expect that just because we are who we are that the world will provide us with whatever we want when we want it. We need to understand that we have to work for our rewards and that there are no freebies.

"Men are challenge oriented, so part of the challenge is to use our own skills and energy to get what we want and, depending on its importance to us, continue to work until we get what we set out to get.

"This whole idea of entitlement is very dangerous because it doesn't provide us with the motivation and the responsibility of taking care of our own business. Too many now assume that certain things will come their way without any effort on their part to make it happen.

"Some think that just because they were born they have rights. After all, they didn't ask to be born, but since they are here they should have this and that. This isn't realistic and yet a good number of males your age feel exactly that way. They steal, cheat, lie, destroy things and generally disrespect themselves and others. Not all but many. They are used to having stuff given to them by parents who seem to be afraid to say no or don't know how to say no, but this is another topic for another day.

"The point is if you want that nice new car, work for it. If you want to go on a trip, work for it. Don't sit back and expect mom or dad to pony up the dollars and get pissed off when they don't, can't or won't. I know that is not where you come from, but many think and feel just this way.

"This also covers relationships and anything else we want. You will not always get what you want, but you usually get what you need, whether you like it or not. Others will have a say in what happens as well, and you don't have any control over them and how they think or what they decide. They may have different wants than you do. Somebody is going to go without.

"Learn from these times and don't pout or whine about it. Handle it and yourself with dignity. Think about how it could have been different so that the next time you find yourself in a similar situation you may well be able to avoid the hurt or the discomfort or the embarrassment, if it gets to that. That's what men do and that is part of what this manhood stuff is about: learning how to do this. You're learning, Jacob. The road may get a little bumpy, but you're not alone. Remember that."

"Any other ideas about what a man brings to the table?" I asked.

"Let me think on this for now," he said. "You know how my head hurts sometimes because it gets so full? Now's one of those times. Thanks. I meant thanks for giving me so much to think about."

With that, he got up and in true Jacobean form gave me something new. It was not a variation of the nod, but rather he held out his closed hand for a fist bump, so I bumped his closed fist with my closed fist and off he went.

Morgan And Jack Made Me Do It. Thanks, Guys

A while back I had the distinct pleasure of watching a movie called The Bucket List. It needs to be on everyone's must-see list. These two gentlemen are two of my favourites and represent all the things that are good about Hollywood actors. They got me thinking about making my own list, so I made the commitment to at least consider the possibility.

I ran the idea by John and he said go for it if I could. He provided me with a bit of scientific assistance and that was that.

I went to bed that night wondering how Jacob would make out at tomorrow's crucial meeting with Sharna's father but also charged with excitement that I hadn't felt in quite some time. I got up early the next morning too 'jacked' to eat anything and went right to the garage to look at her.

There she was. I slowly took the covers from her sculpted frame and moved a bit closer for a better look. Nothing had changed. She still made my heart beat a little more quickly whenever I saw her. I gave her a bath and dried her off and then stood back and marveled. This may well be the last time we would meet like this, so I wanted to take it all in. I ran my hand over her frame. She was as smooth as a baby's backside.

Finally it was time. I put the key in, turned it on, hit the ignition switch and she started up without hesitation. Yowser!

They say you never forget how to ride one of these things, so 15 minutes or so of riding it around the lot of the supermarket down the street assured me I was ready to venture out. I had no idea how far I could go or how long my energy would hold out. I ingested the concoction that John had created for me, hoping that it would help me get the day in.

I pointed my 1996 Yamaha Virago/750cc mint-shape cruiser toward the water and off we went. There is something quite magical that takes over for those who enjoy the ride. There is the man vs. machine thing, of course, but far beyond that it's the freedom that I get from being out there, the sun in my face and the warmth on my body. The sun warmed my skin through my leathers. It was like Mother Nature was holding me in her arms telling me to ride forever. It felt that good. The world is a different place on the back of one of these machines.

Luckily, everyone who was supposed to be at work that day was so I had the road virtually to myself. Up, down, bend to the left, to the right. It was glorious. A bit more confidence and a little more speed through the turns.

I felt a comfort that I had not known for a long time. I didn't spend more than a second trying to figure it out because I didn't want to waste any of this adventure thinking about that stuff.

As my mind does all too often, I thought about Jacob and how he might like this as well. I thought about how he was changing and growing and maturing right before my eyes and what a wonderful thing that was to witness. I felt good about the decision I had made regarding his future. I knew that it was the right thing to do and I took great satisfaction in knowing that he would thrive as I had.

I travelled mountains and valleys, all the while marvelling at the beautiful work of God all around me. How else could this canvas have been created? I stopped for a lunch that I had packed. I sat by a stream with my jacket off and let my bare feet dangle in the icy water that had made its way from the mountains.

Before I knew it and all too fast, the day had come to an end. The sun was setting behind a peak in the distance. It transformed the sky into something that was so indescribable I could not move from my spot for fear of missing something never to be seen again. The dark began to crawl in around me and I knew that I had to leave this place.

The ride home was amazing. It was still warm enough to ride without my leather jacket on. The closer I got to home the more sadness crept into my head, not because it may have been the last ride I would take but because I hadn't bothered to take the time when I was younger to enjoy the true gifts the world has to offer us.

And I thought of Jacob again. I wanted to impress upon him, somehow, that he needs to see as much as he can and do as much as he can to experience the freedom and the majesty and the energy that is his for the taking. The world is abundant. There is enough to go around. I hope that he will find someone who will want to share that with him, someone who has the same thirst for what is out there and that they will help each other get all they can. He needs to ensure that nobody takes away or tries to lessen the importance of the gifts he has to offer the world around him, those that only another male would understand.

He is so desperate to trust someone. He has not had a good experience with that so far in his young life. His father abused the innocent trust that a boy gives his father. The idiot didn't understand the gift he was being presented.

Certainly his mom was and is trustworthy. However, that trust is not the same as the trust earned by and given to a peer. He will need to understand that trust is not the same as permission although they are similar in some ways. There are so many different elements of our lives that require trust as a foundation in order for us to be truly joyful. Not happy, joyful.

Faithfulness and loyalty are two big ones, but there are others. He will realize that he needs to trust someone to keep his secrets and that they will be honoured, and that his hopes, fears and dreams will be respected and kept private and that his thoughts are not judged. They may not be accepted – that's OK – but not judged. He has so much to learn and so little time.

When I got home and put her away for the night, I was immediately cocooned in a coat of exhaustion. I can't remember ever feeling that weak and tired as I did then. I slept well into the next day. I didn't see Jacob the next day nor did I see him for the next three days. This was about the same time it took for me to feel somewhat human again. I had regained some energy, but I knew I wasn't going to be dancing for a while yet.

I sensed things had not gone well for him. I felt sad and concerned for him because I knew how important this whole relationship was to him. I also had to respect his desire for privacy and for him to have a chance to process whatever had happened between him and Sharna's father.

Many men retreat, think, sort, process and decide. Then they will let the rest of the world know what they had decided and they will go about moving on.

Reality Bites Hard Sometimes

I hadn't seen Jacob in over a week. Just as I was thinking about him, he showed up at the bottom of my sidewalk. He, of course, didn't need to be invited, so he just walked up and threw himself into his chair. He looked at me hard and then said, "You knew. How did you know? This is really weird, I gotta tell ya. How did you know?

"How did I know what?"

"How did you know how this whole thing was going to go. You practically told me how it was going to go down not in my favour with Sharna's father. We really didn't hit it off well. I'm not one of his favourite people and I don't see how that is going to change much. No Christmas card for me this year.

"Besides Sharna seems to be too busy to return any calls or to call me. This really sucks and I'm not amused. Talk about a slap in the face. Whoa, this one bites hard. I could have walked into that place with a thousand dollar suit on driving a Jag with gold license plates and a Brinks truck parked at the end of the drive and it would not have mattered a bloody bit. He had already made up his mind about me and that was that. What a prick. He didn't even give me a chance. And she, well, she didn't say a friggin' word. Nada. You knew, so why didn't you clue me in?"

"Well, first of all," I said," I didn't know anything for sure. All I did was outline the possibilities. This isn't about money either. It doesn't matter what you have or don't have. And by the way, why am I responsible for your decision-making? We talked about this, remember? I asked you if you were ready to deal with this. I asked you if you could take what he had to say and move on with it if it didn't favour you and Sharna. I asked you if you could make a decision about how to handle it

137

that didn't result from your being angry and you said you thought you could do that.

"I'm sorry that it went as it did, but it really has nothing to do with you. He has his reasons for his decision and that is that. He might have explained his decision to you, but it sounds as though he didn't feel like he needed to give you an explanation. That's also his prerogative. Stand up, deal with it and move on.

"Feel bad, feel sad, feel whatever you need to feel about it all and then move on. Take this as a learning opportunity and grow from it. It hurts– believe me, I know that – and it hurts me to see you done unto.

"Do you want to talk about it or do you want to carry it around for a while yet? I'm not trying to be a smart ass. I mean what I asked. You have to deal with this in your own way and in your own time. But deal with it you must. If you carry it around, it will fester in you and it will color your judgments and decision-making. Other relationships you will enter into will be affected until you do deal with it. You cannot get into another relationship to get over this one, either. More people do this thinking that if they can't feel anything about the old one then they'll forget about it in time. Wrong, so wrong.

"All you will do if you do that is carry the negatives forward into the new relationship and you will end up punishing your new partner for the sins of the past partner. You will not learn anything from this experience until you deal with it. So what do you need to do to deal with it?"

"I need to understand what happened here: what went wrong, where did I screw up?"

"What makes you think that you screwed up?" I asked him.

"Well, if it wasn't me then who was it?"

"Well, maybe nobody screwed up. Perhaps it just wasn't meant to be what you had hoped it was going to be or perhaps Sharna had a very different agenda than you did and when it played out you got caught in the crossfire. Don't be so quick to punish yourself here or to accuse yourself of being a screw-up. That's what losers do, and you are not a loser. Do you hear me on this? You are not a loser."

He was more crushed than he was angry. That was evident. He is living on the brink of becoming a man in this world, closer to manhood than childhood or adolescence, yet he is child-like in some ways. It's like being in a no-man's land. That's not a criticism but rather an observation. He is vulnerable in many ways and this human relationship stuff is no venue for the faint at heart.

138

He finally looked at me and asked in a steady voice, "Ok, what do I need to be aware of for the next time?"

"Wow! How much time do you have? Just kidding. If I asked you what you think is the most important thing in a relationship, what would you say?"

He thought about that for a minute and then said, "I think it is feeling good about being with each other. Not looking at or wanting to be with another girl. And I think that it is important to show her respect, especially in front of other people."

"Those are really important things, Jacob, that is so true, but I think the word we are looking for here is trust. We need to earn the trust of the person we care about and that person needs to earn our trust before we can take the relationship to the next level. Don't get me wrong here because I am not being critical of you with Sharna, but you gave her your trust and she hadn't earned it.

"Trust is the most important element in any relationship, in my mind, whether it is a friendship or something that runs deeper than that. You didn't know her long enough or well enough to give her your trust. You guys were in the kiss-and-giggle stage. That's the place where everything is wonderful and nothing could go wrong or touch either of you in a negative way. Most everyone else was excluded from your lives. And as we talked about before, this is the time when the only thing you see in each other is the very best. We really only see and hear what we want to see and hear.

"That's why you are feeling so disturbed by what has happened here. I think that you are feeling betrayed by Sharna because you trusted her and maybe you're feeling that she did not honour and value the importance of the trust you gave her.

"The thing is she may not have been aware that you gave her your trust. She may have been operating under the idea that this was just a summer thing and she was going away in the fall, so why get deeply involved here? She may not have felt the same for you as you did for her.

"Another possibility, and it is only a possibility, is that she may have been trying to send a message to her father or both her parents that they need to pay more attention to her than they do. If they aren't going to do that then 'I {meaning Sharna} am about to run amok.' She may have been emotionally blackmailing Dad for a big prize – maybe a new car for school as an example – and you were the bait. It's called a guilt gift.

"I don't think she meant to hurt you intentionally. I really don't. We need to understand that people's behaviour is most often guided by their efforts to get their needs met in ways that make the most sense to them. The point is you didn't know her long enough and you didn't see her in any situations that might have set off some bells for you that said, 'I have never seen that side of her before.' Be more careful about who gets your gift of trust. You need to decide what needs to happen for someone to earn it and how you earn it from them."

I left him with those thoughts for a moment and went in the house. When I returned I looked at him and said, "Does that make sense to you? I mean that is just a small part of the whole relationship thing. I don't mean it to sound like some stiff and unexciting exercise. The truth is that most relationships probably start off by accident more than anything. But for a relationship to grow into something that is special, there are things that need to happen. Otherwise, they become disastrous and hard feelings are often what's left over.

"Let me illustrate how complicated things can get. Let's jump ahead a bit and suppose that you are involved in a meaningful relationship. What do you think you would need to do to make your partner happy?"

I sat back and let him consider the possibilities. I knew it wasn't a fair question to ask him, given his limited experience in relationships. The get-togethers he has been involved in have been more like dictatorships than anything else because of the nature of the people involved.

"Well, I think that I would need to show her that I can be someone she can trust since that is a theme today. I would need to make her understand that I would protect her and care for her. I would also need to be respectful to her and not push her into anything that she doesn't want to do. Not be demanding and try not to stress her out. I would want to treat her special and be someone she could talk to and someone who would keep her secrets. I guess that is part of the trust thing that you talked about. I think it would be important to support her when she needed it and be someone that she could count on to be her most important person. I was going to say 'friend.'

I nodded at him and then said, "That sounds much like how you answered the other question I asked you, but the points are still very valid and important and correct. However, this is where it gets difficult for us guys. The one thing that we can't do is be all things to all people all of the time. During the years of working with many couples and individuals, I came to understand that there are many other things we are expected to be or duties that we are supposed to be able and willing to perform. Things like being a friend, companion, lover, a big brother, a father figure in some circumstances, chef, electrician, carpenter, plumber, mechanic, decorator, stylist, sexologist, gynecologist, psychologist, pest exterminator, psychiatrist, good listener, good father (when the time comes), sympathetic, athletic, warm, attentive, gallant, intelligent, funny, creative, tender, strong, understanding, tolerant, ambitious, capable, courageous, determined, true, dependable, passionate, compassionate. You would need to compliment her regularly, be honest, being rich would help, don't look at other women, give her lots of attention and NEVER, NEVER forget your anniversary."

"Our needs and desires are much less demanding. We just need her to show up looking mighty fine and not be empty handed. That's it. (A slight pause) I'm kidding. Actually there are a few other qualities we look for in our partners. However, we men are not all that complicated. As a matter of fact, men are really quite basic if folks would just try to see it in us. Basic doesn't mean simple minded, either.

"Think of your own basic needs in a relationship. What are they? Doesn't seem like a lot, does it? We need to have our egos massaged on a regular basis. In other words, we need to know that we are respected for something that we do well. Acknowledgment is a key for us. We need to have and experience companionship so that we are connected to someone in a special way and that we have a place in the world. We need to know that our experience and our counsel are valued. I truly believe that if more men were to experience this, there would be far fewer divorces and one-parent families."

"Do I really need to know all this stuff? I mean, I just want to be involved with someone and have it be OK. That's it," he said.

I could hear the exasperation in his voice. "Hey like I said before. You don't have to know any of this stuff. This isn't meant to be like going to school, but if you don't have any idea what is involved and a minimal understanding what each of us is like and how to satisfy our partner's needs and wants, the likelihood of success is really quite small. If you feel you have enough or know enough, then stop. Go try it out and see how it works. Jacob, you won't hurt my feelings, I can assure you."

"I guess I just get tired trying to make sense of it." he said. "I have to try to remember how to do this and if that happens what I am

141

supposed to do with that. This manhood thing is really hard to get. Maybe I'm not going to be good at it."

Not only is he tired or exasperated but he is stuck. And so am I. The one thing that I did know for sure is that this interaction with Jacob has become close to an obsession with me because I desperately want him to have his chance at what he wants, more than anything. But it is also about me achieving my goal and leaving my mark. It can't be that way and that's where it feels it is right now.

Instead of being excited about the process, he is becoming frustrated with it. That's not how learning happens, at least not this kind of learning.

"Let's take a couple of days off and not think about anything. Go play and have some fun in the sun. I've got some stuff I can do anyway, so it will give me a chance to get that done. Come on back when you're ready and we will go from there. Yes?"

"Hey, you're not pissed at me or anything? He was genuinely concerned.

"No Jacob, I'm not pissed at you. I'm proud of you for speaking your mind. That's something else that men do: we speak our minds, as respectfully as we can, so that things get taken care of quickly and then we can move on. If something comes up you know where I am."

"Thanks. I'll catch up with you in a couple of days."

With that he was off on his next adventure. I realized that I had a great deal to do in the next day or two and had no idea how I was going to go at it or pull it together. I just knew that I had to find a way or this whole thing would go down the toilet. The place to start would be with a phone call and a favour. I was also becoming more aware of time. Always time and a growing lack of it.

It really wasn't dawn when Annie rang my doorbell the next morning, but it just felt like it. I made my way downstairs to the door and opened it a bit. The bright light was hard to stare into, so I squinted a bit. She was so apologetic and ready to leave when I said to her, "Where are you going? You got me up for something, so the least you could do is tell me what the hell it is. Then I grinned at her and asked very gently, "Kidding! What's up?"

She was still uncertain how to take me, but she said that she wanted to make a trade with me: brunch for conversation. I asked what time it really was and she told me that it was 10:45 in the morning. I responded with, "Over easy with brown toast if you have it and honey if you have that too." She said she thought she could put that together and I suggested in a half hour at her place. That was fine by her.

After I had ravished brunch, she got down to business, opening with this: "A while back you generously offered to help me understand what Jacob was going through and that you might be able to enlighten me if that were possible. Is that offer still open?"

"Yup. However the degree to which I enlighten may have to do with what your question is or questions are. I can't talk about anything that he and I have talked about without his permission, and right now I don't have that. If you're good with that, I can listen and possibly make comments."

"I think we can do that without compromising what you and Jacob have got going. My question would be about the topic of manhood. He is really struggling with the whole concept. He said that you told him to take a day or two off and go play and not think about any of the stuff you guys have been talking about."

She stopped then, assuming, I guess, that I would confirm that. I did not respond one way or the other, so she carried on.

"OK, then can you explain to me what that is all about so that I can have some idea of what he wrestles with day after day here. He desperately wants to get it right and he does not want to disappoint you either. He is feeling defeated because he doesn't feel as though he is closer now than he was. He's never been one for patience either. For him, now is never soon enough."

I had to be careful here. I wanted to help Annie become more aware of what was happening but not so aware that she would try to explain it to him. Two different hands in the soup usually didn't work out well.

"How about this: did you take math in school?" I asked as I leaned toward her a bit. She indicated that she did. So I asked her, "Would you rather just have the answer to a particular problem or would you want to know the process by which you got the answer so that you could solve another similar problem if you needed to?"

She thought for a moment and then said," I would want to know the process so that I wouldn't have to depend on someone giving me the answer all the time."

Halfway through her answer to me, I could see a light go on. She knew what I was getting at.

"All right, point made. But how does that help me with what I need to know so that I can help him?"

"I'm not sure that I can explain this in words that will make sense to you," I said, "but I'll give it a go. Before I try to do that though, I need you to give me your word you won't talk to him about this or try to explain it to him. My concern is that he would become confused about what each of us is trying to say. He needs to go through the process of putting it all together so that it makes sense to him. Not anyone else but him. He can't do this for anyone else either. Not you and not me.

"That's why I can't just give him the answer that he wants me to give him. He would tell you that we have talked about how part of this process is him going out to 'slay his tiger'. Well, this is his 'tiger.'

"He is oh-so-very close to doing this for himself. He is an exceptional young man who is thirsty to learn. I know that he is impatient, but that's not a bad thing unless it leads him to try to short-circuit the process. I know he's frustrated too. He'll learn to deal with that. The learning that is vital here is not about remembering or retaining information. It is about his using some of that information to determine where and how he will fit into the world as a man. It's knowing and using and understanding his skills and gifts to do it. It is HIS place that he needs to secure and no one else's."

"But . . ." I cut her off in mid-sentence.

"I'm sorry if I am being rude here, Annie. I don't mean to be, but there are no 'buts' here. It's a 'yes' or a 'no' response I need from you. If you want to be a part of this and you want to help Jacob with this, just listen to him. Make yourself available to him if he wants to talk about it. That would be huge if he knew that you cared enough to do that for him. He is not looking for guidance from you. He just wants an ear."

"Alright, OK," she said, sounding put out. "I won't try to explain it to him. I won't repeat whatever it is you tell me. It's more important to me that I understand where he is and what he is dealing with and what he is going through."

"Done. This manhood thing is simply about Jacob learning how to present himself and represent himself in the world that he lives in. He does this by understanding and incorporating the time honoured roles other men in his life have illustrated. These earlier men would have gone through a similar process involving their mentors and guides speaking to how a man lives his life each day according to the roles I referred to. Unfortunately Jacob didn't have any body willing to help him with that. In my mind that's part of the reason why he's struggled to find his way.

"When you mention roles what are you referring to exactly?" asked Annie.

"Things like being a protector, provider, challenge oriented, problem solver and one that takes the 'bullet' for the family. For whatever reasons, men have accepted the responsibility of fulfilling these roles since time began. It's what they do. For many it is their 'reason for being'. How Jacob manages these roles is what will define and describe him and, in large part, drive his behaviour as a man.

"True that his environment will govern, to some degree, how he responds to things that go on around him. That's all I can say about it. At least for now.

"So can you see why you can't try to explain this to him? You can't because you don't know how to do it. Only a man can help another man with this part of the process. You could tell him intellectually, I suppose, but you can't tell him from the core of who you are because your core as a woman and mine as a man are dramatically different."

"Not to change the subject too radically, but I would like it if you and Jacob could come over for a barbecue one night soon, maybe Saturday or sometime next week. No big deal, just quick and easy. I'll take care of everything. Steaks work for you?" It didn't take her long to agree although she pointed out that she can no longer speak for Jacob and his time schedule. Then she threw in that that was partially my fault and that I was helping to create a monster. Then she chuckled and said she thought he would be good with it though.

I wanted to go home and lie down. The last while was really catching up with me. The energy I used to have was not as available as it once was. I said to Annie, "So does that make it a bit easier for you? I don't want to be secretive or anything, but I know what I know about this stuff and it's the best I can do for you right now. You'll just need to trust me on that."

She looked at me carefully and said, "I will trust that you have done and said what you can, for now. You have to know that I'll be back for more. Thanks for what you felt you could give me. I appreciate that much. At least I have some idea of the why of it all. Men!" she said, shaking her head.

She stood and put her hand on my shoulder and wished me well. I got the strangest feeling from her at that time, almost as if she could intuit something was wrong or that something was going on she was not supposed to know about. And then the feeling left me as fast as it had come.

The rest of the day passed quickly as I kept a low-energy profile. I just needed to catch up a bit. The next three days went quickly as well. I found myself feeling much better and actually felt restless, even bored. I took this as a good sign, but knew the feeling wouldn't last for ever.

Epiphanies Can Be So Good

Jacob was back at my porch soon after, looking rested and tanned. He had a comfortable way about him and then he said, "Gimme what you got. I'm ready." I was envious of how fast youth can regenerate.

"Really?" I said. "You sure you're ready?"

He was being playful. "Oh, yeah," he said, "Almost untouchable. You'll never guess who I ran into on my travels?"

Without giving me a chance to even think about it, he burst out with "Sharna. The one and the only."

I have to admit that I didn't see that one coming. Actually Jacob seemed quite OK about it and not upset at all.

"Wow, so how did that go?"

"At first I was a bit pissed. No, that's not true. I was really pissed and angry. We had left things unsaid and unfinished. We really hadn't had an opportunity to go over what went down so we got off to the side and walked the shore for quite a while. I was going to unload on her but rather I heard your voice in my head and I remembered some of what we had talked about. Instead of unloading on her, I got quiet for a minute or two and calmed down and decided that I would not go there. I would give her a chance to explain it to me instead.

"If I really wanted answers, which I did, I knew that I needed to ask the question and then shut up. It wasn't about a short-term feel-good blowup. I needed to know, so I went that way. It was truly amazing to go about things that way because normally I would have downloaded on her and kissed her off.

"The conversation went really well. She asked me out. SHE asked ME to go out. What a change! Of course, I declined her generous offer but I wasn't rude about it. I just said to her that I didn't see the benefit of that for either of us but thanked her.

"Actually I think it stunned her that I would turn her down. I don't think that she is used to being told no. Anyway I said no not to hurt her or to be mean or rude. I just plain didn't see the point in it. It was not in

146

my best interest to do it. There was no up side so I didn't. Shit, it was so cool to do that and do it that way for that reason. It felt so good.

"The bonus of the whole thing is that I think I'm getting more of what it is you are trying to get me to see about this manhood stuff. I could have gone off like a jerk, but instead I felt as if I responded like a more mature person would have, like a man might have. What do you think?"

Here we go, I thought. He has opened the door for me once again. "It's not important what I think as much as it is important what you think about how you handled this. This could not have been easy for you. But you did it and with class, by the sound of it. I feel all warm and fuzzy inside for you. Don't give me that look, either," I joked.

"I do feel good for you though. Perhaps you understand more about what I said to you when I said this isn't about school and your having to memorize all this stuff. Depend on your instincts and intuition. Allow yourself the time to plan your response and you will do just fine most of the time. Sometimes you'll just go off and then have to apologize or something for what happened. That would likely depend on who you were with at the time too."

Jacob nodded and then said, "I spent a great deal of my time this last while just watching other people and thinking about other situations. I don't know why I did this, other than it seemed like fun at the time. Anyway, I came up with some questions for you. Before I head there, though, I'm a bit confused about something. You say that it is not important what you think but rather more important what I think. On the other hand, you suggested that you can't be my father but you can be a mentor. My question is this: don't mentors teach? If they do, then you are asking me to accept what you are saying as correct or the truth as you know it to be. I'm not believing what I think is right or good at that point. I'm doing or believing what you tell me to do. Help me out here because this is really important to me to get this part straight."

Well. I can say that he certainly came back a much different person than when he left. I have to say that the difference is truly impressive. He is asking for clarity not theory.

"Mentors are teachers and guides, "I said. "You know how I feel about giving advice, so that one is out. I can only give you what I believe to be true. I do the best I can to get and give the best, most accurate information that is available to me, mostly through my own experiences and observations and also by my own feelings about what I think is right. I depend greatly on my own instincts and intuition. Some would say that these are spiritual messages but that's another conversation for another day with someone who knows more about that than I. All I know is that I have come to rely almost completely on what I understand and accept as my social and cultural gifts. These are the ones that I received from my mentors and teachers. In the end, however, I always have the final say about how I will proceed and what is in my best interests. I don't seek advice but I do seek solid and trusted information. I try to stick to what my heart tells me and not my head.

"I don't want you to be a clone of me. My hope is that you will be an independent thinker and doer in the world, based on what you believe is truth for you. That is what I pass along to you. You need to take it, look at it and see how it fits for you and how it feels for you as a person, as a man. In other words, you have to believe it as YOUR truth and whether or not it is good for you. You have to buy in in order for it to be something that you can do because it is right for you and not because I or anyone else, for that matter, says that it is true or right. I can say this about all of what you are trying to understand. This manhood thing is not about 'getting it'. It's about 'living it' every day and making it your own way of going about how you choose to live your life.

"Too many of us have made our decisions based on what other people would think or say, and we have to stop doing that. They are not us and we are not them. I'm not sure how else to say it. Does that work for you or can we go at it from a different place?"

"I get that," he said. "I see the difference. Next question: You know I'm liking this way of doing things. I get to put you in the hot seat for a change. Really. It gives me a chance to actually get the parts out that confuse me. I've been trying to sort out stuff that I'm not sure about and trying to listen and take it all in at the same time. Some of it really depends on knowing what you were talking about before, but if I don't understand that part then it all gets jumbled up in my head and then I get nuts. So this is good that I can sort it out before we go on to something else."

He was making a lot of sense but I felt bad for him. I had put my agenda and my need to do this ahead of where he was and just expected he would get it and that he would keep up. For the most part, he had done that, so I had not seen a reason to change what we were doing or how we were doing it. I had completely forgotten about the rule that suggests I needed to meet him where he was at and not expect him to be where I think he should be.

It was a compliment to Jacob, and his true desire to learn how to do it differently that was the remarkable thing. "You are absolutely right and I am so sorry that I let my expectations get way ahead of where you were or are. The other side is you are a pretty quick learner and you have done remarkably well to get it and to keep it together. You didn't give up when you could have said, 'Screw it, I don't need this.' I appreciate your tenacity and your dedication." I grinned at him as I said, "Hey, you're a lot smarter than you look."

"Thanks" was all he said as he grinned back. "Next question: What do you think happened between Sharna and me?"

"I think you got caught up in the romantic idea of being able to attract a girl other than the girls you were used to being around. I also think that you couldn't see the difference between lust and love. I believe that you were in lust with her. Remember the challenge and the chase and the importance of conquering? You got caught up thinking with your other head.

"This was a person who did not respond to the normal rules of the game and you had to find a way to conquer her as you went along. Your usual charm wasn't enough. She was a great challenge."

"You know I like this format as well," I said. "It gives me a chance to say what I really think and feel. You ask and I have to be honest with you. Yes, I like this way of doing things."

"I've got two more questions," he said. I happened to be around a couple who just got engaged. He is 20 and she is 19. I think they're nuts, but watching them together got me thinking about how they were, how I am and what I thought relationships and marriage are supposed to be like.

"Anyway the other day I dropped past his place to pick him up and, he invited me in for some lunch. We got shooting the breeze about stuff and I noticed how he treated his mother and how he spoke to her. He thanked her for her effort at lunch and helped her clean up. He was very respectful and mannerly. But then later on after we had left his place and we had picked up Marsha – that's his fiancé – his manner of talking to her and how he treated her was very different from how he treated his mom.

"I guess I don't understand why some guys treat their mothers better than they treat the person that they are supposed to be in love with, like this guy who is going to marry this person next year. What's that about anyway?"

149

"I should send you away more often. Where've you been anyway? That's a great question. I've wondered the same for years and years. We see it all the time. We used to call these guys 'mommas boys' but I don't think that's it. All I can offer on this is that there is a physical blood connection between mother and son that is stronger than any other bond. The connection between wife, or would-be wife, is an emotional connection. It is one that is or needs to be built on a strong trust for each other. The one with mom has a trust that is built into it. It's there right from the time of birth.

"Junior has a dependency on Mom for the basics from day one. Her caring and nurturing are the foundation for his trust of her. He is locked into her connection with him. Often we can see the same kind of thing between daughters and their fathers, although the connection is built on other factors. Obviously. I would be willing to bet that 99% of guys would choose Mom over the new missus if a choice was necessary.

"I've heard it explained by some that there are many prospective wives out there but we only have one mother. The relationship with Mom also has a built-in respect factor attached to it that doesn't begin with the relationship with his bride-to-be. Sons just don't trash their mothers. This is a taboo from ages past and it still stands today. It's one of those social and cultural values that I have spoken about."

"That makes sense, Jacob said. "When I think about the relationship I have with my mother, all that you have said stands true. Nobody would get between her and me. Nobody."

I needed to finish the thought that we love our mothers but can't let them rule our lives. "That said we can't let our mothers determine the course of our lives or manipulate the choices we make regarding our choice of life partners either. They need to back away when the time is right to allow their sons and their daughters the freedom necessary so that they can continue on with their lives. It is up to us, as sons, to make sure that that happens."

Jacob looked at me for longer than normal and asked, "Are you OK? You look tired. I can do this tomorrow if you want."

"Thanks for the concern. I had a poor nights' sleep, that's all. Not to worry. I've got enough left in me to answer one more. I'm rather enjoying this turn-about." I tried to sound upbeat but I'm not sure I sold it.

"If you're sure. The last one is about the manhood thing. This is a big one, and I have to have a better understanding of it than I have now. Talking about it is difficult because I don't completely understand what it is we are talking about. I want you to tell me about manhood. I need to understand what it is. What do you mean by that word when you say it? Right now, I don't want to know or need to know how to get it. I need to know what it is. I've got a better chance of figuring out how to get it once I know what it is."

If he only knew how much he had taught me today instead of the other way around, it would amaze him, I'm sure. Of course that made perfect sense and again I am impressed by his insight and his grasp of the obvious. Our children can teach us great things.

"OK, let's try this. This manhood thing is simply about you learning how to present yourself and represent yourself in the world that you live in by understanding and honouring the social and cultural values and qualities that you have inherited from men of an earlier time. As I just mentioned it is more about how you live these gifts each day – what part do they play in terms of how you treat the other people around you."

I was set to carry on when Jacob jumped in and said, "Tell me about the social and cultural gifts again. I know we've talked about them before. I just want to know that I got what it is I think I got. That sounds lame, but it makes sense to me."

" If we think about the word 'gift,'" I said, "many of us think about something that we are given that we not likely asked for but were surprised by when we got it. A gift tends to add something to our lives and ideally, a gift can make us feel good. Some can be much more important to us than others. If we think about the words social and cultural we think about our societies and how they exist – how they continue to operate and what the rules are.

"There is much that we are forced to take for granted because we just don't know why or how our bodies do what they do. Our hair colour and our eye colour are determined by genes long before we enter this world. We don't really have a choice about whether our eyes are blue or brown or if our hair will be blond or red. They are what they are, and we live with it. We accept what they are.

"Our gender is decided by the combination of Mom's and Dad's genes and other chemicals. We don't choose to be male or female. We are born and life begins. We are what and who we are. But once we are born into this world a process called socialization begins. Males are treated differently from females and rightly or wrongly are seen to be different as well. There are many differing thoughts about all of this but this is where we are right now.

151

Definition of Manhood

There are certain expectations that come with being male. Our mentors and our guides help us understand what these expectations are and how we are to live our lives. This is true for our mental, emotional and physical development. For instance: Because we are built, generally speaking, with more muscle mass and our bodies are built with larger frames. Therefore, we are assigned – and encouraged to do the more physical types of labour. Certainly in days gone by we have been the hunters and the providers and the builders of homes, the protectors and so on. In many instances this process of socialization and the introduction of cultural expectations helps separate us from the animal kingdom and the other systems that go together to make the world what it is.

"This is where it gets dicey. If you believe in a divine plan, you would believe that there is a plan for how we need to live and honour our lives. If you believe that we came from a one-cell amoeba-type thing, you would have another belief system to consider.

"I can't tell you what to believe or not. How we got this way is for you to sort out by yourself. I might have got away from what you asked but I think it is all connected to us as a species and as a gender. We are special in the world. No doubt. Socially and culturally ingrained gifts are just that: qualities and characteristics that have been ingrained in us that help us co-ordinate our lives according to certain thoughts and feelings. They are generated within us and help us to live our lives, basically to help us survive as a species. They are special in that we can use them to do good or not. The gift of it is that it is our choice as to how we use them and for what purpose."

Jacob sat there, quiet and trance-like. Finally he asked, "So how does this work between us, as males and females?"

"I'm not sure I understand what you are asking me. How does that make us different?"

"Yeah, how does it make us different? I know that we do things and think about things differently. I guess it's about how I am supposed to live with these 'gifts' as you call them. What do they make me do?"

"Well, Jacob, it's not like you have some kind of a disease. They don't make you do anything that you don't want to do. They help us identify the roles that each of us play in our day to day lives. They are a part of what comes naturally to you, just like when Harlan came around. You knew by instinct and intuition how you wanted to respond and what you needed to do. You acted on the protector and the provider

152

roles you are beginning to understand. You always have the choice about how you respond, Jacob.

"I can't speak for how the same processes in women are felt and acted upon, but I know this: You do not need to apologize for being male to anyone. That is not to say that you will not need to apologize for something you do or say, but it will be you, as a person, who, I hope, recognizes the need to do so.

"That is called responsibility. It is about feeling free to be who you are as a man in the world, the community you live in, the home you help build and the family you help to raise both as a parent and as a father. You're not there yet, as a father and a parent I mean, but you will be and you will see that these roles aren't always the same. You'll find that out for yourself.

"It means feeling comfortable enough and free enough to do as you please with no justification necessary, provided that no one else's rights are abused or violated in any way; that no one is hurt or marginalized in any way; and that no one has been lessened or taken advantage of in any way.

"You don't just look like a man but you learn to behave like a man. Being a man is not an excuse for being a pig either. It is about holding an absolute respect for women. It's about recognizing and honouring the gifts they bring to the world as well. They are not toys to play with and they are not here for our use. They don't sign on for a life of servitude, and we don't expect that to be the case either. One of our responsibilities as a man in the world is to encourage our partners to be all they can be and to help bring out the best in them. That's the quick version."

He looked at me with a look of puzzlement then annoyance and then acceptance. "Why didn't you just tell me all that before ? It could have saved me a lot of grief and lots of sleepless nights. I want to be sure that I get it and that you know I get it. Why didn't you just say it this way before?"

"Because as men we each have to make our own decisions about how we will accept our role in the world and what it means to each of us. Our gifts and the value we place on them will help us determine who we become. Making this decision yours and not what someone else says it should be is the only way any of this can happen. This is about how you choose to live your life according to your own beliefs about what is right for you. It is not and cannot be up to me, or anyone else for that matter, to tell you how to do it.

153

"This is the big one, Jacob. This is how you begin the transition from boyhood to manhood, and you have to do this alone. You have to determine for yourself what you will stand for and what you can't or won't stand for. Did I ever mention this old saying: 'If you don't stand for something you will fall for anything.'? This is a strong truth that you can live by if you choose. Now is the time you begin to re-define yourself as a person and as a man in the world. Sound dramatic? It is. It is also vital to your happiness, and there is nothing more I want for you than for you to seek and find your happiness and your peace. To date, you have not had much of that. Now I believe you can."

I looked down to see that my hands were shaking, both from the energy I had spent and the knowledge that he and I were getting close to the end of what I could help him do. I was feeling light-headed and needed to lie down. This was new for me, and it was scary.

"Jacob, I need to lie down. I think I caught a chill or something so I need to lie down. I know that you have many more questions but not today. Think about what you will do now and where you might want to go from here, OK?"

When I looked at him, he looked frightened. He had not seen me like this before, and I knew I would need to tell him the whole truth soon. Not yet, but soon. This internal biological clock was telling me something and I needed to pay attention to it. I would call John in the morning and arrange to see him.

Jacob stood up and opened the door for me. He helped me inside and then asked if I needed anything. I said I would be fine. He nodded, but I could see the sadness in his eyes. He knew, I thought, at least he knew something.

John was able to see me the next day. I dreaded going to see him, yet felt somewhat relieved when I left his office. He was, of course, glad to see me, but the news was the same. Things are progressing. The progressive nature of the illness had slowed again, somewhat, from the last time we had met but the inevitable was happening nonetheless. I pressed him for a time frame, but he would not give me one so I let it be. He added a bit to the potion, as we had come to know it, but he explained there was a limit to how helpful it would be. For now it would likely make some difference in my energy levels and ability to concentrate.

He stipulated a day or two of rest in order for the levels to build back up again and then just go about my business with some common sense thrown in for good measure. I shook his hand as I was leaving and as I was doing so we both looked at one another and hugged each other for what seemed like an eternity. It felt good, for it was the hug of friendship, a closeness and not doctor-to-patient stuff.

Isn't it strange, I thought to myself as I was leaving his office, how a simple thing like impending death could change a lifetime of beliefs and guarded behaviours. There was a time when I wouldn't hug anyone except my kids and my partner. It just wasn't manly. That's what hands were for. I now understand the value of a good hug and a hug makes us human. Real men do hug each other.

Back home, I took John's advice and laid low. My little back yard became my sanctuary and the quiet was rewarding. Before I knew it the day had gone and crickets were in full serenade mode. I laid there in my lawn chair and thought about the next few days: how I hoped they would go and what changes might take place.

All the seeds were sown. Now it was time to sit back to watch and see what would grow. Time. There it was again. Time would tell all.

The Best Laid Plans Of Me And The Universe

Saturday morning came bright and early. There was a warmth in the air that was different. Tropical without the humidity, beautiful. It was a great day for a barbecue, or at least I hoped it would be.

She was due over around 4 and he was due around 5, but neither was aware of the other, not yet. So I took advantage of the opportunity provided me to relax and to think through what I needed to do. I also felt a bit strange, at odds with myself for what I was trying to orchestrate, but I knew in my heart that my motives were honest. It's strange how most things can be justified or reconciled if we try hard enough, I suppose.

At any rate, the morning gave me a chance to sit and listen to some music that I hadn't heard for what seemed like eons. It was great stuff – some smooth jazz, some old Pink Floyd, The Moody Blues – some of the best music ever put together, in my estimation. Where does that come from in people? How do they create melodic emotions like that. To close the set, there was Supertramp and a wee bit of Joe Cocker.

It's wonderful how music can transport us to times and places in our memories. It really is the cheapest way to travel. I remembered concerts when I was a kid, whom I was with and even what was going on at the time. The world seemed a kinder, gentler place then. Not politically I suppose, but personally. It was uncomplicated.

Then I thought about Jacob and what was in store for him in his young life. He was full of questions. He had worked hard to get to this point, given up things and taken monumental personal risks. Would he forgive me for what I'm sure he will see as a deception? I didn't want to leave him in this world feeling that way but that was not up to me to decide.

The morning morphed into afternoon and soon it was time for Annie and Jacob to show up. Annie did, but Jacob was not with her.

"You seem to be flying solo. Is Jacob all right?"

"Oh yeah," she said. "Some things to do and, of course, he waited to the last moment to do them. He said that he would be here as soon as he could make it and not to begin eating until he was here. He hasn't eaten all day, so watch out. The boy can really put it away when the mood comes upon him.

In a way I'm glad that he isn't here. It gives us a chance to catch up. Much seems to have happened in a very short period of time. I can't keep up. Are you OK to chat about business for a bit?"

"As always, that depends, but sure. What is it you want to know?"

"Are you OK? Jacob came home the other day really concerned about you. He said you gave him some story about catching a chill or something. He said you didn't look good. Are you planning on finishing up your – I don't even know what to call it – your work with him soon? I mean you can do what you want. I'm in your debt for eternity. The changes and the insights and all that goes with that are nothing short of miraculous, and I'll never know how to repay you for saving him from himself. But you've got to understand. He has become very attached to you, and I think he is afraid that you are going to tell him that it's time to wrap things up and he will need to fly on his own."

Before she could continue, I put up my hand for her to stop. "Annie, first off, all I did was get him to look at some things from a different perspective. He is the one who has done all the work. He's taken the risks, not me. If he doesn't risk something, he learns nothing. I'll tell him so at the first opportunity. You owe me nothing. I have come to respect him, and I have gotten close to him as well. Perhaps too close, but it is what it is. To be quite honest, I never anticipated any of this when I consented to talk to him. What I saw was a rebellious teenager with a huge mountain of anger and resentment on his shoulder. All he wanted was to have someone come along and try to knock it off. I say that with all due respect for him. He has become an exceptional person. But this will all come to a close at some time. It has to. It is the way of life, isn't it?

"He learns, he test-drives what he has learned and then he goes off to do what he has been created to do. It will happen when he decides it's time to make that happen. However, I can promise you this. I will not see him left without support and someone to continue to bounce things off. That's all I want to say right now. Are we good?"

She looked confused, she looked frustrated and she looked pissed at me because she knew something was up and couldn't get it out of me. She felt as though her son's well-being was at risk somehow and wanted to save him any hurt.

"I guess it will have to be," she said, "but you haven't heard the last from me. Enough business and more relaxation – we could both use it."

"I hear you and I'm in full agreement, and oh," I said, as casually as I could to change the subject and to slide this in, "I hope you don't mind but I took the liberty of inviting a friend of mine for dinner with us. He's a very close friend and I haven't caught up with him for a bit, so I thought it might give us a chance to do that. Besides, he is reputed to be one of the best barbecue guys ever to don a pair of mitts."

She grinned and said that it would be nice to meet any friend of mine.

Leo was due to show up around five o'clock and he is seldom late. Just around that time, Annie went into the house to prepare something she had brought for dinner, and Leo slid around the corner of the house. I welcomed him and sat him down with a cold drink. We chatted for a minute and then Annie re-appeared without knowing that Leo had arrived.

The response was fascinating and completely unrehearsed. She stopped mid-track to look at him, and he stopped midsentence to do the same. The silence lasted only a second or two and then both tried to carry on as though nothing had taken place. It was comical, really. I introduced them to each other and on we went. Small talk about the usual things seemed appropriate, but I knew I needed to disappear for a moment to give them time to chat with each other.

Just then Jacob appeared. I couldn't have staged this better if everyone had known what to do ahead of time. I got him to come in and give me a hand with some things in the fridge that needed to be tended to. We were only gone a minute or two but that was enough. I introduced Jacob to Leo. I hadn't talked about Leo much to either of them, but Jacob knew of him, just not about him. He seemed to be guarded when he spoke to Leo or when Leo spoke to him. They were sizing each other up was my guess. Leo did have the advantage of knowing a great deal more about Jacob, but I was comfortable knowing he would keep our conversations to himself. There was a bit of attitude coming from Jacob and just a bit of testosterone as well. Perfect. I would guess that Jacob sensed some energy between Annie and Leo and assumed his role of guardian.

All the people were here who needed to be. I could only imagine what was going through their heads as we sat in my backyard talking about this and that. Leo would be wondering what he had gotten himself into. I wondered the same when I was in his position not so long ago. He would be thinking about what he had to offer this kid. He had agreed to do this because I had asked him. It was not something he would have offered to do on his own.

But he is a man of his word and he would follow through. The rest would be up to Jacob. That would not be an easy sell. Leo knew that going in. He'd wondered about Annie and how that would work out. In a sense, they would be co-parenting Jacob, although he didn't need much in the way of parenting now. But he would need to know that there were those who loved him and supported him and would be there for him when and if he needed them. He would be a father someday and would need to have that guidance as well. Leo could do that as well as anybody I know. But Leo was also thinking about Annie and what was she like. He had stayed away from relationships in his second life and seemed to be OK with that decision. I saw how he glanced at her every once in a while when he thought no one was looking. There was just a quick shift of his eyes but it was there. Curiosity?

I hadn't thought about a connection between them in a personal or romantic way. I just hoped that they would be able to work together for Jacob. That one was not for me to get involved in. I had my own stuff to deal with, and that time was coming faster than I liked. Leo knew that his life would change forever if this connection was made with Jacob, but he acknowledged that he was good with that. The rest would be his doing, one way or the other.

Annie was interesting to watch. She was a bit nervous, curious, guarded but couldn't quite hide her excitement with having a man there, other than me, who she could relate to. It had been a long time since she had the occasion to be in the company of a man who paid her some attention without being crass or suggestive or demanding in some way.

As the day wore on she seemed to be more comfortable with Leo there. They talked about the music of the day and the good old days' when tunes were tunes and had something to say. It happened that they both enjoyed some of the same artists. She commented on his Jimmy Buffett look and asked if he was a 'wanna-be'. He smiled easily and said he was, so they both enjoyed a laugh at that. There developed an easy comfort between them. They found that there were several things they had in common.

Not to be overlooked in this was Jacob. He sat there very quietly at first. He glanced at me several times during the day for a sign of some kind. Was I seeing this the way he was seeing it? Was I OK with what was going on? What was happening anyway? I could see the concern and the stress growing on him as Leo and his Mom chatted away oblivious sometimes to Jacob and me being there.

At one point, Jacob tried to intervene in the conversation by offering his two cents on a topic that he felt he knew something about. Leo and Annie listened to him, nodded politely at the point he made and then carried on with the conversation that they'd begun prior to his statement of fact. He looked at me again, and I looked back and shrugged at him as if to say, "Hey, it's OK. No big deal."

I nodded to him to follow me into the kitchen and when we got there, I said to him, "You look a little uneasy. What's up?" He said he wondered what Leo was up to. He knew, of course, of my friendship with him but still . . .? He talked about Annie and how well she was doing right now. She was past Harlan and all that was attached to him. He didn't want to see her get taken advantage of in any way. I suggested that he may be jumping the gun just a little bit here. They had just met one another, and by chance at that. They were both very social people and they were both adults. They were capable and free to develop a friendship if they so chose. He shouldn't worry about it. Besides, Annie was a big girl who knew her own mind, so he needed to let her exercise her free will just as he wanted her to do for him.

I gently reminded him that that door swung both ways. He might consider feeling happy for her that she has decided not all men are awful to be around and that she has not lost faith in us as a species. Hadn't he found out the same about the females he had recently known, that they were not all the same?

159

We grinned at each other, and I placed my hand on his shoulder as I said, "You are feeling protective of her and I think you are feeling a bit of a challenge. This guy has come in here and could be trying to horn in on your territory. Maybe it even feels as if he is not respecting who you are or your place. I can assure you that Leo is not like that. He is the most kind and considerate man I have had the good fortune to know. That needs to be the last thing to concern yourself with.

"There are two people sitting in my backyard who are having an interesting conversation about a bunch of stuff and are enjoying each other's company. I do get how you are feeling right now, and it is pretty normal for you to have those feelings. But you also have to keep them in their place. Your mom will be fine. This is where you get to trust her in terms of her knowing what is right and good for her. It looks as though she is really enjoying herself. For the first time in a while she is able to relax a bit and enjoy some down time."

"I guess you're right, but he needs to know that I will be watching him."

I let him have the last word as we went back out to join the happy twosome.

The rest of the day went well. Jacob even allowed himself to get into the tunes a bit, the 'old' ones, as he referred to them. If the truth be known, I think he enjoyed them more than he let on. Leo out-did himself with the steaks, and Annie put all of her concerns aside to enjoy some of the freedom that she so richly deserved.

It was good to be surrounded by positive energy, but, as with all good things, the day came to an end. Leo made his exit but not before saying how much he had enjoyed himself. It was so unlike him to do that. Usually he said his goodbyes and left quietly before anyone really knew that he was gone.

Jacob and Annie left shortly after, but not without Annie giving me a look that said, "We have to talk." Jacob thanked me for the day and said that he too had enjoyed himself but he would be watching to see what was happening with Leo. I just nodded to him in our way that said without words, "yeah, I hear you." I didn't realize how tired I was until I finally sat down. It was a good tired, though.

A Day Of Reckoning

I only hoped that Annie would give me some time in the morning to sleep in a bit before she came knocking. I knew that she would come. At 11 a.m. on the mark there was a tapping on my door. I opened it to see a slightly blurry-eyed woman who had, quickly, run a brush through hair that still ruled the top of her head. Yes, it was Annie.

She started right in with little small talk then said, "OK, we need to chat."

She invited me out to sit on my own porch. I offered a fresh coffee to which she quickly agreed. After I delivered it to her, she wasted no time in saying that she had really enjoyed the previous day. She had been surprised how easy it was to meet Leo and to feel comfortable around him. BUT she did not want me playing Cupid for her. Nor did she want anything more to do with him. Not because she didn't like him or that he didn't appeal to her, but rather because she just didn't need any further complications in her life. So if I didn't mind would I let Leo know all of this just so that he didn't get the wrong idea.

She rattled on, hardly stopping for breath, as though she had been up all night practicing what she wanted to say to me so that she could make herself perfectly clear without any further discussion about the topic.

Then she launched into how she didn't have time to be involved with anyone and that she had Jacob to think about. He was her main and only concern right now and her stuff could and would wait and that was IF she decided anything would ever happen that would include another man in her life.

The guilt and the frustration were evident in her tone of voice and body language. Single parenthood strikes again, I thought. She was so wound up I'm not sure she had taken a breath during the last five minutes so I signaled her to please stop for a moment. She did.

We sat in silence for a time and then she said, "He made me realize how much I missed those simple evenings when people got together and enjoyed each others company and talked and laughed and just had fun without expectation and posturing. It was good. Then I thought that this can't go on any further because of these other things that are going on. OK, I know that you've got something to put in here. I guess that's part of the reason I had to come see you right away."

161

"I'm not sure what it is you want me to comment on," I said, adding with a grin, "That is, IF I have anything to add on the matter. Seriously, I'm not sure what you want from me here. Yes, I too enjoyed the day. It meant a great deal to me to have you and Jacob here and to have Leo join us. He is my best friend and to have him here was special for me. I apologize if you felt uncomfortable in any way. Perhaps I should have asked first, but knowing him I knew he would be a good fit for the day. He too enjoys just what you described."

She was quick to say, "No, don't take this wrong. I enjoyed meeting him, and there was no need to check with me first. As a matter of fact, meeting him was what got me thinking about all of this. He seems a gentle, kind, polite, considerate and interesting man. He's easy on the eyes too, I might add. I didn't have a problem with that at all, believe me.

"My problem is not with him. What surfaced for me, however, was the realization that a whole other world exists and that I have been isolated from it. I was beginning to believe that all men were dogs and that they were, in the end, all the same, just with different fleas. Leo, by just being who he is as a man, helped me see that really isn't true and I could actually enjoy being in this other world. It's just that now is not the time to do that when I have other more important things I need to tend to."

I could see where this was going, but she needed to get there on her own. "So can you tell me what some of those things are? What do you mean, exactly, when you say you have to other more important things to tend to?"

She took a second or two and then began, "Things like being a single mom and having a teenage son to raise. Being careful not to rock the balance that exists now between Jacob and me. Introducing another male into the mix and how will that work between the two of them? Do I have the time to give to someone else? What happens if the relationship gets serious? How do I navigate those waters? What happens if . . .? Then she stopped. Her voice was a bit unsteady when she began again. "I can't deal with all this stuff right now."

"You know, Annie, you may well have the cart before the horse here." I wanted to be sure that my voice didn't sound harsh or angry so I tried to soften it when I said, "First of all, I wouldn't feel comfortable talking to Leo about this, so I think that if you have some concerns about his intentions, or your own for that matter, you need to address them with Leo yourself. I don't want to be involved in that at all. I thought that you would enjoy meeting each other, but that's as far as that goes for me. You really have just met the guy. You don't have any idea what he wants or what he is thinking about unless he said something that would lead you otherwise. I doubt that he has said anything to that end.

"So are we talking about how you feel about him instead? Does that thought frighten you in some way? You have to sort that one out. What I can say about him is that he is a good guy. He is all those things that you mentioned and much more.

"What I heard in your voice is that maybe you don't think anyone else would ever want to be with you because of the baggage that comes along, meaning Jacob. He isn't baggage, number one, and anyone who would see him that way is not worthy of you or him. Number two, he is a small step away from being out in the world on his own. He is close to leaving the emotional nest, if not the physical one. He will want to be making a life of his own soon. I guess what I am trying to say is that he will soon be making his own decisions based on what is in his best interests. Oh, he will still feel responsible for you and your well-being. He will want to protect you from the big bad world, but the balance has shifted now. He will begin to see himself as being less dependent on you for his emotional existence."

"And what you don't see is that I am not sure how I will deal with that. He is my world," she stammered. "He is what I get up for each day and to have that just come and go one day is not something that I could deal with. I'm as frightened for him as I am for me. I feel weird just saying that out loud. It makes me sound like some old shrew that lives through her children. That's not it. I can't explain what it is but I know that it hurts just thinking about it. How do I deal with this? Can you tell me how?"

I was just about to launch into a response to her question when the phone rang. It was Leo. "Hey, Leo, What's up with you? Sure, I can catch up with you around one o'clock if that is good for you. Yeah, OK, same place. See you then."

"Obviously that was Leo. He's asked me to meet with him about something, but I don't want to leave this hanging in the air. I was about to say that Jacob is not walking off the planet, never to be seen again. You don't even know what his plans are. He may be around for another five years before he makes his move. What I can tell you for certain is that he will still need to know that you love him unconditionally, that he has connection and importance to you and your life.

"He will also need to know that you are proud of him for who he has become and that you are willing to step back a bit and let him go his own way. He will want to try out some of the new skills he has been learning about and building. It is close to the time when he needs to fly on his own. You won't have much to say about it, Annie.

"I think the one thing we, as single parents, find the most difficult to establish is the boundary between being our kids' friend and their parent. They don't need us to be a friend. They have all the friends they want. What they do need are parents or, in this case, a parent who loves them and is willing to be consistent in their manner and message. They need boundaries and they need to have someone be clear about what is and is not appropriate behaviour, what is acceptable and what is not."

"And then what?" she asked. "What happens then? How do I go about my business? Do I do it like he was never a part of my life?—like he doesn't exist?" Her voice trembled as she continued. "I can't do that. How do I fit into another lifestyle when my head and my heart are somewhere else most of the time?"

"You do it like many of the other single parents who find themselves in the same place. You are not the first nor last who will struggle with this very same issue. You need to begin to re-construct your life. I'm not sure what that would look like to you. You get to make it whatever you want, and that's exciting or it can be. But it would be one that doesn't feature Jacob as the centerpiece. It's not disrespectful to him or to you. It is the right thing to do, for both of you. You cannot allow him to determine or dictate what and how and with whom you choose to experience your life. This is your life and always has been. You chose to dedicate a big piece of it to Jacob and now you are simply moving to reclaim some of it. That's what's difficult to juggle.

"The question isn't 'should I . . .' but rather 'how much and how fast'. It's not about feeling guilty for sitting around a fire talking and having some fun with other adults. As far as having a man in your life and introducing him into the fabric of your home, perhaps that need not happen until you decide IF you want to have someone in your life, and if you do, both of you have to decide how serious the relationship really is and where it is going.

"To back up a bit, we men are not that difficult to figure out. We basically take our lead from the females around us. You are in control of how much you get involved with Leo or anyone else. Leo is a male. No big surprise there. He will follow leads if he is interested. If you

164

don't want him to follow those leads, then you need to be sure that they aren't out there in the first place.

"We males follow the trail that you females put down. Appearance, mannerisms, responses, innuendo, or not, etc. are all factored in. We're 'chase' oriented, competitors, challenge oriented and conquerors. But we will not chase anyone we are not interested in or anyone who has not shown any interest in us."

"OK, I get that part, but how do I introduce Mr. Right into the mix without risking losing one or both? What happens then?"

I could sense the desperation in her voice again but I needed to cut this off. "I have to go to meet with Leo soon. My best suggestion would be to sit down with Jacob and ask him these same questions. He is much better suited to answer you than I am. I would only be giving you what I think. He will give you what he feels. That's much better than I could ever do. Trust your instincts. Ask him. You'll do OK. He's likely thinking about the same things as you are anyway."

With that I got up and Annie reluctantly followed my lead. "We can carry on with this later if you want. Just let me know." She nodded to me and slowly made her way toward home.

I finished up with what I needed to do that morning, took a wee power nap and met up with Leo at the park as we had agreed. He'd brought a couple of coffees with him and so did I, so we were amply armed. We grabbed a bench in the sun and just sat in the quiet enjoying the penetrating rays on our bodies. It was glorious with the warmth going right to my bones. It was as if Mother Nature had enveloped me in her arms and was holding me close. I felt assured that the day was going to be a good one.

"And so you called because . . .?" I asked.

"You know damned well why I phoned, so don't play Mr. Innocent with me," he said it with a mixture of light heartedness and concern. "The question is, and you know what the question is, now what?"

"Leo, I truly do not know exactly what you are referring to. What is it I'm supposed to know?"

He looked at me for a bit and then, resigned, blurted, "Annie, that's what."

I thought he sounded cautious or guarded. That was not like Leo at all. I hoped it was nothing beyond how the stability of his world and its future may be threatened by my next door neighbour. He usually took things in stride and approached them in an organized, practical manner. Now, it seemed, he was turned around a bit and it was disturbing for

165

him. I had not seen him like this before. He was completely off guard. The tables had turned on him. He was treading on unfamiliar ground.

Now he was looking to me for feedback, for those pearls of wisdom that he had been so comfortable providing me with over the years that I had known him. I had asked him once if we could take our relationship to a different place, one that was based on equality instead of mentorship. Here we were and, although I didn't like to see my friend squirming like a worm on a hook, it was gratifying that he trusted what we had developed and honoured our maleness. This type of true trust is often rare in men.

"What about her?" I said, eyeing him closely.

"Oh, come on. Are you going to make this so difficult for me?"

I looked at him without saying a word.

"I'm pretty new at this relationship stuff," he said, "and I have come to understand that I know very little about this part of life. It was much different years ago. To be honest, I had given up on the thought of having a relationship with anyone because I didn't believe that it would be important anymore. I have other missions in my life that require my time and energy. I have managed to keep it simple, certainly not complicated, up to this point at least. I didn't think – and I still don't think – that I have the time or the energy to do both. I'm not sure that I want the challenge of balancing both, the 'missions' and a relationship I mean."

He stopped to gather his thoughts or perhaps to measure how far he would go with me regarding this declaration of his feelings. This was still new to him. Then he looked over and continued.

"It's seldom that I feel as relaxed around someone as quickly as I did after meeting her at your place. She is funny and articulate. She has an energy about her and around her that is irresistible. It just draws you in - to be close to her. I don't think she is even aware of it. I can tell you that it exists, though. There is a vulnerability to her and yet I think she is what you see. There is no pretext and there are no games here. Wow, how often do you find that in someone these days? It seems that everyone has an agenda of some kind to play out. I know that I have a good sense about people, so I know this about her. She knows how to play and have fun, and she sure is easy on the eyes too. And to top it all off she gets 'Jimmy B.' I would like to ask her out but I'm not sure that I should."

"Well, are you going to tell me the rest of it or leave me to fill in the blanks?" I said, gently.

"It's not about being turned down or anything like that, but I go back to our conversation regarding Jacob. I gave you my word and you know that I will honour that unless it becomes evident he doesn't want any type of connection to happen. If I'm connected to his mother in some way or if he knows that I am interested in her, I'm concerned that will influence what we might have otherwise accomplished.

"I have no way of knowing what Annie thinks of me or feels about seeing me. I don't even know if she is seeing anyone else right now. She may not want to be involved with anyone because of how Jacob might feel about that. Tough being a single parent and juggling all this stuff. Why can't it just be simple?

"You know, there was a time not long ago when I thought that my life was finally settled. I had direction and purpose and I knew what I was about. One evening of gentle conversation and relaxation and it's all shot to hell. What's that about anyway? How do I connect with Jacob if he senses any or all of this? What does that do to him? What does that do to their relationship if, by some miracle, she consents to go out with me or that something develops between us? Where do you stand in all of this? You set this up, didn't you? I know you did. It's just like you to do that."

I sensed he was done, at least for the moment. "Think about what you just said. How could I have set anything up. That would mean that I would be able to manipulate both you and Annie, emotionally, and we know that I can't do that. All I did was introduce you to each other and provide a place where we could get to know one another better. Nature will take its course.

"At some point you two were going to have to meet, so I decided that my place would be the best middle ground and the least awkward place to do that. That's it. Believe me when I say that it's better now than later. I don't know how long later is. What goes on between you guys is up to you. A wise man once said to me – you may even know this guy – that I need to be careful not to let my heart get in the way of my head, that I need to allow my thinking process to outweigh my emotional process. Perhaps you could take a page from your own book and take that advice too.

"If I had come to you with the same situation, what would you have suggested to me? I'm thinking that you would have said something like first of all is this lady available? All of this may be moot. Second, if she is, what's the worst thing that could happen if you asked her out on a date and she said, "thanks but no thanks"? Would you survive? Yes, we know you would. Third, If you do decide to ask her out, why not let her decide what would be best for her and Jacob? You don't have any idea whatsoever what thoughts they may have around this very same thinking, do you? Fourth, if it gets to a point where you think it may become something more serious, ask Jacob to sit down and have a heart-to-heart with him. I know him pretty well. He would be tough at first. He would want to stake out his position because he is the alpha male in his family unit. He is really taking to understanding this socialization stuff and he has a good idea of how the 'gifts' play a role in how he lives his life now and how he is to treat those around him.

"Jacob is a good guy and he is moving into this manhood thing quickly. But perhaps, and most important, you need to decide if she scares you. If you have or develop feelings for her, she may, just by her being, force you to change how you see the world you live in, to change your goals.

"We all understand about change, right? We don't do it well at the best of times. Perhaps she intrigues you? What is it you want anyway, in a partner, I mean? What if she could give you what you have always wanted in a partner, mate or friend? You've got some work to do my friend. And hey, you just met her and have known her for a whole four to five hours. What's that all about? Maybe a rush to judgment?"

I reminded Leo how long it had been since he was fully engaged in the dating game. Affairs of the heart were not something he dealt with easily. Since he had been clean and sober all these years, he had not allowed or looked for anyone else to be an integral part of his life. Now, he knew if he wasn't careful, that could change, and quickly. He knew he had met someone that struck a chord in him almost from the moment they met—from when he first saw her come out of the door at my place. He had thoroughly enjoyed his time with Annie, especially her intellect. She even liked his Jimmy Buffett look. How great was that.

He had known her for about four hours and never had anyone made an impression on him as she had. It was not something or anything that she did—just simply who she was. She had a presence that was very attractive to him. He felt, a bit, like a school kid with a crush, but he couldn't deny that her affect on him was unmistakable. The smell of her hair as he got close enough on the way past her, the way she wore her clothes and the style she chose, the shine in her eyes and the pleasure and ease in her laugh. He liked her self-assurance when she danced with her son.

"Let's get back to Jacob for a minute," I said. It's possible that he may feel good about someone wanting to be with his mom. He would be ultra protective of her no doubt. You would need to prove yourself to him, but I think that part gets taken care of along the way.

"Let's say that something happens between you and Annie and that it gets serious. You just may be the father figure that he craves, and he may just adopt you and see you as someone who will look after his mom for him so that he can be free to carry on with his own life. This is a bit of a minefield, I know, but it could really work out well for all concerned. Could."

I knew I was done and he was done too, for now. "I don't know much more, and I don't want to be involved in what, if anything, happens next. I'll say this much. She came over this morning to chat and seems as turned around as you are. That's all I'm going to say. I told her the same as I told you just now. I want an arm's length here. I don't want to be involved in any 'he said, she said' stuff. And if you are thinking about him, no. I haven't talked to Jacob about any of this, but I'll bet that's not far off."

Again the quiet returned, and we just sat there in the sun. When we next spoke, it was about how I was doing, some baseball stuff and a book he had read. We then agreed to get together in the next few days. Leo suggested a day away, just to enjoy a cruise down the coast. He knew I loved riding with the top down and feeling the sun on me. I thanked him for his thought and made the short journey back home.

I was, once again, overwhelmed by how much he meant to me and how much I would miss him.

Although some daylight was left by the time I got home, I was exhausted. I laid down just to close my eyes and didn't know a thing until the next day. As good as it felt, I wondered if this was a harbinger of sorts.

While I was visiting with Leo, Jacob had spent his time stewing about all that had taken place. Annie had gone for a walk instead of going straight home. She, too, was trying to make some sense of how she felt and what was to come.

She walked into the house to find Jacob staring out the kitchen window. She wasn't even sure he had heard her enter the room, so she cleared her throat a bit and he turned to see her there.

Jacob sat at the table and said to Annie, "Mom, I need to talk to you and now would be the best time. Please . . ." Jacob motioned to a chair for her to sit on and then began.

"For the last while I have noticed that you have been . . . different. Not in a bad way or anything but just different. It began when I started to meet with Jim, as a matter of fact, and I need to know if I have done anything to upset you or to anger you in some way. I need you to explain to me what is happening between us and why you are so sketchy, especially today. What happened to bring that on? Are you OK? Did something happen to you?

"I'm not a kid anymore and I need to know what is happening so I can help deal with whatever it is. Did Leo do anything or say anything that upset you? IF that happened, I'll deal with it. I know that this is weird because you always carry stuff around with you and never let on that things, other things, are happening. I want to be a part of what happens in this family and I want to look out for us. It's important for me to do that, but I can't if I don't know what's going on. I'll shut up now and let you talk."

Annie sat there, stupefied. She wanted to say things are fine. Don't worry. No problem, sweetheart. She also came to the rapid assessment that there had been a change in her relationship with Jacob sometime between yesterday and today, and they would never be the same again.

She was overcome with emotion and thoughts and had no idea where to begin. Her mouth was so dry she could not speak any words. How does she say that she is proud of the man he was becoming, that he is five times the man his father ever was or hoped to be but that she was scared for him and happy for him and frightened that their relationship would change forever and somehow she would lose him or get left behind; that she didn't know if she could let go of him; that for herself she was afraid to be alone and she was sad and angry and excited about her own possibilities and nervous and unsure and confused and feeling guilty that she couldn't be all things to him; that he missed out on a great deal and she was sorry that she could never make up for the lost good times he should have had and . . .

She drank enough water to drown a camel, but at last she was able to compose herself and sit down across from Jacob. She looked at him with awe and pure love, and with admiration and pride in her heart for who he had become.

Finally she said, "This is probably a conversation that we should have had quite a while ago although I can't honestly say we were ready for it before today. It's funny how the universe just makes things happen when the right time comes. I don't know where to start, so I'll jump in and wherever it goes I hope it will make sense. If it doesn't then stop me so that I can make it make sense. My hope is that this will be the first of many talks that you and I will share.

"To clarify something right off the bat, this has absolutely nothing to do with anything that Leo said or did or anything like that. However, he is the reason I'm where I am right now, and I really appreciate him for it. The odd thing about this is he has no idea what is going on here. Things are different for me now just because of who he is. It's nothing that he did or said. I'll explain that later or some other time, but I need you to know that he is not at fault here in any way. OK?"

Jacob nodded, cautiously, as if he was willing to listen but not sure she was leveling with him.

"When I asked Jim to meet with you, I had no idea what would happen. I was so desperate and worried about you and of who you were becoming. You were angry and could not be trusted. I didn't know how to help you. I was very frustrated.

"I understand much better today why that happened and why I couldn't help with certain things. When I see you today and when I watch how you interact with others and how you conduct yourself and how you treat and think about others and the respect that you have for not only yourself but others, it literally makes my heart sing.

"You are becoming a man in the world, and someday you will be a dad. I think that you will make a great dad. I would not have said that last year at this time, believe me. You have much to offer, yet when I think of letting you go so that you can make a life for yourself, I get fearful. I have always looked out after you and now I am seeing that I don't need to do that anymore.

"I worry about the mistakes that you will make and who will help you through that. But then I remind myself you will have you and whomever you decide to have around you. You and I are all each of us has had for all these years. Unfortunately for you, Harlan had no idea of what being a father meant. I'm afraid that if you move on, as you need to, I will be alone in the world to face whatever comes my way. This is not to make you feel guilty, Jacob, but these are the feelings I'm trying to deal with. I know that you have to move on, and I want you to be able to do that with excitement, wonder and freedom. But I also want to remain a big part of your life. I feel that you have become this wonderful person and I want to be a part of that: to know and to share that part of you because I always knew that that's who you really were. Maybe that's selfish on my part, but I'm afraid that I won't have a chance to do that and so I don't want you to go yet."

171

She had to stop for a moment to gather her thoughts about her again. She could feel herself coming unglued, and she didn't want to do that – not here and certainly not now.

"Does any of this make sense to you, Jacob? Can you understand what it is I'm trying to say to you?"

"Sure it does but you have to . . ."

As she put up her hand to signal him to stop, she said, "Please let me get the rest of this out before I get to be a blubbering fool and not say what it is I need to say. I appreciate where you were going, I really do, and I need to hear it, but I must finish this while I'm on a roll."

Jacob had the makings of tears in his eyes but he just nodded and sat back to let her continue.

"The part that Leo plays in this creates a whole new set of issues for me. He is a good man. I can tell just by the way he is. I believe him to be kind, gentle, considerate, bright and interesting – all the things that interest me in a mate. Before you jump to any erroneous conclusions, no, he hasn't proposed or anything. Just kidding. He is someone I could see myself wanting to know better though. I felt relaxed around him last night, and for me to feel like that around any man after my experiences says a great deal for that person. He knows who he is and is settled in his thoughts.

"All of this has made me aware there is much life out there to experience. There are good people out there that I would like to be around. Again I go back to Leo. Just in those few hours I felt like I knew him fairly well. He allowed me to voice opinions on things, and we didn't agree on everything but he was secure in that. I could be myself and not apologize for it. It seems we enjoy the same things: music and movies and hiking and being near the water. I do like the Jimmy Buffett thing he has going there too.

"I guess what I am saying is that he granted me, and I him, the opportunity to talk openly and freely about how we saw the world without concerns as to how that would be received by the other. For me that represents stability and safety. I know that I can't base a lifetime on a few hours of time together, but he represents what it is I need. I felt like an equal in the world for the first time in a very long time. And it felt good. It felt as if I could strive to be anyone I wanted to be and it would be all right.

He wasn't going to laugh at me or criticize me for what I thought or for how I saw things. I'd forgotten that existed out there, and now I know that there is more of it for me to tap into – maybe with him but maybe with someone else.

"I'm saying all of this because I want you to understand what and why it's important to me. I also need to know how you feel about what I have just said. You have this thought in your head that you need to watch out over me, to protect me from the big bad world and all of its characters. I love you for that too. It feels good to know that someone has my back and that someone is you. But I can look after myself. I really can, I and want you to know that that is the truth of it.

"What I do need to know is that we are tight, that we are always going to be a vital part of each other's lives. I also know that it is time for me to get back on the horse after a bit of an absence. It's time for me to get back in the world.

"Please hear me when I say to you that I never –not for a second – ever regretted taking myself out of that world so that you and I could make a life together. I know that you can look after yourself now. That's sad for me, on one hand, because you aren't my little one anymore, but it's wonderful, on the other hand, because I know that you have grown into a fine man."

She paused here. She wanted to go into all of it so there were no secret thoughts and feelings to get trapped by, but she didn't know if she had gone too far already.

He looked at her and said, "I know there is more, so why don't we get to it. OK?"

She exhaled slowly and said, "OK. Still, I wonder how you will deal with my dating someone or having someone around the house more often. It's your house too, and you have a say in what and who comes and goes. I don't want to do anything that would jeopardize our relationship because it is the most important and the most sacred to me. It always, always will be."

She paused long enough to look him square in the eyes for the last questions she had for him to think about.

"How would we be if I found someone that I wanted to marry? When you are a papa, would you want to share your children with me and my partner? These are the things that have overwhelmed me today. These are some of things that have come up since you decided to share your life with Jim. I can see the changes that you are accepting into your life. You took a huge risk then, and I love you so much for caring enough about yourself to swallow your ego and your pride to help yourself. I know it wasn't easy for you, but you did it and you are better for it."

She stopped and then trying to inject a bit of humour: "So you see, it's just another day. How has yours been?"

Jacob didn't even hesitate but started to finish what he had begun to say a while ago.

"It all makes perfect sense to me. You are my mom. You are the most important person in my life. You stuck by me when everyone else was willing to kick me to the curb. There is nothing that you could do or say that would turn me away from you. I appreciate your talking to me like this.

"For the last month or so I have been thinking about some of the same things that you just mentioned. I was feeling guilty about thinking about how to say that time is moving and I have to move with it. I'm not saying tomorrow or anything like that, but I want to check out things too. I don't think that it means that we have to write off who we are to each other. I love you: you are my mom. That's that. Nothing is going to change that. I hope that feels better for you knowing that's how it is with me?"

Annie welled up and burst into tears. She could not hold back any longer. Jacob had the good sense to let her go until she stopped on her own. It seemed longer, but it was closer to a few minutes.

Then he continued, "I understand that you need to get back into the world and check it out. I shouldn't tell you this, but some of my friends think you're a good-looking lady, for a mom, so I doubt you will have any trouble getting to know people. You'll have them beating down the door. That's why I'll stay a bit closer for a while. Closer doesn't mean that I will interfere, but I will offer my two cents if I think the guy is a putz.

"I trust your judgment about who comes around and how long he stays. I also trust that you will be honest and tell me what's going on, one way or another. You are one of two people in the world that I can say I trust. That is something that is non-negotiable for me. This guessing thing isn't fun at all. And you need to know that if someone hurts you, they will deal with me. By the way, does this mean that we will have to create some kind of signals to let each other know who gets the house on which nights?"

Annie burst into laughter, trying to shake her head "no" but not having a great deal of success. Unseen weights had been lifted from her, and the world seemed much brighter for her now. Finally, as she was gasping for air, she managed to say, "No, I don't think that will be necessary, but thanks for the thought."

She looked at him and then walked across the room with her arms open to him. He walked into them as he did when he was small. They each knew that when all else was flying around them, there was security, love and honesty that would always exist between them. Today was no different.

He decided he needed to walk. It was 'tree time' and he needed to process all that had happened in the last day or two. He didn't know whether to be angry, upset, cautious, bold, out front, protective, quiet or to stay in the back ground and see what happened next. Certainly a part of him wanted to stake out his territory, meaning marking the territory that was off limits: his mom.

He felt like that but he knew he didn't have the right to speak for her? Not now anyway. The one thing that he did know was that he hadn't seen his Mom so relaxed and at ease in a very long time, and it looked good on her. She had had some fun. He saw her in a different light, and Leo seemed to have enjoyed her company as well.

And what about Leo? What was he about? Did he have some kind of an agenda? Maybe he was just having a good time and saw something about his mom that interested him. Actually he liked Leo. There was something about him – he didn't know exactly what it was – that made him feel that what you saw of him was what you got. He even liked the Jimmy Buffett thing. He seemed real, authentic.

And what about Jim? What was he up to? Was he trying to set up his mom with Leo, or was this nothing more than inviting people over for some food and a few beers. He knew Leo was his best and closest friend.

So would that be a bad thing? He trusted Jim. Would Jim set up his mom with someone who wasn't a solid guy? Likely not.

This was all new to him and he wasn't sure how to deal with what he was feeling. He knew it wasn't bad, just that it was not something he knew much about. He had enough to concern himself with in his own life. How far should he stick his neck out here? There were so many questions and he knew that he needed some answers to many of them before he decided what his next move was.

Maybe instead of driving himself crazy with questions, he would just ask the questions he needed answers to. Isn't that what he had learned so far? Isn't that what a man in his position would do? Ask questions, get information and then make a decision. When he thought about it like that, it seemed a much simpler task. Yes, that's what he would do. Tomorrow he would visit with Jim and sort out some stuff.

He reached for his iPod and realized he had left it behind. He turned around and headed back home again. He had plenty of time, so it was no big deal going back for it.

Harlan waited until Jacob had walked away, and then he crept to the back door of Annie's house and let himself in. Annie thought she heard the door close and came into the kitchen to ask what Jacob had forgotten when she saw Harlan standing there with that same dangerous sneer on his face.

She knew that look well from days gone by, and ice shot through her veins. She knew where this was going and she was terrified. Harlan could smell her fear and just smiled.

He slowly made his way closer until he was a foot or two away from her. "Not so tough now, eh? Not quite so sure of yourself now?"

With the speed of a coiled snake, he struck her. She managed to side-step his hand just enough to miss most of the sting but got enough to know that the next one would really hurt. He grabbed her by the front of her shirt and tore it half open. She screamed at him, but he just clamped his hand over her mouth. She could see the malice in his face, the hate.

As he drew back to hit her again Jacob grabbed at his hand. He didn't get all of it but enough to let Harlan know that he was not alone any longer. Harlan spun around and backhanded Jacob, all in one move. He hit him hard enough to knock him down. "I'll deal with you in a minute, you little prick. I owe you big. You think you can just dust me off and that's that?"

He turned back to Annie and slapped her hard this time, driving her to her knees. He grabbed her hair and pulled her back up again, ready to hit strike her again. Jacob had recovered enough to jump him and wrestle him away from Annie. He got between them, so that Harlan could not get at her any more. Without taking his eyes from him, he told her to get out: "Go to Jim's. Go. Now. Daddy and I have something to finish up here. I'll be over in a bit."

She worried that Jacob would trade his future for a few moments of revenge. She began to protest and then Jacob said, "Don't worry. I won't do anything stupid, but this piece of shit will know that when he leaves here today he will not be welcome to return, ever. Now go. I'll be fine."

She had not seen or heard Jacob like this before. It was a bit un-
nerving but she knew that he was determined to close the book on this
chapter of his life. She gathered her torn and tattered shirt together in
front of herself, hesitated until she realized that he would just keep
insisting she leave. She ran for the front door, went out and headed
next door.

She had just cleared the door when Harlan charged at Jacob like a
raging, seething bull. Jacob knew he would, somehow, and was ready
for the move. A slight step to one side and a push on Harlan's back as
he came for him had Harlan stumbling into the wall of the kitchen. He
was half down when he turned and came back at him. Jacob smashed
him in the face, hitting him hard enough to hear the bone of his nose
crack. Blood spewed everywhere it seemed.

Still Harlan kept coming at him. They grappled around the kitchen
until they fell over the table. Unfortunately, Jacob ended up on the
bottom with Harlan hammering away at his ribs and chest. He managed
to get in a few good hits, enough to take the breath out of Jacob. They
both got to their feet. He came at Jacob again, this time with something
in his hand. He swung it with all his strength. Jacob just managed to get
his arm up in time to stop from being hit in the head.

Harlan had opened himself up, briefly, and Jacob took advantage.
With the skill of a placekicker, a perfectly aimed kick to the groin took
Harlan right off his feet. The groan that followed indicated he was
done. He fell in a heap by the door. Jacob went to him and drew back
to hit him in the face again. It was all he could do to stop himself.

Harlan looked at him with mixture of astonishment and fright. Jacob
looked at him and knew that this man was beaten, that it was finished
now. He could see the resignation in Harlan's eyes.

Instead of hitting him, he looked at him and leaned over far enough
to spit in his face. Then he got close and said to him, "If you ever come
close to her again, I will hurt you like you have never been hurt in your
miserable life. If you show up anywhere near this house or the house of
anyone I know. I will hurt you like you have never been hurt before.
Are we clear?"

There was no response. Jacob reached over and grabbed his broken
nose. The scream that came out of Harlan was unlike anything Jacob
had ever heard but he continued. "I didn't get your answer. Are we
clear?"

All Harlan could do was groan and nod his assent.

"Good. Now get up and get out. Oh, before you leave give me your wallet."

Harlan had a puzzled look on his bloodied face. "Why? What for?" he mumbled through his teeth.

"Just give it to me or I'll get it myself."

As Jacob made a move toward Harlan, Harlan tossed it to him. "You owe mom for a nice new blouse. It seems that you damaged the other one."

He took the hundred dollars that was in the wallet as Harlan was complaining that that was all the money he had. "Sucks to be you. I guess this just wasn't your lucky day." With that he put ten dollars back in the wallet and tossed it to him. "I'll call the cab. You've got enough for cab fare. Now get the hell out and lose this address."

He watched as Harlan got into the cab that would take him away from the house for the last time. He needed to calm down a bit and let the adrenaline settle before he made sure his mom was OK. He took some time to straighten up the kitchen and then cleaned himself up as well.

His arm was black and blue. The swelling had started and it hurt like hell. Jacob recognized that the rolling pin Annie had been using was what Harlan had hit him with. That surely would have done some serious damage.

However, he was more interested at how peaceful he felt despite the shock and the outrage and the shear, pure violence he felt when he saw Harlan assaulting his Mother.

This thing with his father had finally been dealt with, as far as he was concerned, and he had no more feelings for him one way or the other. It was as though he didn't exist anymore. No regret, no anger, no nothing. It was done and he could move on from it.

But many questions arose from what just happened. This was another one of those teachable moments that Jim often spoke of. It brought up questions about parenting and how that works. How do you know what to do? How do you know if you're doing it right? What happens if it doesn't work out? What happens if your kid gets angry with you? Look at how it worked out with Harlan? He would not want to do that to his kids. It was all so confusing.

Maybe he wouldn't have any kids and then he wouldn't have to worry about any of this. Maybe he just wasn't parent material. Well, he knew a couple of things for sure. If he chose to be a parent at some time, he would do all the things that his father never did. He would never be who his father was and he would make sure that his kids always knew they were safe. Beyond that he hadn't a clue.

Meanwhile Annie had run up the front stairs two at a time and pounded on the door. I hurried to the door to see her standing there trying to catch her breath pointing to her home. "He's there. The bastard is there. Jacob is there too." She kept pointing saying, "Need to do something" and "Have to hurry." She made no sense. I opened the door and brought her inside. I noticed the torn shirt and the bruise starting to form on the side of her face.

I gasped at her, "Annie, what happened to you? Are you OK? Do you need to go to the hospital? Who did this to you?" I sat her down and she got right back up again. I sat her down again and told her that she needed to slow down so that I could understand what she was saying. I got her to take a few deep breaths and then she said, "He's back. The bastard is back and Jacob is over there with him right now."

"Whose back, Annie? Who?"

"Harlan, that's who, and I'm afraid that Jacob is going to hurt him or kill him. I've never seen him with that look on his face, but I can tell you it was frightening."

All kinds of things raced through my head. I wasn't prepared to hear any of this. Harlan. What was he doing there? What was he doing out?

By the time I could get my head together and slow Annie down, I heard footsteps on the front porch again. This time it was Jacob. He let himself in and walked through to the kitchen. I took one look at him and knew he was hurt. He had blood on him and his face was white, but there was a quiet, almost peaceful look about him that was incongruous.

I didn't how to react to him, so I said, "I hope that the other guy looks worse than you."

He replied with a grin, "Oh yeah. He won't be smelling any roses for a bit. He won't be around anymore either. Let's just say that we came to an arrangement that I think we can both live with. The fine art of negotiation you once called it. Any Aspirins?"

I hadn't even noticed that he was holding his arm. I had focused on the blood but realized that most of it was not his. "So? So what did you agree upon?"

"Basically that there is no need for him to come back because I was sure that the feelings we, that mom and I shared, were not going to change any. The funny thing about what just happened is I don't feel anything like I thought I would after busting him up a bit. I don't feel all that great about it.

"Oh, don't get me wrong. I loved putting his lights out, but the satisfaction of beating him up for all the years that he trashed us? I have no great satisfaction about that. I thought if I ever got the chance to go at him that I would be all pumped, jacked up about it, but I'm not. I actually feel sad that it had to come to this.

"It was not fun to see him all bloodied. I thought it would be. He really isn't much of a man. I guess that is what struck me the most about him. He's got no balls. Would I do it again? Probably, but I think that the outcome would be the same. That said, I'm glad it happened."

Jacob turned to look at his mom. "He's gone, Mom. He won't bother you or me anymore. We both know that it's done. We're free of him."

I needed to let him know that violence is seldom the answer but ... so I said to him, "I don't condone or advocate violence as a solution but sometimes there is no choice. Sometimes the fight comes to you with little choice and, as a man, you stand your ground and do what needs to be done.

"Such was the case for you today, Jacob. Now you have a better sense of what it's truly like, literally, to fight for your home and your family."

I was happy to see and to hear that he didn't accept the violence as a good thing but rather a necessary thing. "Sometimes you just can't walk away." This experience had been another giant step to where he wants and needs to be, I thought.

I motioned him over with my head to have a look. "Let's have a look at that arm." Upon closer scrutiny I suggested that Annie take him down to the hospital for an X-ray. It was black and blue and swollen up like a balloon. She agreed and off they went, but as he got to the door he turned and grinned his special grin and said, "By the way I have a few questions for you if you're around later. Nothing like a good go-to to get the brain working, eh?"

After they had left, I called Leo and asked him to drop over if he could. He was there inside 30 minutes, which is a record of some kind for him. I wasn't sure if it was because he wanted to respond to my request right away or that there was a chance he might bump into a certain female person who lived close by. I strongly suspected the latter. Nonetheless, he was soon here.

I started right in. "I know that things have moved along quickly for you and that you are somewhat confused about many things but I've got to tell you that things are moving along quickly for me as well and I don't know how much time and energy I can give him. I don't want to rush our process, Leo, but I'm afraid of running out of time. Whether I want to think about what is coming or not, I know that I need to spend time with just me too.

"So I might need you to step up before we had planned and I wanted you to know what was going on. I'm sorry if it clouds things for you. Believe me, I wish it was different."

He reached out to put his hand on my shoulder and just looked at me with a somber look that said, "I'm sorry to hear that. I had forgotten that there is a great deal at stake here, and my situation is really secondary to all that right now."

I didn't need to hear the words. I could tell by the look and the quick squeeze of his hand that he was with me. "Thanks, Leo. It means a lot that you are here."

We spoke of many things that afternoon and by the time Annie and Jacob had returned, Leo had gone.

I greeted Annie and Jacob at the door. "Well, are you going to live or what?"

"Yeah, just a hairline fracture they said. Maybe four to five weeks in this cast and that's it, no biggie. About those questions I mentioned? Maybe we could put those over to tomorrow. I've got the mother of all headaches going on up here. Is tomorrow OK for you?"

"That works for me. It's good to hear you are going to be all right. Besides, there's nothing like a battle scar or a cast to score points with the ladies. Try not to take too much advantage of that. See you tomorrow."

Annie was turning away to go down the stairs when she looked at me and winked.

Sometimes Confusion Can Be A Good Thing

Jacob poked his head up against the screen and asked if I could "come out and play." I knew he would be around, just not as quickly as this. But here he was. I told him to relax on the porch because I needed about 15 minutes to do some things and then I could join him. Really I just needed to sit down and re-group a bit.

When I did join him he was ready for me.

"I haven't seen Mom this twisted in a while. She's over there now walking around mumbling to her self. She repeats things that she's done. I don't know how many times the floor got swept. I asked her if she was good, and she said, sure, no problem. Did something happen that I'm not aware of? I understand that having a run in with Harlan would be trying for anyone, but I think that it's more than that."

"Why jump to that conclusion?" I asked. "How does your Mom being out of sorts translate into something that anyone else did? If there is something bothering you about what's happening in your home, then ask her.

"Think about what we've talked about, think about what you have learned and think about what you are feeling and where that comes from so that you recognize it for what it is the next time it comes up.

"I think that before we go any further you need to sort out what's going on at home. So why don't you go have a chat with your Mom and ask her straight out?"

"We already had that chat," Jacob said. "We went through lots of those questions yesterday. She said she was over here, so I'm sure you've some idea of what she had on her mind, in fact what we each had on our minds. We had just finished talking about a bunch of stuff and I had headed out for a walk when Harlan showed up."

"How'd that go, I mean, really?"

"I think it went really well," he said, turning his eyes away from me.

He switched gears and went to another topic. "You know, being a kid is not as difficult as being an adult. At least it feels that way. As a kid I didn't have to think about much other than who it was I was going to hook up with that night and where to pick her up. The basics.

"To get along in the adult world, there are so many rules and things to remember, what you call "processes." Just as soon as I get one thing sorted out, three other things pop up and just like that I get all sketchy about what's going on.

"I mentioned yesterday that I have more questions especially after what happened between Harlan and me. I mean how could he be that kind of person and what does that say about me? Am I going to be just like him? What happened there? The guy is just a jerk but to go at Mom like that? What kind of a man does that? That's not the kind of man I want to be. So how do I not be like him? Knowing what I know and feeling what I feel, how do I not be like him?"

I saw a pleading in his eyes that I'd not seen before. He was genuinely frightened that he would somehow turn out to be just like Harlan.

"You are nothing like Harlan, Jacob. You are much more aware of who you are and what you want. You have learned much already and will continue to learn how to be a man in this world because you care. I can promise you this Jacob: there is no greater privilege or honour than to be a parent. When your time comes to step up I have absolutely no doubt in my mind that you will do it with love in your heart and that you will be very good at it?"

A Man's Work Is Never Done

PARENTING:
The Fourth Cornerstone

Time To Be Seen And Not Just Heard

Parenting is very similar to golf in that golf is the easiest game to teach and the toughest game to play. It is easy to tell people how to parent but very difficult to actually do the job yourself. The slightest miscalculation can result in major catastrophes with life-long repercussions. It's really a game of best guess, instincts, intuition and being true to our natural characteristics, and not trying to be something or someone we aren't. There are some things that we can do, as parents, to help develop and build strong relationships with our kids. Basically, however, the rest is really up to them. I can share some of that with you if you like"

"What kind of stuff?" he asked me.

"What I learned from parenting my own children. I have the benefit, now, of witnessing the outcomes of what I tried to do. I can speak about what worked out and what didn't work as well as I had hoped. That's not to say that I know everything from what happened with my kids, but it may point you in a direction that has some merit.

"I know that we agreed you would ask the questions now and you have raised some great questions already. But if I am going to get to your questions and your thoughts and try to answer them as best I can so that those answers make sense to you, we need to start at the beginning. Yes? You want me to carry on or do you want to take it from here for a while?"

He thought about that for a moment and then said he wanted me to go on but if something came up he would say something. I handed him a piece of paper and a pencil and asked him to write down anything he wanted me to clarify for him.

"When you are out there with your friends, what do you see and what do you hear? What I mean by that is what's going on that makes you wonder what is happening with you?"

"I used to be there with these guys. Some were and are my friends, but I get frustrated around them because they seem so negative. Some

185

have given up on trying to do anything with their lives. Everything seems to be a joke, and they get on other kids who want to do well in school or who don't fit with their way of seeing the world around them. They actually give them a hard time. They act out these attitudes that say, 'I am entitled to this and I deserve that,' but they don't want to work for anything. They expect their parents to take care of things because they have the money to give them things. Kids have the 'right' and the parents have the 'responsibility'. I don't know if this is making any sense to you."

"Hey, I'm on the hill, not over it. I said. "Sure it makes sense to me. I see much the same as you do. It's not a secret. There is a whole generation of kids who have this distorted sense of entitlement and are in trouble, yet no one seems to care much about that. If they do, they are at a loss as to what to do about it. What else?"

Jacob looked at me and said, "In a minute. I want to know what else you see?"

"I see kids out there who want to be different and I understand that. I do. That's been going on for a long time, long before my generation, so this isn't a new phenomenon. But in doing so, they have become what they don't want to be. That is, just like each other. Most are all tattooed up. By the way where do the kids get the money to get the tattoos? I know they are pretty expensive but if they aren't working, where does the money come from? And how do they pay for a Blackberry or the cell phone?

"Many kids wear the same type of clothing in the same style, too. It's like a uniform of sorts.

"There are lots who have little respect for females. Many of the females have little or no respect for other females. The language they both use, especially in public places, is nothing but disrespectful, but by doing so they believe they are showing how independent they are – how much they really don't care, or how cool and outrageous they are.

"When I was a kid, the question parents would ask is 'would you talk like that around your grandmother?' I know it sounds silly, but when you think about it, would you? Would you talk like that around or to your mother? If the answer is no, then why not? Why use that language in public in front of strangers and families with little ones. Shock value? To me the only thing it demonstrates is how ignorant they are and how little class they have.

"If I were to sum it up, I would say that what I see out there is a lack of self-respect and disrespect for other people's rights and property in general.

"I also know that there are lots of kids who are doing great things and want to do important things in the world. They go to school and work at part-time jobs. But I think there are just as many, perhaps more, who don't care about any of that.

"There's a good number of reasons for that, but at the end of it they just don't seem to care about any of it. They are self-absorbed and self-centered. They are angry, frustrated and confused about their roles and their place in the world, so they are busy creating a place – a culture really – where they can feel connected and a part of something with other kids who feel the same way."

I could have gone on for quite a while but didn't. I wanted to hear from Jacob, so I said to him, "This is supposed to be about you, not me. Wind me up and I could go on for hours about this. So? What else?"

Jacob started right in. "I agree that most of the people I know have a strange idea of how things should be. I also agree that there are lots of kids doing interesting things that are different. It seems to work well for them. They are excited about what the future holds for them. I guess that's what started me thinking about my own situation. I had to decide if what I had was all I wanted and the answer was no. But like my friends I get lost and confused about how I get more of what I want.

"It's easy to get locked into the lifestyle that a good number of my friends live. It's free and it's easy. Parents and other adults are basically oblivious to what is happening. For one thing, parents are too busy trying to be like their kids. They want to be friends, but all the kids do is take advantage of them.

"We have enough friends. We don't need anymore and, if we did, we would just go and find them. I know that we have talked about this before, but it is more real now. The other adults are too busy trying to survive or more likely trying to keep the toys they have bought. Either way kids now, at least many of the ones I know, haven't got parents who are around much so they carry on like they are the adults. The kids write their own rules.

"Take sex, for example. It's just a game for many. For some it's fun. For some it's an experiment. For others it's a way of gaining some control in their lives. They decide who gets what from them and when and where. Either way, many are getting messed up making stupid decisions about what to do. There's lots of pressure out there to do things that easily, and usually, gets them into trouble. Half these kids, and I mean the 13- and 14-year-olds, are trying so hard to find a place where they fit in that they will do almost anything sexually to be accepted. It's like a bargaining chip.

"We've talked before about 'babies bringing up babies'. What do they know about being parents? Nothing, yet there they are. To some, these little babies are like having a pet. I know this one girl who's part of the crowd I hung out with. She's 17. I was talking to her the other day and she as much as said that her baby was just like having a kitten to play with, but that she had to look after it all the time. She sounded really put out by that because she didn't have any time to have fun for herself. What's going to happen when she gets tired or bored and begins to resent the baby? Then what? I'm thinking that babies should be important and not a novelty. I mean, they are little people. I know that I am not ready for that, but I hope some day I will be."

And I thought I was wound up. Jacob had certainly been doing a great deal of thinking about parenting since his incident with Harlan. It wasn't as if he was angry but rather aware of just how much he didn't know about being responsible for another life. He knew what not to do and how not to do it.

"You're pretty wired up about all of this," I commented. "And true enough, I'm really afraid for the 'little people', as you called them, as well. They should be a focus, not a distraction or a toy."

Watching Jacob now reminded me of a caged cat. He couldn't stay still. He was up and walking around as he spoke. There was more going on here than just wondering about what had just happened. "So are you going to tell me what's really going on for you?" I asked.

He began to say, "What do you mean?" but then obviously decided not to go there. "It's everything, everything that you and I have talked about. Everything that Harlan means or reminds me of, all the negatives connected to him and how that says I'll be messed up too. My thoughts don't shut down. More questions keep coming up. I feel as if I'm not getting a grip on all this stuff.

"I guess I'm just frustrated. Then I begin to think that I'll never get it and that I'll always be a screw-up. I want more than I think I'll get and that's not good enough. Don't get me wrong, Jim, I've learned a lot about who I am and see the benefits of that. There just seems to be so much to learn and my head feels full."

I thought for a moment and then said, "It is difficult to trust your instincts, especially when you are used to living only for the exact moment you are in. You have the skills, Jacob, and you have the passion to have all you want. Please trust me on that. I know it. I can see it in you. But you are approaching this as if you were in school or something. There are no tests to write and no memory work for tomorrow. You're becoming a man in the world, and it's hard to let go of being a kid in the world.

"Make a choice. Which world do you want to be a part of? Once you do, then you will know how to respond to what happens to you in your life. Things will begin to happen because of the choices you make. Use your gifts and don't be afraid. They will guide you to where you want to be.

"You will make some mistakes. You don't have to remember any of this stuff; just rely on what your intuition and instincts tell you. Be true to your natural qualities – the protector and the provider – and accept the challenges as learning tools.

"Answer me this: Let's say you were a father right now and your son wouldn't do what you wanted him to do. Would you beat him until he did?"

"Of course not," he responded with some surprise in his voice.

"Why not"? I asked him

"Because that doesn't help him learn anything. Besides, I know from experience that he would get pissed off and fight me more. Probably nail me when he got big enough. So what . . ." he stopped in mid-sentence.

"That's right, Jacob. You know that that wouldn't do anything to help either one of you, and you know that that isn't who you are. You didn't have to think about it too much, did you? You didn't have to remember anything that I said to you. Your instincts told you all you needed to know. You can't beat kids into good behaviour. You learned that from your father and you won't act the way he did."

"OK," he said. "Point made."

"No," I said, "point proven. Another thing to remember is that you have and will have good people around you who will help you and guide you on your way. We always need good men around us to talk to and to exchange ideas with. You will never know it all. None of us does, but there are those who know a bit more than others only because they have been around a bit longer, have had good mentors themselves and have paid attention. That's what Leo is to me."

189

He nodded, so I knew he was buying in.

"Speaking of him, what's he up to these days? And don't play dumb. You know what I mean."

"I really don't know," I said, "but he'll surface soon enough."

Jacob had let me know he had had enough for now. He needed to process all this, so I suggested we get together later if he wanted. Again, he just nodded.

Time Moves On And So Does Leo

Leo had finally made a decision about how he wanted to approach Annie. Once he found Annie's phone number in the directory, he called her and asked her to go for a coffee. "You pick a spot and I'll meet you there," he suggested. Annie responded by saying, "That's such a nice offer, but I'm not sure I have enough time." Ever quick on his feet, Leo stated that he would have her home before she could turn into a pumpkin. He added that he thought it was important but if she couldn't, would tomorrow be better? Now he had piqued her interest. She agreed with some reservation in her voice. Twenty minutes later they were sitting in the park with a coffee.

Leo looked at her and got all flustered, so he tried to make some small talk. He isn't very good at it, so Annie saw right through him. She began the conversation: "Leo, you didn't ask me here for a talk about the weather and how I was doing. You have something on your mind and I'd like to hear it, so spit it out, whatever it is."

He took a deep breath. "Well, OK, I guess that's best. The other night, I really enjoyed myself. I mean I enjoyed your company and your easy way. You made it comfortable to be there and to talk about all sorts of things. That hasn't happened to me for quite a while.

"I'm not usually this forward, by the way, but I have to say that I have been unable to think of much else besides you and what it was like just being there in your company. I'd like to get to know you better, maybe ask you out for a bite to eat and maybe a walk on the beach if you like. But, number one, I don't even know if you are seeing someone right now. The other thing is Jacob.

"Maybe that didn't come out right, so please don't get me wrong here. I think he is a good kid, and Jim tells me that he has really worked hard to change things for himself, but he also seems very protective of you and I understand that. I don't want to cause any grief here between

190

you two, so I'm not sure if asking you out is a good thing or not. I can't seem to decide on this one way or the other. I don't even know if you want to go out anywhere with me and I'm not asking for an answer right now. But I thought that if I didn't let you know what I was thinking you would never be able to tell me to move on or not. If you have any ideas about any of this and you feel OK about letting me know, I'd appreciate it."

Annie didn't know how to respond. She was attracted to Leo, no doubt. She did enjoy his company as well, true enough. Was she ready to go out with someone? Should she jump at the first offer? Jacob said he'd be OK with that, but would he if the reality hit? Did she really want or need a complication in her life right now?

"Well how can I put this. I enjoyed my evening at Jim's too. I will say that I was surprised at how easy you were to be around as well. And you're right, Jacob is a good kid. I'm very proud of him and what he is doing and has done to change how his life is going. I wouldn't jeopardize his happiness and his peace for anything or anyone.

"He and I discussed this very thing just the other day – not you specifically but my getting on with my life in general – and he agrees that that's something I should do. He'd find it difficult, but he said he would handle it.

"I'm not sure what I want to do, though. Do I want to play the field to see what life is about? This is all new to me. I'm coming from a relationship that was so distorted and so awful that I'm not sure what I want. Could you give me a couple of days to think about it and call me? I'm not trying to string you out. This is coming at me from left field."

"Sure, I can do that."

With that Annie started to leave then stopped and said, with a big grin, over her shoulder, "I do like the Jimmy Buffett thing," and off she went. He watched her go across the lawn but hung back to enjoy the sun for a while longer before going home. Had he handled this all right? He had spoken his truth, and that was all he could do.

Getting To It

To my surprise, Jacob was back later that day for more. He returned with a new vigour I thought. He looked full of questions and ideas. As he sat down on the porch, he looked at

191

me with an inquiring eye and asked me if I was all right. I said I was and he just looked at me as though he knew something, but didn't push.

For the first time I started to say that I had something to talk about that was, perhaps, going to be uncomfortable to hear, but I stopped short. Not yet. Soon. Also for the first time, a large lump formed in my throat, but I had to keep it together so I just said, "I'm good. What's up?"

He hesitated but moved on. I knew he wasn't going to let this drop, however.

"I'd like a buck for every mile I've put on these shoes lately. I've been thinking and trying to answer my own questions. I'm trying to put together the pieces between what we have talked about and what you have helped me understand. I'm trying to figure how all this fits into where I want to go and who I want to be.

"I don't know enough—not nearly enough about how we, how males, got to this place. When I hear you talk about it, I get an idea of how it was for you. When I look around now at what my friends and their fathers are doing, it isn't anywhere close to how it was for you. I don't think it was like this when you were a kid. Was it better or easier? What happened? For me to make sense of what is happening now, I need to know how we got here."

"First of all, I can't say it was easier or better then than it is now," I said. "My generation, as with all generations, had issues and experiences that were unique to them at the time. I was born right after the war ended, and there was a large group of young men who were returning from Europe and the Pacific Islands that had seen unspeakable acts and, in some cases, were forced to do unspeakable things.

"Those change a man forever, so those who left as boys came back as men. During the war, the women were forced out of their homes and their traditional roles and into the armed services and the factories to help with the war effort. The roles of men and women changed significantly. This is not to say this was good or bad. I was just the way it was.

"However, it did mean that men would now have to share the stage with their female counterparts concerning jobs and opportunities in the workplace. Some men were OK with that. There was lots of work for everyone, some were OK with that but would have preferred something else. Some resented the changes and were downright against them happening and tried hard to make sure the situation didn't stay that way for long. They wanted to go back to the way it had been. They wanted their wives to be in the home taking care of the family while they went out to work and provided for them.

"The roles and expectations had been basic and simple. Each understood what the other would do, what the tasks were and what their responsibilities were. Homes were harmonious and not chaotic, or at least not as much. Most kids always had one parent around all or most of the time. There was structure and guidance, both of which are often lacking today. You pointed that out earlier. Kids are writing their own rules, I think you said."

"So what you're talking about, Jim, is the nest and the castle stuff we talked about before?"

"Exactly," I said. "I'm impressed that you put that together that quickly. But then again, I always thought that you were a quick study. Both sides have good arguments for changing roles and for keeping those roles the same. It depends on whom you talk too.

"Anyway, the ladies of that day and those days that followed were not going to go back to their old roles. So women fought hard for change to take place and it did, albeit slowly, but it did and it continues today. The problem isn't about the changes as much as it's about the rate or speed of change. There has been no other time as important as this time for men to honour their natural characteristics and to teach their sons about what they mean. But we have talked about this before as well."

He was so eager to understand this change process and the 'hows' and the 'whys' so he could understand the 'what nows' more clearly. He needed to get what was happening today. Part of me thought he needed to understand it so that he could make sense out of his relationship with Harlan. He wanted and needed to know that it wasn't about him, as a son, but rather the time and therefore the choices that Harlan made as his father.

"So what changed?" he asked. "What is different for the boys and men now? I mean, I can only go by what I see and hear with the guys I hang around and what they say about their fathers and brothers and uncles. What I see is that there are many men who don't care much about what you and I have talked about. I mention some of the stuff we talk about like 'socially and culturally ingrained gifts' and they look at me as if I'm from another solar system. They have no clue and don't seem to care much about any of it."

"That's a great observation, Jacob, and it's true too. I don't think that it's ALL men who don't care, but certainly a good number of them have just said, "There is only me and what I want or need that matters. The rest can kiss my . . ." Nothing matters to them. They don't care too much about looking after themselves. Why should I care?" they ask. They have given up trying to cope with what is happening. They are confused about the roles they are to play now, especially when it comes to parenting their children and how the house is supposed to run now that two parents are out working more often.

For instance, who has the last say? Someone has to; otherwise, nothing would get decided - home would be very contradictory at best – for everyone.

"There are lots of mixed messages and double standards to deal with. Other roles in the community and at work have changed as well. Many men are not thinking about being fathers or being solid members of society or their communities. They don't aspire to anything or to be anyone of consequence.

"What's changed? Expectations of who we are supposed to be and how we are supposed to act, for starters. Be more compassionate but more aggressive at work. Be more caring and nurturing at home and tougher out there. It's a very confusing world for men right now. There are many who still live by the natural gifts that guide us and our instincts, but social circumstances more often dictate that we should stop paying attention to those things and fall into line here with the new program. Many are not prepared to do that and have responded in very different ways.

"As a consequence to these rapidly changing and pressure-filled times, we are trying to be something or someone other than who we naturally are, and we have lost our way. We no longer have male role models that we can aspire to be like. Think about who those role models have been in the last 20 years and how disappointing they have been not only to young boys but to the world in general.

"Is there really any one male you could honestly say you would like to be like? There are few, if any. It used to be that sons grew up wanting to be like their fathers and their grandfathers. You don't hear or see that much anymore."

I was starting to get tired, and as much as I was enjoying the questions and answers, I was losing focus. I said to Jacob that I had to be somewhere soon and that we could pick this up tomorrow, but in the meantime I wanted him to think about what or who he wanted to be like as a man in the world: What kind of father he wanted to be, what he wanted others to see and think when they saw him, how he would know when the time comes to take responsibility for and to guide a new life, what kind of a life he wanted for his kids, how he would like his kids to see the world they live in, how he would like his kids to see him and how he wanted them to treat other people. So much to talk about and so little time! It seemed to me that "man's' work is never done."

Over the past week I had managed to squirrel away an hour here and an hour there so that I could give myself a little time to begin to wrestle with what was coming. After several introspective consultations and conversations with myself, I decided that the time was near for me to explain to Annie and Jacob what was happening with my health. I still couldn't find the words, but I was getting closer all the time. I figured another week would work out best.

I had made a number of decisions including ones regarding the work that I felt I had left to do with Jacob. He had asked me many questions and I knew there'd be more to come, but I also knew I needed to have some time on my own. The physical and formal preparations were complete, save one, and that would be taken care of today, hence my needing to be somewhere else, as I had told Jacob. Now what was left concerned the emotional and the spiritual parts that only I could deal with.

John finally returned my call. He'd been away and had just got back. He was very concerned by my call and wondered what had happened. He was more upset than I was, so it took a bit of time to assure him that not much had changed other than I was getting tired more quickly. We talked about what could be done. He pointed out that we couldn't do much more because we were near the max in terms of dosages. It is the nature of what is going on with you now, he said.

When John gets emotionally challenged, he tends to become philosophical so he ended our conversation quietly: "It saddens me to say that not much more can be done, Jim. Time is the supreme arbiter now."

I said that my hope was God would fill that space in the process, but I understood what he was trying to say. As we hung up the realization that I was alone in this became more of a reality and I must say it hit me hard. No matter how much support I would receive from those around me, it really was just me and my Maker now.

Friend Or Parent? Can't Be Both

Jacob wasted little time showing up the next day, looking as if he hadn't slept much either. He sat down and began immediately. "Before we get to what you asked me to think about, I need to get your take on some questions that came up for me when I was doing what you asked me to do. I don't want the questions to get lost somehow."

This wasn't the way I thought it would go, but he was in the driver's seat now. I had given him permission to do that and couldn't take it back.

"OK, so what came up for you?"

He pulled out a piece of paper, studied it for a moment and then started. "Well, we got to where I get what happened and the 'how,' but I need to get the 'where to now?' part. I want to know how we men fix this. I want you to tell me what I need to know so that I don't do what the other guys are doing, or not doing. Something isn't working out too well. I'm the newbie, so I get to start from scratch here and I just can't count on my past alone to tell me much."

All I could manage was, "Wow. I mean this is so huge and you want me to just do what? How do I know how to fix it? I can tell you what I have seen, what I think happened and is happening so something different can happen, but I don't know how to fix it. All I know is that we males are in danger of forfeiting our natural place in the scheme of things. If we don't do something soon, we all will pay an awful price for our inaction or our failure to pull our heads out of the sand and say what's going on. How's that?"

"I'll settle for that right now. I thought about what you asked me to do and realized that I can't do it, what you asked. Not yet anyway."

"Jacob, when you analyze what is going on around you and the crew you know, what stands out for you? What one thing is common among many of your buddies and their buddies?"

He didn't have to think about it for long. "A lot of the guys are in trouble with the law. Lots of them don't go to school or don't go often. Most of them smoke, drink or do drugs of some kind. A few are parents already, mostly the girls though."

"Why do you think that is going on?"

"Obviously they don't give a shit. Sorry. I guess they don't care about what happens to them."

196

"Anything else?"

He thought for a moment and said, "Many of them come from single-parent homes. I'd say that quite a few of them have a mom looking after them, but the old man has taken off. Sounds familiar."

"Unfortunately, it's true," I pointed out. "A large number of single parent families are parented by the mom. Dads are either out of the picture altogether or have very limited contact with the kids. The last time I checked around 80 percent of single family homes have Mom running things. This is not a knock against Mom. This is just to say that fathers tend to be the ones that leave, for a variety of reasons.

"I can't talk about how that affects the daughters in the house, but I suspect it has a huge impact on the sons in the house. I also know that the families that have Mom as the head of the house tend to have sons who are more violent and aggressive than otherwise. Again, this is not to be critical of Mom. This is not about what she is or isn't doing. It is simply the fact.

"I also suspect that single-parent homes where Dad is the parent have difficulties with daughters. Single parenthood lacks the alternate perspective if there are both males and females in the house. If the kid is male and the parent is female, she cannot teach her son the ways of the male world and how he can function in it – what it means to be male. The same is true for daughters with a father as the parent. They can teach their kids about being human and the expectations of that, but that's it. Kids need to have the perspective and the input of both parents, at least, in order to have a balanced view of how the world works and how we can better understand each other as males and females."

"OK, so I get that part, but what I still don't get is the 'why.' Why do you think that's how it is. You just can't say, 'That's just the way it is.' There has to be a reason why it's like that. You said once that you feel the last two generations of young men were in trouble. You pointed out how they dress and don't seem to care how they are seen by others. They don't want to go to school, but they want all the perks that come to those who do bother to be educated. 'Entitlement' you called it."

Jacob continued, "They are more violent and less caring about other people's rights, whether that has to do with their belongings or their human rights. Maybe they feel as though they don't fit in anywhere. You also said that they are confused or struggling in some way with how to be male and that they aren't aware or don't understand the importance of our natural gifts,' that we are in danger of losing sight of how important they are. I heard someone say they were like a light in the darkness.

"My question is still 'why?' Why do you feel that way and if that's how it is now, then what do you think the reason for that is? If I can get this part then I hope I'll know what I should do and what I should not do as a man and as a parent."

I thought for a moment and then said, "I'm not sure where to start all of this. Would you agree that we, as people in general, act on what we believe is real, that our perceptions become our realities? In other words, if we see that violence is the only solution to solving a problem, then that's what we believe is true. If we believe that women are second-class citizens or not to be respected, then we are likely to treat them that way. If we think or are told that it is better to steal than to work for things, then we are likely to adopt that attitude and follow that path. Are you following me so far?"

"So what that means is that what we see is how we think things are, true or not."

"That would be a loose translation, but yeah, that's about it," I said.

"OK"

I continued. "For the last two generations of young men, fathers have been more absent than ever before. Some have left, just walked away and left for a better deal somewhere else where they don't have the responsibility of being a father. They leave their wives or ex-wives to play both roles, apparently uncaring about the outcomes for their children, especially their sons.

"Some have left because it is easier to get along somewhere else where the world of political correctness is basically non-existent. Life's rules and the expectations of others are simple, uncomplicated. The most recent generation of young men has not had any male guidance to help them because their fathers had little or no direction either. Fathers are not there to hold their sons accountable for their decisions. In so many cases there has been no parental consistency to teaching responsibility or even basic social conventions – manners and respect, for instance. And even if dad is at home many have abdicated their father role and the sons suffer for it.

"Parents often parent as they themselves were parented, unless someone helps them realize otherwise. You have realized otherwise, Jacob, and that's why you will be a good parent to your children when that time comes. You know that you have much to learn, but you are willing to do the work. You have proven that already.

"You have had and will have good teachers around you. Many young men have no one to look up to these days, especially anyone who understands what is needed. Those young men have no one to learn from and no one to hold them accountable for the choices they make. They run free with no boundaries, they are not concerned about consequences for the decisions they make and they have no sense of direction. They spend far too much time in front of computers playing violent games and often carry that violence into their real lives. Life becomes a game of sorts.

"We also need to be careful not to put all young men into the same category because there are a good number of them who are doing really well for themselves. But not all, and the numbers of those who aren't doing well is growing. That's what is disturbing to me. If you couple that with the pressure to ignore their natural characteristics, trouble is right around the corner big time.

"Here's the quick summary: many males today have not developed the attachments and the relationships they need with their fathers or any other strong male influences in their lives. They are not connected or don't feel attached to the community they live in: to their neighbours, coaches and teachers. They have no sense of purpose, worth or importance.

"When you think about your friends, how do their parents, especially their fathers, spend time with them? How much time do they actually spend with them and doing what? Is it more like 'Here's 20 bucks, Have a nice day.'

"This happens with kids who have both parents at home too. Both parents are physically there but emotionally absent or unavailable. Both parents are too busy in their own lives trying to make ends meet and trying to have or keep all the toys they believe are needed in order to be happy. In doing so, they are ignoring the real needs of their children – in this case, their sons. They give them the latest Xbox program or Blackberry or computer game, thinking and hoping that they are being good parents. They don't get that you can't buy love and respect. And just because the kids are given all the latest gadgets that doesn't ensure or guarantee their good behaviour will come as part of the deal. They don't need stuff; they need their parents to be parents, and that means sharing their time and being their children's teachers and role models."

My energy was fading quickly now, and I needed to be quiet. I let the silence play itself out. Jacob was quiet too. He was trying to grasp what I had said and then apply it to what he had asked of me. I knew he'd get it. It was really about everything he never got as a kid, a boy neglected and abused by his father.

Finally he said, "Not to repeat myself, but are you OK? You look tired again. What's up?"

"I have been tired lately, you're right," I said. "I'm seeing John tomorrow for a checkup. Thanks for asking."

"Speaking of checking up, I should go see what Mom is doing. Something is going on, but she is trying to let on that nothing's happening. I can see through her like a pane of glass. Anyway, I'll stop by tomorrow if that's good."

I gave him one of our famous nods and off he went.

He walked into the house and could see his mom in the kitchen. Standing the kitchen doorway, he said to Annie, "I realize this is new territory for both of us. I don't want to appear nosy or prying, especially after the understanding we reached, but I know that something's up. I was trying to figure out how to ask you about this but in the end decided the front-on approach was best."

She offered him a cold drink and motioned for him to have a seat. As he was sitting down, she said, "Leo called and asked me out." She stopped to gauge his reaction.

When there wasn't one, she began again. "I thought abo. . ." At the same time he began to ask, "What did yo. . ." They both stopped and grinned. He said, "You first." As casually as she could, she said, "Leo called earlier and asked me if I wanted to catch some cover band down at the beach tonight."

"Well, what did you say?" He already knew the answer but asked the question anyway.

"I said that I would be delighted. He's coming by to pick me up about 7:00 tonight."

"That's great. I'm glad that you said yes. Shall I wait up—do I need to be on the porch when you get home? And what time can I expect you home, by the way?"

Her face became very concerned and then Jacob grinned, "Hey, just kidding. Really. Hope you have a good time."

"You little . . .," she began. He raised his hands, covered the sides of his head and said, "Careful now. Be careful of my tender ears," and they both laughed heartily.

After talking with John, I realized that the time had come. I could not keep hiding the complete truth from Jacob, or from Annie, for that matter. I would need to tell them in the next day or two. Before telling them, though, there were a few matters that I needed to straighten out with Jacob. He had some questions that he wanted answers to. I would do that first. He was very close now to understanding . He was full of energy for finding the answers and determining his own way. I couldn't and wouldn't take that from him. Not after all the time he had invested and the risks he had taken building the relationship we had built. I prayed that Leo was up to the challenge and that the timing was right. It had to be.

Is Truth Always The Best Policy??

I knew that Jacob would be around fairly early today, so I had to run my two errands before he showed up. Because the jewelry store and the ticket outlet were close enough together, I felt I could cover both and get home again in good time. Jacob, being very perceptive, had put together the idea that I had more energy earlier in the day than the latter part of the day so that's when he tended to show himself.

Leo called to let me know he had been out with Annie the night before. Hey, good for you I said to him. I suggested he come around later because I needed to speak with him and I had something I wanted to give him. I also mentioned that Jacob might be here, and it was OK for him to join us if he was confortable with that.

By mid-afternoon Jacob was bounding up my walk to the porch. He had a grin on his face as if he had a secret he couldn't wait to share.

"I don't know if you know this, but Mom was out with Leo last night. They went to some little bar near the beach to catch a band or something. Anyway, I was in bed when she got home, but first thing this morning she was up and busy. I haven't heard her hum along with the radio tunes for a while, so she must have had a good time. It looked good on her too. Maybe this Leo guy is all right. If he can put a smile on her face like that, he's good in my book."

"Oh to be a fly on the wall, eh?"

"Nah," he said, "I don't think I want to know. Too much information maybe. She's happy and that's all that matters to me."

Then he put on his serious face. "I've been thinking about what you said yesterday and it's starting to make sense to me. I mean I always think about what you say, but the stuff yesterday cleared a lot up for me that had been bothering me for a long time. I'm thinking that if I get to know the rest of the story, most of it will fall into place. It may be working ass backwards but, to me, it makes sense that way."

"I need to make a point to you that I meant to make the other day, Jacob. I think that it may be helpful to you when you look at the whole story, as you call it. You OK with that?"

"Yeah, sure. What is it?"

"I know that you have hopes and dreams just as most other people do, and I know that you don't like to talk about them very much. It's as if you don't want to jinx them or something. The past is something that will always be with us. We can't forget the past. It is imprinted on our memory.

What is true about you, Jacob, is this: yes, you are your fathers' son. Does that make you just like him? No. Because he believed certain things, you don't have to believe them to be true also. You are not the same person you once were. You have learned what Harlan was never taught or shown. So what is it you think you need to know or understand, now, to bring it all together?"

"Nice segue," he managed to squeeze out. I had tapped into a dark place for him, and he was truly uncomfortable, but he soldiered on. "I guess what I need to know now is how I make it different. When the time comes for me to be a father, what is it I have to do to make it different for my kids than it was for me? I can see now why there are so many guys who struggle with being in the world today. I don't want that for my kids."

I hesitated for just a bit and then began, "Before anything else, you have to decide if you are ready and able to accept the responsibility that goes with creating another life." I gave that a second to sink in. "Not after the fact, but before the fact. If you can't commit to that, then keep it zipped up until you are mature enough and responsible enough to make that choice. That's what men do. And they don't abandon their families. They don't trade their kids for the bling. Besides, those children didn't ask to be born, but should expect that you or someone else will take care of them once they arrive.

"You can't parent all children the same way. They are like snowflakes. Not one is exactly the same as another. They all have individual personalities. You can't do it exactly the same way that I did it or how your friends' fathers did it or how your mom did it.

"Right from the time they are little people to the time they are grown and gone, as parents, we need to treat our children with the respect and dignity they deserve. We are their teachers, so we need to help them understand that they have worth, they are appreciated and valued and they are loved. We need to develop an environment for them to live in where they feel that they have purpose and that they feel attached to the family and community they spend their time with. They need to feel secure and that they always have a home to return to where they are safe both emotionally and physically.

This is where your instincts and intuition come into play. What would you want from your father? It may not be a fair question for you right now, but I think you know the answers. Trust those to guide you. And if you want your children to trust you, then you have to earn that trust from them. Nobody gets on that ride for free. You earn their trust and they have to earn yours.

"Validate your sons' behaviour and his feelings. Help him know that boys and men have feelings too. When he is old enough help him know that it's OK for men to express them and if they do that they are not showing weakness. Help him understand that it's not cool to hurt other people because he's angry, for instance, but it's OK to express that anger in an appropriate way. It's OK to feel it.

"An interesting point here is that kids never seem to forget things they have been told, especially if it's the first time they have heard it. They learn from us by watching and listening to us deal with everyday issues. What do you want them to learn? If you don't have a handle on your emotions, then what can you teach your children, especially your son? Get your work done first.

"From all the things I've mentioned, what are the three things that most kids – sons in this case because, as I've said, I can't speak for the women of the world – want from us as parents?"

He was locked in, but was struggling to answer the question I put to him. I don't think he expected it, so he stumbled with it a bit. "What they want? I guess to know that you love them, that they are important and that they need to know they are safe. I get all of those, so it won't be hard to remember them later."

"So you were listening. Sorry if this turned into a seminar, Jacob, but there is so much to share with you and so little time. I wanted to make sure that I covered your question about what you could do differently as well as I could. You want me to keep going? Have you got anywhere you need to be?"

"No, I don't have to be anywhere. I came here looking for answers and I don't want to leave until I get what I need. I hope that's not selfish, but it is really important because I see my friends struggling.

Some are trying to make sense of what happened to them as well. The ones with kids already are still just kids themselves. I can hear them talking about not knowing what to do and how to do it. Maybe some of this can help them too. What are these three things they want?"

"There's nothing selfish about wanting to learn something. I just didn't want to overwhelm you. From my point of view these are what they want: love, – for your children to know that you love them and they are valued and important to you; time – that you spend as much time as you can with them playing and teaching and helping them see the world as a place of opportunity, accountability and responsibility; and consistency coupled with honesty. This one is, in my mind, is the most important of the three. It is by being consistent and honest that trust is developed. Without trust then nothing else will matter so trust is the most important. Think about how consistent Harlan was with you. How difficult was it for you to believe anything he said to you about anything? If there is no consistency and honesty then how will your children know what to believe when you are trying to tell them something important? Saying one thing and then doing another or changing what you said in mid-stream is very difficult for kids to handle. After a while they just give up trying to figure out which one of you will show up today.

"You also have to teach them that there will be times that you can't do what you said you would because surprises happen and you can't always see them coming. They will know the difference if you have done your job well, even if it is something they don't want to hear.

"You can't buy trust and you can't buy love no matter how many toys you give them. If you only have an hour to spend with them then, be sure that that hour is spent just with them with no interruptions or distractions. Often it's about quality and not quantity.

"Too many parents try to be friends with their kids. They dress the same and talk the same. If the kids are small, some parents dress them up to look just like dad with the same haircut and the same kind of jeans so they look like mini-me's. Some even party and drink with their kids when they get older, with the silly belief that if they do, the kids are more likely to want to get along with them because they'll think Mom or Dad are cool. All they teach them is to be unlawful and it's OK as long as you are at home or with an adult.

"Kids need parents, not grown-up adolescents to hang around with. Many kids see themselves as the equals of their parents because the parents don't try to separate themselves from their children. They don't maintain the necessary boundaries. There is little respect for parents who try to be their kids' friend because there is no balance in the relationship that some parents have with their kids. If there is no balance, there are big problems.

"Kids are not equal to their parents. Someone needs to be in charge. Part of that is about saying 'no.' Saying 'no' is OK. Our kids need to be reminded, consistently, about guidelines, boundaries and expectations to live by. That's how they learn to live in society.

"They learn nothing from parents who are permissive and expect no accountability from their kids for their behaviour. Letting them act like adults before their brains are ready is not a good idea.

"As men, we need to parent our sons by depending more on our natural characteristics – our instincts and our intuitions.

"Sons don't want to disappoint their fathers. They don't want to hurt their mothers either. They are attached to Mom and respectful of her. They want to be like Dad and are proud of him. Our sons give us a lot of power until we don't live up to who and what they want us to be.

"Never make a promise that you can't or don't plan to keep. If you want your kids to trust you, you have to be consistent with them in everything that you do. They need to be able to count on you to do that.

"Teach your sons to respect other people's rights as human beings along with their property. And that includes girls too, especially mothers and grandmothers. We, as fathers, have to set the example by being our sons' teachers. Where do you want your son to learn about how to act like a man in the world? Who do you want him to learn these things from? What do you want him to know and understand about maleness and the natural gifts we have talked about? That has to be passed on to your sons and to their sons.

"You must be their main source of accurate information and intelligence. Don't leave that to someone else to do. It is one of our basic responsibilities to our children. Be their teachers.

"Our son's and daughters need to know there are logical and natural consequences for all the decisions they make. Make one that isn't a good one and the consequence will be unpleasant. Make good decisions and the consequences are usually pretty good. It's up to them to learn how to deal with consequences. This is how they learn so that they don't repeat their mistakes over and over again. It is up to us to teach them how to think, not what to think. As hard as it is sometimes, as a parent we have to stand back and watch them go through the hard times and not rescue them."

Just as I was finishing up with my response to Jacob's questions Leo showed up as if queued. He hesitated a bit at the bottom of the stairs when he saw Jacob but proceeded anyway. I offered him a chair and explained that we were just concluding a chat about being a father and how important it was to be involved in our son's lives. It was a topic that he said he didn't have a great deal of experience with and that he regrets that lack of opportunity.

Then Jacob did something he hadn't done before. He said, "Thanks for taking the time to do this with me. It means a lot and it makes so much more sense to me. The whole thing does, so thanks."

There was an eerie feeling as though he knew we were done or close to it.

Finally the conversation got around to last night and Jacob started that ball rolling by asking how the band was. For the briefest of moments, Leo looked uneasy, but then said, "They were really good, a cover band called "The West End Boys. Ever hear of them?"

Jacob looked amused by Leo's unease, and then said, "Nope, I've never heard of them. What kind of stuff did they play?"

I was out of the conversation so I had a cat-bird's seat as I witnessed the interaction between the two of them. It was the perfect dance. Jacob was leading and Leo was following beautifully. "Oh, they did a set of Eagles music, a set of Top 25 stuff and then they finished up with some of my favourite Jimmy B tunes."

After a few minutes of silence, Leo said to Jacob, "I'd like to talk to you about last night. Got a minute?"

"Sure," Jacob said. "It's really none of my business though. Mom and I have already cleared that air. All I would ask is that you don't mess with her. She's a big girl now, so she can decide who she sees and what she does. You seem like a good guy and she seems to like you." Then he chuckled and said, "I shouldn't say that maybe but, hey, we're all guys here right. We need to stick together."

"I'm glad you feel like that. She's a lot of fun to be around, and I wouldn't do anything to mess with her. Just so you know, I mentioned to her that I would like to see her again and if she wanted to see me again that would be great. She said she was so . . . "

Again there was a silence, but I didn't let it go on for long. "Hey, Leo, remember I said that the Yanks were coming into town to play this weekend. I picked up a couple of tickets for you and me to go, but just found out that I've got something else that I have to do and can't get out of it. Jacob here is a Mets fan, if you can believe that, and he even admits to that out loud. So I know he hates the Yanks and I know that you are a Yanks fan, too, so why don't you guys go to the game on me. My treat."

Neither of them said anything. Perhaps I was pushing too hard too fast, but time was a factor and if I left it to these two, the situation would never get better. "Well, what do you say?"

They just looked at each other, neither knowing exactly how to respond in case the other didn't want to go. Finally Jacob said, "Sure, why not. It doesn't make a difference to me if I trash you or him," he said as he looked at me.

Leo jumped in with, "You only get to trash me if the Yanks lose, which isn't likely to happen," Leo said, "so I wouldn't get excited about that."

"Friendly wager?" grinned Jacob. "Dogs are on you if they aren't winning at the stretch." He held out his hand to shake on it.

"Just like taking candy from a baby, I believe, is the saying. Done." Leo shook his hand and smiled.

Then Jacob asked, as an afterthought, "Whose throwing for you guys?"

"The Big Fella's going, I think."

"Shit," was all he could say.

"Good," I said. "I'll leave the rest up to you guys."

"Hey, Jacob if I lend you my digital camera would you get a few good pics for me?" I asked. "Homerun trots, that sort of stuff. Maybe some shots down in the pit before the game."

"No problem."

Jacob was soon off, and Leo sat down. "I'm going to tell him and Annie this weekend. I needed you to know because I think he is really going to be angry with me, and I'm not sure how he will respond. Thanks for taking him to the game, by the way. I didn't mean to drop that one on you but . . . " I was having some trouble going on.

"I had a chance to speak with Annie when we were out, Jim. I stopped just short of telling her what's going on. I didn't, of course, but it was difficult. She knows something is in the wind but not quite what. I don't want her to think that my interest in Jacob has anything to do with my interest in her. I don't want her to think that I have an ulterior motive or anything. You know how some guys would use the kids to get to Mom. Anyway, thanks for the tickets. I was going to say the timing was good, but I wish we were all going. Do you really have anything to do that keeps you from the game?"

"No, not really," I replied, "I just thought that it would give you guys a chance to spend some time together, to see how it goes without me around. There needs to be some transition of some kind, and that might as well start now. He's quick, Leo. Don't underestimate him because he's 18. I made that mistake a few times. He likes to give and take too. And he gives as good as he gets, so heads up. He's a good kid and I found that he loves to learn. You'll be good for him. I know you will be. Enjoy the game tomorrow. I'll watch it on TV. Tomorrow needs to be a low-key day.

"Oh yeah, there's one other thing. Try not to get on the Jumbo Tron. You are not that photogenic, especially when you're cramming a foot-long in your mouth."

I started to rise and so did he. Before I knew it, he had me in a bear hug. He half-whispered to me, "I love you my man." This was so unlike him. Maybe this whole thing was good for him too.

I needed to lie down. The next day or two were not going to be pleasant for me or for anyone else, I suspected, but there were things that had to be said and done.

I went to bed early and got up late the next day. I was sleeping more now than I had in a long time, but I was getting up feeling as though I could sleep for another twelve hours. I tuned in the game just as it started and by the third inning I was lost to the world in sleep. I awoke by the sixth just in time to see them on the big stadium screen. There they were, big as life and there was Leo with a grin on his face that said, "I told you so."

That grin told me the Yanks were up in the game but not by how many. That meant that Jacob was likely on the hook for the dogs and drinks. If I could go by the facial expressions and their body language, it looked as though they were having a good time. Interestingly enough, however, I felt a pang of jealousy watching them. That should be me. I wanted to do that. I wanted to be there with Jacob.

For the first time since John had presented the news to me, I could feel the anger building in me. I wasn't angry at Leo but, oddly enough, with Jacob. If I hadn't gotten involved with him in the first place, would I be feeling this way right now? I couldn't say yes or no to that question. I just didn't know. What I did know was that he had become an integral part of my life and my family. It was as though I had three kids now and not two.

I had chosen to tell Jacob and Annie first, not because they were more important to me but simply because of proximity. Jacob had provided me with the opportunity to care for him and about him. He had ascribed to me the position of father, and I had accepted the challenge, the responsibility and the privilege of the role of mentor and of teacher.

He risked trusting that I would guide him as best I could. That was a mammoth undertaking on his part. The reality was I would not have had it any other way. The truth? The real truth was I was angry because I would not be around long enough to see him become the man I knew he would be.

He knew all he needed to know. He had been a willing and able student. He had also been energetic, enthusiastic and dedicated to the process, no matter how uncomfortable it had been for him at times. He was ready to begin his journey as a man in the world, and Leo could teach him and guide him through the rest. A man's work was never done when it came to helping and supporting and teaching another male in the world.

And once Jacob had all he needed, he would do the same for his sons and they would do the same for their sons, all because Jacob understood the importance of carrying on that tradition of one male helping another into the state of manhood.

My own kids know nothing about what is happening. They are a bit older and are so busy developing and planning their own lives and careers that I have become a back-burner item. I get cards or phone calls on the appropriate days and the I-love-yous too. There is nothing like hearing that from your kids and knowing that they truly mean it. Those are the things that keep you going some times. But that's how it's supposed to be.

As parents, we raise them and teach them to be self-sufficient so that they can and will eventually leave us. That's our job. My kids live so far away that we hardly ever see one another. I guess they think I will be around forever and that one day soon they will come for a visit and catch up with all things family.

This news is not something that I can share with them over the phone or in an e-mail. I know I will see them soon enough. Anyway, they will be the next to know.

Life Is Rarely Fair

S leep did not come easily. I woke up several times during the night going over what I would say. How would I phrase the news? My mind had started to race now. The what ifs and the how-tos had taken over. I had many decisions to make, and time was moving quickly ahead. I had called Annie last night to invite her and Jacob over in the early afternoon. I had left the same message for Leo. Today was going to be a life-changer for all of us. I just hoped that it would all end well.

Jacob and Annie showed up before Leo did, so it gave me some time to talk with Jacob about the game and how it went. He gave me back my camera with some great shots of my favourite players: Jeter, Tex, Swish and Brett. These guys knew how to play the game. They understood how the game is supposed to be played – flat out and not afraid to get their uniforms dirty. To his chagrin, the Yanks were victorious and, true to his word, he'd bought the dogs and sodas. I told him he could come over to the right side anytime, but he would hear none of it.

Leo was not long in showing up, so the time had come.

There would be no easy way to do this so I started in where it had started for me.

There is no easy way of telling you this, so I will tell you what I know and how I know it. Some time ago I had begun to notice a drop in my energy levels, and I since I pay close attention to my health, I went to John and asked for an in-depth physical exam, including blood work, etc. Two weeks later I got a call from him to say that an anomaly of some sort had shown up, and he needed me to come back to see him to sort it out. He didn't think it was anything to be concerned about, but he wanted to be thorough so I went.

"Two weeks after that visit, I got a call from him telling me that I had contracted a very rare blood disease and that the prognosis was not good. He insisted that I pay him yet another visit, which I did. Three days after that, I received a phone call from him confirming his diagnosis and the news was the worst possible. I won't go into all the details, but the bottom line is I won't likely see another springtime."

I could hear the insects moving on the floor it was so quiet. I could hear my own heart pounding in my chest. I looked up to see them all staring at me as though I was a creature from another world. I looked at Annie and I could see tears forming in her eyes. Jacob was staring at me with a mixture of sadness and anger and disbelief. Leo, my trusted and beloved friend, was watching me with eyes that radiated his love for me. We knew, we understood, how important each of us was to the other.

It was Jacob who spoke first. His voice shook and his lips quivered, but his words were strong. "So that's what has been going on all this time. I asked you what the deal was, and you lied to me. You gave me some bullshit excuses about not sleeping well. You freakin' lied to me. What kind of shit is this? You talk about trust and yet you couldn't tell me the truth about this? What the hell is that? Why should I believe anything you said? It was all bullshit. The whole freakin' thing. I bought into this thinking that, for the first time, I could actually believe that someone cared enough to be my friend, that you didn't want anything from me, that you just wanted to help me."

Leo began to say something to Jacob, but I looked him down and shook my head ever so slightly. He knew to let him go on. I thought that this might be the way it was going to go and I – we – had to let him do what he needed to do. He started to rant again and then just kicked over the chair and stormed off the porch.

There was nothing I could say now that he would hear. I just hoped that he would give me a chance at explaining why I did what I did. The time for that conversation, however, was not now. He needed to go off on his own and begin to think it through. I could only hope that some of what he had learned would come to him and that he would use it to help himself through his feelings and his thoughts.

Annie was stunned by all of this. She wanted to know the how and the why and the what-now. What could she do to help? She said all the usual things that one would expect to hear from someone who cared about you. She wanted to feel useful and helpful in some way because the alternative was too difficult for her to consider right now.

The sudden quiet seemed to create a calm and a peacefulness that was surely welcome. Finally she said that she should check on Jacob to make sure he is OK.

Now it was just Leo and I. I said to him, "Well, that went well don't you think?" He just looked at me and smiled a bit and then said in return, "Oh, yeah. Real well."

I felt exhausted yet relieved and at peace. The anxiety and the stress had been building for days, maybe weeks, and the elephant in the room had finally been identified. The secrets were out.

I also recognized that my connection to Jacob may have been damaged considerably so we might not get the chance to finish what we had started many months before. If ever there was a possibility of divine intervention taking place, now would be a good time for it to happen, I thought.

Leo stayed well into the evening. We talked about many things, as only true best friends are able to do. He wanted to know if I was comfortable and what he could do to help me in the coming days. He said he didn't want to intrude, but wanted me to know that he had nothing but time to give me.

Finally I said to him, "What I need is to know that Jacob is OK and that you will try to reach out to him. If he doesn't want to be a part of that, that's on him. I think that he'll be OK, but it'll take some time and it will be on his terms."

Several days went by with no word from Jacob and no sight of him anywhere. I spoke with Annie several times to see what was going on, but she had little to share with me. She seemed to be more accepting of what was going on, but still teared up when she saw me.

I wasn't sure if I should stay away or what but chose instead to say to her, "Can we sit down and talk about this? Are you going to be OK? What needs to happen here so that you can feel better? It's not as though I'm going tomorrow. I would like it to be like it was before you knew what was going on – you and I being able to share tea and conversation, I mean. I know that's difficult to do, but I'd like if we could."

"I need to say a few things and then I think I'll be better."

"OK, Annie, whenever you're ready." I sat and watched her.

She fussed around her kitchen putting on the kettle for tea. She straightened up things that I am sure she had straightened up several times already this day, but she needed to stay busy doing something. At last Annie sat down opposite me and poured the tea.

"I feel so sad, Jim, and I don't know how to deal with that. I feel sad for Jacob because I know how much he respects you and cares about you and how much he admires how you live your life and how you have come from where you did to here and now. I feel bad for you because I know how much life means to you and how connected you are to Jacob and to Leo. I think I know that you are going to miss not seeing him continue to grow into this manhood thing. I feel sad because you spent so much time with Jacob and me, for that matter, talking to us and reaching out to us when you could have been doing things that meant more to you.

212

"I know you made the commitment to us after you found out about your health but you could have ended that commitment at any time, with no hard feelings from either Jacob or me, but you didn't. You honoured your word.

"I feel sad for Leo because he will be lost without you in his life day to day. He is a really good person, and if I'm not careful I could really get to feel deeply for him. You are his true friend, as he calls you.

"And I feel sad for me. That may be selfish on my part, but so be it. You are someone truly special to me. You are someone I trust and count on and learn from. I enjoy our conversations. You listen to me and accept that I have a point of view that matters. You are a good man, Jim and you've helped me to see that not all men are bad and that I need to be sure not to judge everyone by my past experiences. I'll be eternally grateful to you for that. So you see I am sad and I don't know how to deal with it all."

"I'm not sure how to respond to you, Annie," I said. "About Jacob, all I can say is that I hope he will give me the opportunity to tell him some things that he needs to know and to hear from me. He is very special to me. He was not supposed to become this important to me. The relationship between us was not supposed to get to this but it did and now I'll deal with it.

"He is like my own in many ways. It's true I want to see him grow into manhood, to be the kind of man that other men look to and can learn from just by how he chooses to live his life. He deserves a good life, and I believe he will have it.

"About my choices? I didn't give you two anything that I didn't want to give you. I have my own reasons for what I chose to do and why. I did it because it was the right thing for me to do and the right time to do it. Besides, that's what men do. They honour their commitments.

"About Leo, you are right. He is a remarkable man and I am much the better for knowing him. You couldn't do much better in my estimation, but I don't want to play matchmaker. One thing I will tell you, if he already hasn't, is that I asked him to watch out for Jacob. I asked if he would step in and guide him or help him out if that was something that Jacob wanted or needed him to do. He said he would be more than pleased and honoured to do that. He was also concerned – and I am probably saying more than I should here – that if he wanted to date you that that might interfere with what I had asked him to do. He didn't want to be seen as someone who was chasing you around so that he could get closer to Jacob or vice-versa. He didn't want to take on a

213

mentoring role with Jacob so that you might see him more favourably. I told him to do what his soul told him to do and that the cards would fall from there. I'm counting on you to never tell him I told you that . . . Deal?"

She nodded her agreement.

I finished my tea and went back home. I stood in my little back yard and watched the sun set. My days and nights were different now. At times I felt I was just marking time, standing around waiting for something to happen. At other times, I wanted to take off, to go for a ride or a drive. Maybe I was hoping I could out run the inevitable. My energy or lack of it became my enemy.

Legacies Are Not That Important In The Grand Scheme

When this whole thing got started, it was mostly about me and what I wanted. That seemed to be the driving force behind my decision to connect with Jacob initially. What has happened is that my reasons for taking this on have changed. Oh, the idea of leaving my mark, my footprint on the world, is still important. I cannot tell a lie.

But the idea that I could help to influence another human being in a way that would help him make choices that would enhance the quality of this life and the lives of his children is much more important. It is about doing what I could to help one young man become more of what he could be.

It's not important to know who did what but rather that it was done and things are better because of it. I hope that history would record the generational changes for the better, so that a small corner of the world is safer, kinder, more free, more generous and more friendly than the previous generation was.

Leo gave to me of himself. I gave of myself to Jacob. Jacob will give to his sons and so on. A man's work is never done.

As I sat down at the table and began to think about what I wanted to write Jacob, I heard a soft knock at the door. As I approached it, I could see who it was. Jacob opened the door and stepped in just as I was reaching for the handle. I stopped and moved back a step to let him in and we just looked at one another. He moved forward a half step as if to say, "Am I still welcome here?"

I didn't know whether I should hug him or shake his hand so I opted for the hug. I was happy to see him because I knew not only that he was all right but also because I knew that we were going to be all right.

"Have you got some time?" he asked tentatively.

As I turned to walk back into the kitchen I said over my shoulder, "I've got all the time you need."

If body language was an indicator of how he felt, I understood that he wanted to be angry but couldn't do it. I believed what he came for and what he needed from me was an explanation of what was happening and what was to come next.

"When you first dropped your news on us, I wanted to run. I wanted to get high so that you and everybody who knew about what was going on would say look what we made him do. But you taught me that that's not the way it works. Like it or not, that wasn't going to work out well. I wanted . . . No, I needed to hurt somebody so that they would know how I was feeling.

"All my life I have wanted what I thought we had: somebody who cared and somebody who saw me as something other than a screw-up who didn't deserve any happiness or for things to be normal like other guys seemed to have.

"I know that my mom loves me, but I needed to know that someone else would miss me if I wasn't around and that I meant something to someone else. That I was important. Mothers are supposed to love you. I wanted to know that I had a place in someone else's life besides hers.

"I wanted to believe that that person was you. Why else would you do what you did? Why else would you take your time and share it with me the way you did? I thought that I had it, finally, and then this. It's like being told, 'Got you again, sucker.' I slept a couple of days at a buddy's house so that no one would bother me because I needed to think this out before I just trashed what I thought I had. In the end I decided that's not at all what I wanted to do but I need to know why you lied to me. You told me one thing and did another. Why?"

"I'm not sure how you came up with the idea that I lied to you, Jacob."

"I asked you to be open and honest with me, Jim, and I would be with you. That was the agreement that we came to a while ago, and you said you would live by that. I asked you if you were OK because I could see there were times when you weren't. You thought that you were hiding it well, but after a while I could see something was happening. I didn't know, but I knew something. Maybe those instincts you talk about. I don't know. When I asked you, you gave me some bullshit excuse about not sleeping well or having caught a bug. There was always something, but not the truth about what was really going on."

I knew that all we had done together – what he had challenged within himself and what he had bought into, the changes he'd made and the risks he'd taken in good faith, and the trust he placed in me – all of it came down to how I explained this to him right now.

"It saddens me that you feel this way. I understand how you could feel this way, but I have never lied to you. Because of the nature of my illness, there were many days that I was not able to sleep. I got exhausted quickly and just plain ran out of energy. I was being honest when I said I was having difficulty sleeping.

"John, my friend the doctor, has been very helpful to me by providing a protein/energy concoction that boosted my system so that I could carry on with my life. In this case it was about my being able to meet with you each day. There wasn't much more important to me than that. I looked forward to seeing you and talking with you. There were times when knowing you were coming by was the only reason I got out of bed. I always knew – and he'd told me straight up – that it wouldn't last forever, but it would do the trick for a certain amount of time.

"Along with that, my immune system has been compromised so that the longer this goes the more susceptible I become to bugs that ordinarily wouldn't affect me. That's the truth of that.

"In the natural order of things, you were always going to be here longer than I and that hasn't changed except that my time will be somewhat less than I had planned or hoped for.

"I'll admit that I left some things up to interpretation, but I never meant to deceive you and I didn't lie to you. I wouldn't do that to you, and I'm sorry that that is what has come out of this for you."

I paused to let that sink in. He wasn't angry. He was hurt and frightened.

"I will also admit that when I first was asked by your mom to speak to you, I didn't think much would come of it. I was wrong about that and I was also off base in terms of what I thought you could or would bring to the process.

"You have become very important to me, Jacob. You are like family to me, and the importance that you speak of is certainly there, as far as I am concerned. I didn't tell you directly about my illness because I was concerned that it would influence, in some way, the learning and the focus of what I wanted to share with you. I wasn't sure if you would see me the same way if you knew that something was wrong with me. I didn't say anything because of my hopes of what might be possible and I didn't want to risk that being compromised in some way.

"The other thing is, quite frankly, what is happening is a deeply personal thing. It is really no one else's business until I say it is, and I am still having some difficulty coming to grips with what is going on.

"The truth is you are like a son to me in many ways, and I am proud of who you have chosen to become. I feel good knowing that you will be a father yourself some day and you will pass on this learning to your sons. There is always much more to learn, as I am finding out. There are many things that we didn't speak about, but you got what you need in order to live as a man in this world.

"There's one other thing I will mention to you, since honesty and openness is the topic of the hour. Leo has said he would be honoured to be there for you if at any time you needed to talk to someone who is also interested in seeing you become all you can be. I know of no man who would be better for you than he. He is smart and discreet. He's also a great teacher and an intuitive and thoughtful human being who I am fortunate to say is my best friend. He taught me about how to be a man in this world when I had no idea. Some of what I learned I passed on to you so that you can do the same one day. All I am and most of what I experienced I owe to him.

"And just for the record, the relationship that may or may not develop between your mom and Leo has nothing to do with his commitment to you. He will do it because I asked him and because he sees what I see in you. If you want him to do that for you all you need to do is ask him. In other words, it doesn't matter what happens between them; he will be there for you. He is as good as his word.

"I am not sure what else I can say to you to help you with all of this. Is there anything else that you feel you need to say to me about what I said the other day? It is what it is, Jacob, and I don't like it any more than any one else. But I can't spend my days angry at the way things have turned out.

"I want to see you grow and mature as a man, but we can't always have what we want. This is one of those times. I honestly don't know how many days, weeks or months are left, but what I do know is that nothing would mean more to me than to spend a great deal of that time with you just talking about what we want to talk about and to spend some time with my own kids. There are things that I need to say to them as well while I still can."

He got up abruptly and started to move toward the stairs and then stopped and turned around. I had no idea what was coming when he started to speak.

"I think it sucks and I'm pissed off about what is going on, but I'm not mad at you, Jim. I'm angry at the idea that you won't be there for me if I need to sort things out and I'm still not sure about Leo either. I guess I'm feeling alone and maybe scared a bit and really sad for you. I'm not used to feeling these things and not doing something to make them go away."

"Welcome to the real world," I said. "Awful things happen, and they aren't always fair. As you learn to handle these feelings, the ones that bring you joy will be that much more important to you."

"See you tomorrow?" He said as a question and not as a statement.

I looked at him and just nodded. He looked at me with a grin. He knew what the nod meant. It was my way of removing the tension a bit. It was our way, something just between us. Personal.

I also knew that he and I were done. There was a feeling that washed over me that we'd gone to where we needed to go and we'd talked about the things that needed to be talked about in order for Jacob to grow into the state of manhood. He knew what he needed to know. Now he had to live it each day. He would continue to learn as we all do and I thought that he would eventually turn to Leo for that guidance. I felt some peace about those things. I also knew that my job wasn't done altogether. There was still a piece to finish.

I would get started on that tomorrow.

Happy Birth Day, Jacob: Welcome To Manhood

I was up a little later than I wanted to be but found that I needed the rest. When Jacob came by, we just sat in the front room and watched the game together. The run for the playoffs was on and, of course, my Yanks were in the thick of it. Jacob wasn't amused that they had 'bought' their way to the top again. We trash-talked and discussed baseball strategies for the duration of the game.

It was a great afternoon in that we didn't talk about anything heavy. We exchanged barbs and sarcasms with ease, knowing that none of it was serious, as is the case with true fans of the game.

There was something different about Jacob today, though. He had a maturity that seemed to have grown over time, and a self-assuredness that wasn't quite as evident a few days ago. Maybe I just hadn't noticed.

As he was preparing to leave, I asked him if he was busy on Saturday evening because I was having a few friends over for a pot-luck supper. Would he ask Annie to come as well? He said he would be there and was sure that his mom would want to come as well unless Leo was taking her out somewhere. I mentioned that Leo was also invited so they would probably show up, one way or the other.

Saturday came and all the people I wanted to attend had arrived or were on their way. Officer O'Hanagan was the first to appear, followed by John and Jacob's two aunts. Then Leo, Annie and Jacob arrived. These were the people who had the most to do with why I had organized this evening.

When everyone was seated, I told them how pleased I was at seeing everyone. There were, however, two other people on their way and if we could wait another 15 minutes, I would appreciate their patience. Of course no one minded, but they were uncertain who it was they were waiting for.

Ten minutes later, my two children walked into the room and I made the introductions. I had asked them to come because I really wanted to see them while I had the energy and I wanted them to meet Jacob. He was as close as anyone could be to being a part of my family without actually being that part.

When I looked at my son I wondered what was going through his mind. Did he feel like he had missed out on something important in his life? Did he realize that I had not done what I was supposed to do? Did he even care after all this time? Was he angry? Was he disappointed? Did he come because he was curious about who this Jacob person was? I felt so disconnected from him and I knew I had to address that before he left to go back home. I wanted him to know that he was important to me too and that I felt like our relationship had been damaged because I didn't make the effort with him that I had made with Jacob.

My daughter was a bit more hesitant but also agreed to come. She and Jacob would likely meet again at some time in the near future, so I wanted them to have a sense of each other before that time came.

Now that everyone was here, I began. "I guess this is more of a surprise birthday party than anything else. It's a surprise in that Jacob has no idea of what this about." I could see the surprise and the wariness in his eyes, but I continued. "Some months ago, I was asked to have a word with this character who lived next door because his mom was at her wit's end and didn't know what to do with him. Reluctantly, I agreed, and one way or another we found ourselves engaged in a process that has led us to today. It was a most unlikely connection with an unforeseeable outcome. I am very pleased that it turned out as it has.

"I have always believed in the 'rite of passage' idea for young men. Simply, it is a ceremony that marks the transition for a male from adolescence to manhood. It has gone the way of the dodo bird, but the importance and the significance have not diminished. As a matter of fact, I believe there is even more need for this ceremony and the public acknowledgement of it today than ever before.

"I have referred to this day as a birthday, and it is, of sorts. This is the day that Jacob gets to experience a 're-birth.' He leaves behind the experience of boyhood and is now seen and accepted by his fellow men as achieving a state of manhood. He has proven himself worthy and deserves our respect and our acceptance. He knows and understands how to live among us as a man in the world and what that means.

"He demonstrated this recently when he intervened in an assault on his mother by his father. He did what a man does: he protected his family home and those most precious to him. In this case it was his mother, Annie. It could have been his children or his aunts. The point is that he did what was necessary. He followed his instincts. He acted upon his natural gifts. Jacob now understands what those gifts are, how they shape his life on a day to day basis and how to honour and accept them as an integral part of who he is in the world. He showed a maturity and courage in the face of danger and unknowns. He put his own well-being second to defend the integrity and safety of his home.

"He also demonstrated a sense of compassion, although his father and his broken nose may not agree. When he had got the best of his father in the fight, he could have done real damage and no one would have been critical. However, he didn't do that. He assessed the situation and stopped where he did because to continue to beat his father would have only surrendered him to anger and rage. He chose compassion. He knew his father was defeated and left it there.

"I also want to thank Jacob for granting me the opportunity to help him learn and understand why we do what we do and how we are different from the other half of the people who also inhabit the planet. We're not better, but we are definitely different. We spoke at length about why it is important that we, as men, never let anyone discount, diminish or try to take from us the gifts that have been a traditional part of us as men since time began. We have passed them on from generation to generation. They are an integral part of who we are as human beings and always will be. They do not need to be justified or defended. I believe that Jacob will do that with determination and with dedication. It's the mark of a man."

I had to stop. I could have gone on for a long time, but it was not my place to do that. This was Jacob's day, and I wanted him to feel the significance and the importance of what was happening. I had looked at him when I finished my little speech and he just stood there looking at me. I saw a mixture of pride, of shock, of uncertainty and of satisfaction. He realized that he was truly loved, appreciated and cared for and that's really all he ever wanted. I looked at Annie and thought that she was going to explode with love and admiration for her son. I also stole a quick look at my son. I thought I noticed a sadness in his eyes but couldn't say for sure.

I looked back at Jacob and asked him to step up beside me for a moment. I put my hand on his shoulder and said, "I want you to have this as a reminder of today and what it means. There will be days when you are frustrated and challenged. You will forget some of what you have learned. Hold this in your hand, rub it, look at it and it will help to remind you of who you are and what you need to do."

I presented him with a small box. He looked at it and then at me and then back at the box. He opened it and removed what I had placed inside. He turned it over and then back again. He looked at me once more and a tear rolled down his face. He didn't try to hide it but rather reached out to me and lovingly embraced me as he had never done before. It was done with love in his heart. Of this I was sure. I knew that he finally had found what he was looking for and knowing how to receive it was the greatest gift of all for him.

He faced the group formed in front of him and said, "I usually have some smart reply to stuff like this but not today. I thank all of you for coming. You have no idea how important it is to me to see all of you here."

Then he looked at Officer O'Hanagan and said, "Even you." He couldn't resist the opportunity. The two of them laughed at each other, and then everyone else joined in.

Annie spoke up and asked, "What does it say? On your gift, what does it say?"

Jacob again looked at me and then at the gift and held it up for all to see. It was a sterling silver medallion about the size of a dollar. "On this side it says 'Remember Where You Came From' and on the other side it says, 'Always Pass It On' with today's date at the bottom."

As the celebration moved on to the next phase, I said to the group, "I have one other gift to present to Jacob." I pulled out the leather-bound journal I had been writing in and said to Jacob, "This is for you. I have written a few things in there already but it is for you to keep track of those thoughts and ideas that will come to you. My hope is that you will use those thoughts and others to help you map out your journey. They are meant to be private and only shared with those you trust and those you believe will grant you the freedom to claim who you are. Should anything happen that would prevent you from telling your sons or showing them who you are as a man and what you are about, this will serve as the next best thing. Your sons will be glad you did. When the time comes, you can pass it on to them to do the same with their sons. It becomes a journal of knowledge. Enjoy it, use it and share it, if you wish."

The formal part of the ceremony was now complete. He had been seen and accepted by his peers as a man into the world. It was time to celebrate this day. He still looked a bit shocked by it all, but he stood in the middle of the group and accepted their good wishes.

As for my kids, I helped them understand where all things stood regarding my health. It was sad; it was life affirming; it was a relief. It's ironic that the very issue that has become so important—time—was washed away in an instant. I told them how much I loved them and how important they were to me. We hugged one another with sincerity and intensity. I am very proud of who they are and of what they represent in and to the world.

As I thought back to the time when I, too, began my march to independence one of my great disappointments was not making the time to say the things to my parents or caregivers that needed to be said before they were gone from me. I just never got around to it.

I feel very fortunate, not only to have children, but to have had the privilege to be a part of their life experience. What an honour to have been a part of the direction and choices they made. We did promise to dedicate more of our time to just 'be' with one another in the time I have left. I look forward to that.

I watched Jacob as he made his way to every person in the room. He engaged each in a one-to-one conversation off to the side so that he had some privacy with each one. He had begun with Officer O'Hanagan. As I watched I could see gestures and grins that ended with a heartfelt hand shake between them. And the famous nod. Jacob went to the aunts next, and then to John and then to Annie. This one was more personal, of course, and was marked by several hugs and demonstrations of gentleness that only existed between a proud Mom and her son.

He had left Leo to the last. The conversation they had lasted much longer than the others. As much as I dearly wanted to know what they discussed, it was none of my business. I was determined not to ask either of them. It was theirs to share if they wanted. It did finish with a solid handshake and a very quick, man-hug.

As the day wore on and I began to tire, Jacob came to me when all except Leo had gone and said, "I have no idea what to say to you now. This has been the greatest day of my life for so many reasons, and I can't even think about all of them. I just know that's how it is. It's the best birthday ever. I want to say thank you but it doesn't seem to be nearly enough. I mean, what is it I'm thanking you for anyway? You have done so much for me that I can't think of just one or two things. There are too many. I'll just say that you are the most important person, next to my mom, that I have ever known. I hope that you know how much you mean to me."

He offered me his hand, I offered him mine, we shook hands and then he hugged me once again. I could get used to this.

Jacob left and there was just Leo and I. He said, "That's going to be a tough act to follow. Jacob and I agreed to see how things go. He's not sure about how much he needs me to be fooling around in his life right now. He's a good kid. You're right about that. He is proud too, and that may slow him down a bit, but I get the feeling when he needs an ear he'll knock on my door."

As I walked him toward the door, he looked at me and asked, "How are you? Are you OK? What's going through your mind right now?"

I replied, "You know, I'm not sure about anything right now. I know I'm going to be OK for the rest of this day and likely tomorrow, but after that I plain don't know."

"Cool," was all he said. Then he asked, "Two out of three crib?"

"Cool," I said.

There's Nothing Like Good Friends

In the end, nothing is as important as good friends. I once read that a man is not judged by what he has or how much he accumulated over the span of his life but rather by the quality of the friendships he was involved in. That being the case, I find myself wealthy beyond compare and truly blessed.

Over the next week or so, Leo managed to hang my hammock out on the front porch so we could spend time there just talking and working in a few games of cribbage. My children were true to their word and visited often. It was good to see them and to have that time with them. Both Annie and John came by often and usually stayed long enough to have a bite with me and talk about everything from politics to baseball to motorcycles and the trips we had gone on. It was a great way of staying connected and saying good-bye all at the same time.

Leo and Jacob were around most days from morning to night. We never got into any heavy conversations, just light and easy ones.

And I had my nights. Some were long and lonely but most were filled with a sense of well-being. I had actually come to some peace because I had dealt with most of my misgivings. I had been given the opportunity to make peace with myself before I saw my last sunset.

Afterword

Her name was Rebecca but I called her 'Becky'. She was beautiful to look at but even more beautiful on the inside. She was compassionate, loving, a free spirit, serious when needed, funny and at peace most of the time. She had long dark hair to her shoulders. She had big beautiful eyes that didn't miss anything that happened around her. She walked along with happiness in her stride—not a care in the world. And my wife was very pregnant. I was going to be a 'daddy' in about two month's time. She was every man's dream—certainly mine.

We already knew that we were going to have a boy to love and care for. We had already agreed that his name was going to be Jimmy. The really cool thing was that Mom loved Becky almost as much as I did and Leo was always looking out for her. It was like I always thought a family would be.

Becky and I often came to the park to spend time. Jim Sr. and I talked endlessly about how this place was his salvation and how he would come here to gather himself. He would watch the kids play; he would fly his kite and just let it hang up there in the air hundreds of feet up. He loved the quiet and the peace and the freedom that was found here. It's difficult to believe that five years have passed since our last conversation and I miss him more than I can say but as he said—'life goes on don't waste it on me'.

Becky said, "Hey where've you been? You seem a thousand miles away."

"I guess I drifted away for a bit but I'm back. I was just thinking about Jim and how he really enjoyed this place. How was your walk?"

"Great," she said with emphasis. "It will be good to bring Jimmy here to enjoy the days. Did you bring it with you?"

"Yup," was all I said. She was referring to my journal. I always bring it with me when I come here because the thoughts usually come to me here in the peace and tranquility. I love reading through what he had written especially the stuff he shared during his final days. It's almost like I can hear him talking to me still.

I undid the leather tie-strap and turned to the front page. I read it out loud as I usually did: "To Jacob—a journal of random thoughts". I turned to the next page where a single paragraph had been written.

225

Here it said, "These are thoughts written in no particular order of importance. I felt like I needed to share these with you for what they may be worth to you. My hope is that you will glance at them from time to time and take from them what you will—Love Jim." I closed it and put it down. Then I picked it up again—opened it to a random page where I began to read: ". . . then reconsider your decision to have a family. A man's family and his home and his children should be his first and last priority. If you are going to father children then you accept this premise as the truth and you do what you can to show it and to live it every day."

I continued to turn the pages and read the words as I had done a hundred times before:

"To be effective as a parent there are many things that need to be done. But there are two that stand out as more important than some of the others: 1. Show your children that you can be counted on to provide solid guidance, to establish appropriate boundaries for behaviour and to satisfy the developmental needs of your child and 2. Show your child, every chance you get, that you love them for who he or she is as a person. Show them compassion, that they have your undivided attention and that you are giving them your time. Take them to a ball game; go fly a kite, play catch or just go for a ride to the ice cream stand. They need to know that they are important to you and as a member of the family they are valued and have a place—a safe place in all aspects. They need to be reminded of this often."

"Kids need these things. They will seek them from their parents first. But if they are denied they will look elsewhere. That's why it is so much more difficult for kids in single parent homes where Mom is the primary care giver and for males who grow up in a fatherless environment. A son needs to feel attached to his father and the father needs to encourage that attachment. Once that has been cemented the father then has a chance to become the teacher. The son will watch and learn by example. He will open himself to the lessons of being male. The father needs to protect and encourage the son and to help him recognize and understand maleness tempered with compassion and acceptance of others . . ."

"Dad's most often provide the 'authority' figure in the home. Not always the 'authoritarian' but usually the authority. You'll make a good father Jacob . . ."

"As a man you may be a competitor, for instance, but you still have to learn how to compete. There are skills to learn so that you can be the best you can be with each of your gifts. As you become aware of your gifts you need to learn how to use them for the greater good . . ."

"Kids don't do or behave any better if they feel powerless. They become more problematic if anything. Don't belittle them and call them names. That just adds to their sense of having no relevance, no place, no connection to the world and no power. They feel as though there is nothing they can do to change anything or to stop anything bad from happening to them . . ."

"Young men are less and less interested in participating in higher education. They view their opportunities to succeed or even to find meaningful work as shrinking. It may be true. However, with less education comes diminished work skills and a distorted work ethic. There comes that 'entitlement' problem again. If they cannot compete for better jobs they are more likely to be unemployed for greater periods of time. With that comes a whole new set of social problems among them: substance use and abuse, criminal activity and more abdication of parental responsibility. Make sure your son understands the importance of an education. Encourage him to learn—make it fun for him or at least rewarding in some way that encourages him to continue . . ."

"Equality and sameness are not even close to being or meaning the same thing. The argument does not take into account the principles of your physical and emotional differences—your histories and your natural gifts. As a man or a woman in the world you are not the same but you need to be seen and treated as equals by each other. You need to encourage each other to be all you each can be and to enjoy freedom of opportunity equally. But at what cost and to who? You begin by accepting who you are as men and women and that you are not the same. Therefore, you cannot expect each other to think, act and respond like you would. 'We' are not 'them' and 'them' are not 'we' . . ."

"Encouragement vs. praise. Encouragement builds independence and choice while praise supports the kids' choice to please his/her parents--to win their love and acceptance. Eg. To encourage you need to recognize the hard work that your kids put into something regardless of the outcome. It is the hard work that they put into it that matters. They will learn how to make it better the next time. Or when they make a tough decision you need to comment on how difficult that must have been for them to decide that. When you say 'I'm proud of what you did there' you are saying that what they did was more for you so if you want to keep making me happy keep doing what you are doing. It's not supposed to be about you. It's supposed to be about them . . ."

"The two things men fear the most is being alone and losing their minds . . ."

"If you, as a man, want to change the perception of who you are, and perception does become reality, then you need to ask yourself the question: what am I doing, what have I done, what can I do to do that—to change the perception of who I am as a man?. . ."

"Not all men are born equal. Not every man will fit the stereotype that has been suggested. Some are wired differently meaning that some men have different skill sets. Some are great athletes while some are great artists. Some are great musicians while others are great actors. The common denominator is that you are all men and you will utilize your natural gifts to promote those skills you possess . . ."

"I have learned that not all women are born to be great cooks. They are not born to be 'kitchen help' either. Likewise, not all men are born to be handymen nor are they born to be beasts of burden. But they seem to assimilate the roles of providers and protectors, predators, hunters, warriors and challenge oriented quite naturally. Women do seem to have a natural ability to be caregivers, nurturers, teachers and negotiators. This doesn't mean that a woman cannot be a hunter any more than it does not mean that a man cannot be a caregiver. What we need to recognize is what are natural characteristics to both of us and acknowledge and accept that they are real for each of us. Once we do that, we can move ahead . . ."

"When we are pushed to make a decision, we often push back. . ."

"The question remains: can each of you – both men and women - do what comes naturally to you and still manage your way through your lives together? I believe you can, but not the way you are currently trying to do it. Does one have to give in or give up before you make any progress? That's the point: No is the answer. It will never work that way. First, there has to be a desire, on both sides, to get it done. Do you have enough energy to support one another without having to sacrifice your natural gifts as a gender species?. . ."

"For some men, sex is just sex. There does not have to be a feeling of love involved. Sometimes it is just primal. As I have said I have not been a woman in this lifetime so I can't say what they think or feel about this topic. Men will often decide if and for how long they will stick around with one partner based on a first sexual encounter or if they have been stimulated enough physically or mentally. Love will often follow, but I'm not sure that we are cut out to be monogamous. We each need to pay attention to what the other is saying if we want our relationships to succeed . . ."

"In order to have a successful relationship, do we always have to see the same issues in the same way or can we agree to disagree? I'd like to think that we can disagree and carry on. Find someone who works this way and you are half way to the Promised Land . . ."

"Do you want to be right or do you want to be happy? We have to learn how to accommodate and accept what we don't want, sometimes, so that we can receive the same consideration. It can't always go the way we want it to or think it should . . ."

"Being secure in yourself is not the same as telling the world how right you are or how smart you are . . ."

"Is trust, once given, absolute? I don't think it should be . . ."

"I have learned that to ignore the facts of something doesn't change them . . ."

"It's not the amount of stress that is deadly as much as it is the length of time you try to carry it around with you that is deadly . . ."

"Time is not something you have as much as it is something you manage. Time is finite, so there is only so much of it. How are you going to spend it? I read somewhere that there are things which, once done, can't be recovered: the stone after it has been thrown, the word after it has been spoken, the occasion after it has been missed, a person after they pass away and time once it is spent. As I grow older, I can only say that this is the truth and the essence of living a life you don't regret. You have absolutely no idea of what is to come. You can only hope that most of it is good. You can't live in fear of what you don't know about. To waste any time worrying about what may or may not happen or to try to solve the problems or issues, before they even transpire, is simply crazy making. You can plan for the future and do what you think you need to do to make that happen. To worry yourself into paralysis over what may or may not happen or to try to anticipate future events or future developments involving others just doesn't work well. When I was working I used to call this kind of event a 'planned crisis'. Decide if that's the way you want to spend your time. My suggestion would be don't do it. To do so will rob you of the day to day joy that is part of what we live for. Surprises can be blessings too . . ."

"My hope is that over time, you will add to these thoughts. Challenge them if you like, but make sure you teach your sons so that they can teach theirs. Read this every once in a while and know that I will always be with you . . ."

"P.S. Go Yanks!"

I took some time to read a few of my own insights as well, what I have come to understand more clearly with time and experience but I always go back to what Jim had written. I still wanted – no, I still needed – to know what more there was I could learn and whether I could add anything new, any new insight?

As I read, I looked at Becky from time to time and knew that had I not taken the chance and the risk to listen then and that had I not been able or ready to give up my anger and my rage I never would have connected with Jim and, in turn, I never would have met Becky. Had I not, finally, spoken with Leo I wouldn't have been able to work through whatever was standing in my way of being at peace.

Jim knew these things would haunt me, and he made sure I was prepared to deal with them. It's interesting how the circle goes around.

Hindsight being what it is, it seems as though Jim was right about many things. Experience is a wise teacher, indeed.

I closed the journal and sat in the quiet for a bit. I took out my cell phone and entered Leo's phone number. It had been too long since we last chatted.

Maybe Jim was right about this as well: Maybe a man's work is never done.

"The quality of my journey is largely defined by the quality of my companions."
Earnie Larsen

How To Live With Us And Survive It: 30 Best Suggestions

1. Try to understand that we are not the enemy and that the ills of the world are not always our doing.

2. We need to accept each other's time honoured qualities as real and of great value and importance to each of us. We need to celebrate them as gifts to share.

3. If you don't want to hear the answer, don't ask the question (see #13 for example).

4. Know that there is little more fragile than a male ego.

5. The difference between receiving a direct order and receiving an invitation is co-operation and success.

6. Never mistake gentility and compassion in a man for weakness. We have feelings, too, just like other people.

7. Three things that every man needs: 1. companionship, (2) knowing that he is admired and respected for something that he does well, and (3) knowing his knowledge and his counsel have value.

8. If you feel you need to know, then just ask. (See #3)

9. If we walk away, it's because we need time to think and not because we don't care. Leave us alone and well get back to you.

10. Understand that we will get angry. Don't accept any abuse that we say is driven by anger. We all need to be accountable for our actions. Men are no different in this regard.

11. Say what you mean and mean what you say. Let's keep it simple.

12. If you want the "seat down," then learn to put it up when YOU are done.

13. Please, if you think you are carrying a couple of extra pounds, you probably are. Don't ask us to lie and then question our honesty. (Refer to #3)

14. Coercion is a poor motivator for lasting change. Instilling or creating fear is not a long-lasting solution either. Please don't push and threaten.

15. If you already know how to do it, then do it. Don't ask me to do it then tell me how.

16. If we ask what's wrong and you say nothing, that's good enough for us. (See # 11)

17. When making a point, don't make it about winning. If someone wins, someone also loses. State your piece, and I'll do the same. Now we both have heard it, so let's move on.

18. Don't make me responsible for your happiness, and I'll not expect that from you. We each need to take care of that one for ourselves.

19. Don't tell me how to think and feel, and I won't do that to you. And let's leave the "shoulds" out of it.

20. If we are going to have words, let's be sure that we both get to use them and not at the same time.

21. Wait until I'm done before you judge it or me.

22. We think of hair rollers, fuzzy slippers, old terry cloth housecoats and knee-highs as natural birth control devices.

23. Don't be critical of another man's possessions or provisions. It's demeaning. The likelihood is what he has is the best he can do right now.

24. At the very least, try treating us as well as you treat your friends.

25. Understand that everything has the potential to be a competition of some kind.

26. We don't have toys; we have hobbies.

27. Understand that double standards do exist, and, yes, we ALL use them.

28. Some men grow old gracefully; others don't. Make sure you know which one you got (see #4). And here are two more of my favourite bits of advice from a very wise man, Will Rogers:

29. Lettin' the cat outta the bag is a lot easier'n puttin' it back. (It's a great deal easier to say it than to take it back)

30. There are three kinds of men: the ones that learn by reading; the few who learn by observation; and the rest of them have to pee on the electric fence and find out for themselves. (Most of us tend to be experiential by nature, so let us be.)

About The Author

Jim has worked in the human services field for 20 years. Having done so, he has developed a keen understanding of the differing ways both genders see the world they live in. Some of that time included working with men and women, as singles and couples, whose lives and families had been ravaged by alcoholism and drug addiction. Having been a single parent for several years, Jim can now add a personal level of experience to the insights he shares in this book.

He is especially proud of his son and daughter and the human beings they have become in the world.

**Are you an Evolutionary Leader with a message
and interested in becoming an Author of Influence?**

James Cloughley is a graduate of the InspireABook program and a member of the Inspired Authors Circle. If you want to get on the path to be a published author by Influence Publishing please go to **www.InspireABook.com**

For information on the Authors circle and other Authors of Influence please go to **www.InspiredAuthorsCircle.com**

Each month a new book title is released that "Inspires Higher Knowledge" Each pre-launch campaign is supported by the other Authors of Influence with Free E-Books, Audio Books, Mp3's and other gifts. For each book you purchase from the Influence Publishing family you will receive $100's of Free gifts if you support our launches by pre-ordering the books. Take a look at the gifts offered at: **www.SpiritualAuthorsCircle.com/book-launch-gifts/**

Influence Publishing

More information on our other titles and how to submit your own proposal can be found at **www.InfluencePublishing.com**

A Man's Work Is Never Done

CPSIA information can be obtained at www.ICGtesting.com
Printed in the USA
LVOW112056190312

273798LV00006B/5/P